Research Supporting Middle Grades Practice

A volume in
Middle Grades Research Journal Top Studies

Series Editor:
Vicki L. Schmitt, *The University of Alabama*

Middle Grades Research Journal
Top Studies

Vicki L. Schmitt, Series Editor

Model Minority Myth Revisited: An Interdisciplinary Approach to Demystifying Asian American Educational Experiences (2008)
edited by Guofang Li and Lihshing Wang

Research Supporting Middle Grades Practice

edited by

David L. Hough
Missouri State University

Information Age Publishing, Inc.
Charlotte, North Carolina • www.infoagepub.com

Library of Congress Cataloging-in-Publication Data

Research supporting middle grades practice / edited by David L. Hough.
    p. cm. — (Middle grades research journal top studies)
  Includes bibliographical references.
  ISBN 978-1-61735-079-5 (paperback) — ISBN 978-1-61735-080-1 (hardcover) —
ISBN 978-1-61735-081-8 (e-book)
  1. Middle school teaching—United States—Case studies. 2. Middle school
education—United States—Case studies. 3. English language—Study and
teaching (Middle school)—United States—Foreign speakers—Case studies. I.
Hough, David L.
  LB1623.5.R48 2010
  373.1102—dc22

                                             2010021948

Printed in the United States of America

Review Board

We thank all our *MGRJ* reviewers who spend time examining the many submissions we receive for consideration.

CONTENTS

EDITOR'S PREFACE

Welcome to the *Middle Grades Research Journal's* second book featuring the crème de la crème of research focusing on middle grades educational issues. Our first book, *Middle Grades Research: Exemplary Studies Linking Theory to Practice*, featured the 10 top studies published in 2006, 2007, and 2008 as identified by the *MGRJ* Editorial and Review Boards. *Research Supporting Middle Grades Practice* features research published throughout 2009 in *MGRJ* that has been identified by our review board as the most useful in terms of assisting educators with making practical applications from evidence-based studies to classroom and school settings. The editorial team is pleased to present these studies under one cover, trusting each will contribute to the existing body of knowledge on middle grades education in ways that will enable readers to develop theories more fully and apply findings and implications to a variety of settings.

Studies are presented in chronological order as they appeared in each of the four issues published during the fourth volume year (2009). Our first three issues 4(1), 4(2), and 4(3) were special themes wherein guest editors provided the oversight for selection and substantive editorial revisions. Guest editors' introductory comments regarding previously published manuscripts appear first, followed by the editor-in-chief's comments.

We would again like to thank the many people who made this book possible. Mr. George Johnson and his staff at Information Age Publishing (IAP) have made the publishing transition of *MGRJ* smooth and seamless.

Research Supporting Middle Grades Practice,
pp. ix–xv

Their work to promote middle grades education and its research under-girding the development of both theory and policy has become recognized globally. We thank IAP for supporting the annual publication of books comprised of collections of the very finest scholarship in the field of middle grades education. The *MGRJ* Review Board has contributed untold hours evaluating manuscripts, and the Editorial Board has done likewise in addition to meeting semiannually to develop policy. Guest editors have done yeomen's work to effect very fine theme issues, and of course no journal could exist and no collection could be produced were it not for the contributions made by scores of researchers who have focused their agendas and studies on important middle grades issues. We thank you all!

"Using 'ESOL Rounds' to Prepare Middle Level Candidates for Work With English Language Learners" is an action research study conducted with pre-service interns by David Virtue, an assistant professor of middle level education at the University of South Carolina. Interns participated in "rounds" within middle school settings designed to encourage observation of ELLs in classrooms and during transitions to further their understanding of the learning needs of ELLs. Through guided inquiry, interns challenged their assumptions regarding students from diverse linguistic and cultural backgrounds, resulting in the perception among interns that the "rounds" model yielded positive learning outcomes.

This study from volume 4, number 1, provides a practical approach both to preparing future middle grades teachers for working effectively with children who are English Language Learners and for collecting useful information to address ELL instructional approaches for the "here and now" in middle grades classrooms. Action research of this nature continues to grow in popularity among middle school scholars. This study would be a welcome contribution to college textbooks that focus on middle grades teacher preparation.

In "Marginalization or Collaboration: First Year ESL Teachers and the Middle School Context," Courtney George, a recent graduate of the University of North Carolina at Chapel Hill's Culture, Curriculum, and Change program, presents the results of an ethnographic study that explored the first-year experiences of three middle school teachers working with ELLs in North Carolina. Issues of marginalization and collaboration with non-ELL teachers in the middle school context were illustrated through analysis of dialogue during new teacher meetings, and commonalities emerged between ELLs and their teachers, and their relationships and status within the larger middle school context.

Also from volume 4, number 1, George's inquiry is guided by a conceptual framework linking "Caring Theory," "Political and Ideological Clarity," and "Politically Situated Culturally Responsive Caring Theory," to create a culture of "Political and Ideological Clarity and Care." In sum, this framework leads to a practical conclusion: Teachers with expertise in ELL / ESL can and should collaborate with teachers lacking such expertise to meet an ever-growing demand created by a burgeoning number of ELL students in classrooms across the United States.

"The Impact of a Professional Development Program to Improve Urban Middle-Level English Language Learner Achievement" is a collaborative study conducted by Jennifer Friend of the University of Missouri-Kansas City; Ryan Most of the Kansas City, Kansas Public School District; and Kenneth McCrary of the Belton, Missouri School District that examined changes in teachers' perceptions regarding ELL instruction and the impact on ELL academic achievement. Data were gathered related to a professional development program designed to improve instruction for ELLs over a two-year period in two urban middle schools, with quantitative analysis of state reading and math assessment results for ELLs demonstrating significant results, and qualitative analysis of teacher surveys providing implications for professional development to improve instruction for ELLs.

This research team's mixed methods design included 70 teachers and 235 ELL students in two high-poverty, urban Kansas middle schools. Utilizing paired-samples t tests to examine the state's reading and mathematics assessments from 2006 and 2007, the researchers found that ELL student scores improved significantly over time. In tandem with their qualitative data the study led to the general conclusions that "improved instruction for ELLs includes the value of multiculturalism, the need for first language support, and the effectiveness of professional development." This study has the potential to guide practical applications in a variety of educational settings to support improvement of ELL students' state assessment scores and, thus, helping schools meet and exceed AYP requirements. It was originally published in volume 4, number 1, as well.

"Quantitative Reporting Practices in Middle-Grades Research Journals: Lessons to Learn" by Robert M. Capraro and Mary Margaret Capraro appears in volume 4, number 2, another special edition...to provide a baseline for quantitative reporting and facilitate the accumulation of knowledge across studies for those who depend on this research to build or improve middle-grades programs.

This brief treatise addresses various reporting strengths and weaknesses found in articles published in three middle grades journals: the *Middle Grades Research Journal, Middle School Journal,* and *Research in Middle Level Education.* The article is included, here, because it adds value to practical applications of research to middle grades settings. Specifically, because it is unrealistic to presume that all middle grades educators (educators at any level, for that matter) are expert consumers of research, it is incumbent upon the Academy or community of researchers in any specialized field or subspecialty area to ensure that what is reported meets expectations. Ergo, the authors target original, empirical quantitative studies published from spring 2006 to May 2009 to determine what types of statistics were used and what types of reporting standards were met. This is an important contribution to a field in need of empirical data to develop theory more precisely and guide practice more appropriately.

Recognizing that the t test is a common statistical approach for determining the significance of mean differences between two groups, Guili Zhang addresses its appropriate use, its shortcomings, and its deficiencies in another volume 4, number 2 articles titled "t Test: The Good, the Bad, the Ugly, & the Remedy." Because the t test is dependent on sample size, the research community generally agrees that effect sizes and confidence intervals should be used to support, supplement, and/or replace t-test results. Only then, argues Zhang, can we judge practical significance and draw inferences of value to educational research.

The application, here, is relevant to all research including the social sciences in which education is prominently featured. In tandem with the previous study, one can readily see that middle grades educational research should take note and address issues in more sophisticated ways. While the relative merits and usefulness of quantitative versus qualitative methodologies remains a subject of debate, it is hard to argue against more robust studies to inform middle grades practice. Hence, the need for all consumers of research to understand better the technical intricacies of statistical procedures such as the t test, effect sizes, and confidence intervals. Only then can educators make truly informed decisions, develop appropriate policies, and implement promising or "best" practices in middle grades classrooms.

Appearing in a third theme issue, volume 4, number 3, is "Effective Alternative Urban Middle Schools: Findings from Research on NativityMiguel Schools," research on the success of alternative programs in urban middle schools via the NativityMiguel model from leading alternative school and middle school researcher, Mickey Fenzel. These schools have utilized proven practices in serving students who are economically disadvantaged.

Poverty continues to be one of the most serious threats to our society and to our educational system, in particular. Few studies I have reviewed hold as much promise for helping young adolescent learners achieve academic success as this one. To understand the approach, one needs to read this article in context from beginning to end with no interruptions. After doing so, it should be evident that public, private, parochial, and charter schools have much to gain by applying many of the strategies discussed herein. Concerns and questions will always be a part of educational approaches; however, experimentation, innovation, and exploration (hall-marks of the middle school movement) can be expertly explored through careful examination of this very fine study.

Included in the discussion on alternative schools is research about juvenile justice schools by Cynthia Calderone, Susan Bennett, Susan Homan, Robert F. Dedrick, and Anne Chatfield. These authors examine reading interventions for students in six juvenile justice schools located in a large school district in Florida.

Again, just as the previous article demonstrates, much can be learned from scientific study of schooling in alternative settings; and much can be applied to public, private, parochial, and charter school settings in "Reaching the Hard to Reach: A Comparison of Two Reading Interventions With Incarcerated Youth." Specifically, here, the evidenced-based evaluation of a reading intervention program in Florida addresses a number of issues that impact teaching and learning in most every educational setting. Much can be learned both in terms of effective program evaluation and in terms of practical application to middle grades settings. Of value as well is the manner in which this study addresses young adolescent literacy issues that continue to be critical components associated with student success in middle grades schools. This article appeared first in volume 4, number 3.

I first began studying the relationship between middle grades organizational structures and student outcomes in 1988 while working as a Research Fellow at the University of California. While I expected to find that middle schools organized as 6-8 and/or 5-8 grade spans would be related to more positive student outcomes, i.e., higher academic achievement and attendance rates accompanied by lower incidents of behavior infractions, referral, and suspensions, for example, the data could not support such findings. In fact, data collected from 1988 to 1991 indicated that K-8 school organizational structures were associated with more positive student outcomes than the 6-8 middle school, 7-8/7-9 junior high school, or 7-12 middle-high school counterparts.

For those K-8, PK-8, and 1-8 schools that were implementing the so-called middle school "signature" practices at the highest levels, data indicated positive high relationships to higher academic achievement, better attendance rates, and fewer behavior incidents, referrals, and suspensions. I coined a new name for such schools—"Elemiddles"—and about ten years later with the passage of the No Child Left Behind (NCLB) legislation of 2001, public school systems across the United States began examining that research more carefully than ever before in efforts to meet AYP. This career-long research agenda now spanning two decades and growing daily as additional data are collected, has spawned a national movement that continues to gather momentum from coast to coast—

from Portland to New York City, from Los Angeles to Miami, and in the nation's mid-section in areas such as Kansas City, Cincinnati, Cleveland, and Minneapolis. Philadelphia's much publicized wholesale restructuring from 6-8 to K-8 schools is now complete and can be studied even more robustly, for example. Many other school districts across the country are also studying the feasibility of restructuring their grade span configurations to accommodate better the needs of young adolescents, where sudden "dips" in achievement have been made glaringly evident in 6-8 middle schools ever since systems began scrutinizing such data, per NCLB.

Published as an addendum to volume 4, number 3, "Findings From the First and Only National Database on Elemiddle and Middle Schools" is an executive summary from the most recent findings on a national level—the first ever data base of its kind that took two years to amass. Work continues en route to publication of findings as a number of preliminary reports have been issued over the past 5 years as new and additional data have been made available. Even in high poverty elemiddle schools, student achievement is significantly higher, attendance rates are better, and incidents of behavior problems are lower than in more affluent middle schools and junior highs. Parents are more engaged in their children's schooling, and the overall school climate is higher in elemiddle schools than in middle schools and junior highs. Most interesting, is the fact that more "signature" middle school practices are implemented at higher levels in elemiddle schools than in middle schools or junior highs. This latter finding begs the question, "why?" which is fodder for future study. At present, conventional wisdom holds a very simple conjecture: perhaps K-8 elemiddle schools, while generally smaller in size, foster a more nurturing, caring environment in which children feel safer and more secure as they cope with a very difficult stage of human growth and development known as young adolescence. Stay tuned.

"Impact of Environment-Based Teaching on Student Achievement: A Study of Washington State Middle Schools" is a correlational study of the relationship between environmental education programs and student achievement in mathematics and the language arts that was published in volume 4, number 4. Oksana Bartosh, University of British Columbia & the Pacific Education Institute, Olympia, Washington; Margaret Tudor and Lynn Ferguson, Pacific Education Institute; and Catherine Taylor, University of Washington; found that "providing a universal context for learning, environmental education could support schools' accountability efforts to integrate discipline standards and improve student performance." Their methods include two phases involving 77 pairs of schools in the former and 10 pairs in the latter. The bottom line for this fine bit of research is an affirmation of what many educators hold as conventional wisdom: teaching environmental education within the context of a middle grades curriculum helps young adolescent learners become more engaged in learning.

Six researchers contributed to the last study included in this book from volume 4, number 4. Christopher O. Walker, Tina D. Winn, Blakely N. Adams, Misty R. Shepard, Chelsea D. Huddleston, and Kayce L. Godwin, all from the University of Science & Arts of Oklahoma, Chickasha, Oklahoma. Their study of "Hope and Achievement Goals as Predictors of Student Behavior and Academic Achievement in a Rural Middle School" resulted in a couple of important, yet not unexpected findings: (1) student perceptions of available pathways were related to academic achievement, and (2) goals were predictive of behavior. This study of 314 rural middle grades students is precisely the type of inquiry that should be taking place across all middle grades schools to test other theories related to teaching, student demographics, and educational outcomes.

POSTSCRIPT

I trust readers will find practical application drawn from the research presented herein. It has been my privilege to be associated with the *Middle Grades Research Journal* as founding editor-in-chief since 2006. As I pass the baton to Dr. Vicki Schmitt, University of Alabama, she becomes the new editor-in-chief as of January 2010. I will remain on staff in an advisory role as founding editor. The future for *MGRJ* as the premiere outlet for the highest quality research on middle grades issues is, indeed, very bright; and I hope you join me in embracing the legacy that is being created.

David L. Hough
Founding Editor-in-Chief

ACKNOWLEDGMENT

This book is dedicated to Ms. Cassie Hanson who has worked for the Institute for School Improvement (ISI) at Missouri State University for 5 years. During that time she also served as the *Middle Grades Research Journal* Editorial Assistant since its inception in 2006. Cassie has worked diligently throughout our review processes to ensure contributing authors' manuscripts were handled with professional care, communicating with the *MGRJ* Editorial and Review Boards and working very closely with our editorial staff. In addition, Cassie has managed and coordinated the publication of the first 12 issues of *MGRJ*, contributed to the development of two books, and facilitated semiannual editorial board meetings. Throughout our transition to a new publisher and editor-in-chief, Cassie has provided expert assistance organizing files and maintaining the highest degree of integrity. Her future career in the field of human resources has been shaped, in part, by her work for ISI and *MGRJ*, but in a reciprocal manner her contributions to the field of middle grades educational research should be noted here. Thank you for your many years of service Ms. Cassie Hanson.

CHAPTER 1

USING "ESOL ROUNDS" TO PREPARE MIDDLE-LEVEL CANDIDATES FOR WORK WITH ENGLISH LANGUAGE LEARNERS

David C. Virtue

This chapter presents findings from an action research study that investigates the impact of an inquiry project designed to help better prepare preservice middle level teacher interns for their work with English language learners (ELLs). The inquiry project combined a "rounds" approach with ethnographic observation to help preservice interns see beneath the surface of school life and to better understand the kinds of multilayered transitions that middle level ELLs navigate on a daily basis. Three questions guide this ongoing action research project: (1) What do the interns tend to see and hear during the ESOL rounds experience? (2) What do the interns learn from or value in the ESOL rounds experience? and (3) In what ways can the ESOL rounds experience be improved? Data suggest that interns view the rounds inquiry project as a valuable learning experience; their assumptions about ELLs are challenged during the experience; they notice differences in behavior as ELLs transition from one class to another; and they tend to

Research Supporting Middle Grades Practice,
pp. 1–25
Copyright © 2010 by Information Age Publishing
All rights of reproduction in any form reserved.

focus on language use during their observations. Recommendations for implementing rounds in teacher education programs are provided, and further implications of this research for teacher education are discussed.

INTRODUCTION

Young adolescence is a time of intense and rapid transitions for all middle school students (Dryfoos, 1990; Santrock, 2005). These "transitional events" include the rapid physical, cognitive, and emotional changes associated with puberty; moves between schools (i.e., elementary, middle school, high school); dating; increased academic demands; and, in many cases, engagement in risk behaviors (Brooks-Gunn, 1988, p. 189). These transitions may be especially difficult for immigrant and refugee students who are learning a new language and culture while they are simultaneously expected to learn social studies, math, and science content and demonstrate progress on state assessments as required by the federal No Child Left Behind Act (Miller & Endo, 2004; Olsen, 1997; Pryor, 2001).

In addition to the academic learning that is required, many immigrant and refugee students must also learn "how to be American middle school students" as the school culture and academic norms in the United States may be quite different than in their country of origin (Valdés, 1998, p. 5). As Valdés (1998) observed in her case study of two Latina middle school students:

> They knew little about school spirit. They were not sure why being in band or in chorus or in the computer club might be important. They frequently confused teachers' friendly demeanor with permissiveness, and they quickly found themselves in trouble. They understood little of what went on around them and often they became discouraged and disinterested. (p. 5)

This passage highlights just a few aspects of a rigorous "hidden curriculum" that immigrant and refugee students must master as they transition into American middle schools (Jackson, 1968).

The number of English language learners (ELLs) in South Carolina, as elsewhere in the southeastern United States, is rapidly growing. The latest U.S. Census reports that the Hispanic population in the state grew by more than 200% during the 1990s. Moreover, school report card data from 2001 to 2007 reveal how the student populations in individual schools have been affected by this demographic shift. For example, at Northside Middle School in West Columbia the Hispanic student enrollment grew from 11 students in 2001 to 68 students in 2007. While the Hispanic population is the largest and most rapidly growing ethnic group in South Carolina, schools throughout the state have ELLs from diverse places including East Asia, Africa, and Central Europe.

Candidates in teacher education programs throughout South Carolina will likely teach some children who speak a language other than English at home. However, few programs leading to certification in English for Speakers of Other Languages (ESOL) exist in the state, and few opportunities exist for teacher candidates at all grade levels to get specialized preparation for working with ELLs. In many states experiencing rapid growth in ELL populations, ESOL is becoming the proverbial "elephant in the sitting room" as the need for services far outstrips the level of services government is willing or able to provide (see Colton, 2006; Santos, 2007). The situation is particularly acute in South Carolina, where ESOL can be considered an acronym for "the elephant sitting on our lap." As a middle level teacher educator in South Carolina working under these constraints, I have asked myself, *What can I do in my courses to better prepare preservice teachers for their work with English language learners in content area classrooms?*

The body of literature addressing the needs of ELLs in content area classrooms has expanded in recent years (e.g., Abrams & Ferguson, 2005; Anstrom, 1999; Carrier, 2005; Case & Obenchain, 2006; Hudelson, 2002; Reiss, 2005). However, this body of work, which emphasizes second language acquisition, tends to reduce the complex processes of acculturation and identity development to English language learning. In reality, classroom success for ELLs involves much more than English language acquisition. Educators must also address the social and psychological development of the student, while affirming and respecting his or her cultural background (see Virtue, 2007a).

In successful schools for young adolescents, "every student—no matter what creed, color, or uniqueness—serves as a genuine part of the community and contributes based on individual strengths" (National Middle School Association, 2003, p. 13). Exemplary middle schools educate the whole young adolescent child and address the academic, social, and psychological needs of every student. Such schools create structures to ensure that every student has at least one adult advocate who knows him or her very well, and they establish high expectations for every learner. Thus, schools that are implementing the design elements outlined in *Turning Points 2000* (Jackson & Davis, 2000) or the characteristics of successful schools for young adolescents described in *This We Believe* (National Middle School Association, 2003) should be places where ELLs will not "slip through the cracks." However, researchers have only begun to explore how specific middle school practices, such as teaming, help to create positive educational experiences for ELLs (see e.g., Brinegar, 2007). These relationships need to be explored and examined more closely.

To help pre-service middle level candidates better understand aspects of ELL education and how it connects with middle school culture and organization, I have developed an inquiry project in my social studies methods course that combines a "rounds" approach (Del Prete, 1997; Elmore, 2007; Thompson & Cooner, 2001) with ethnographic observation (Frank, 1999; Frank & Uy, 2004). My goal is to help the candidates see beneath the surface of school life and to better understand the kinds of multilayered transitions that middle level ELLs navigate on a daily basis. I believe that such an understanding may strengthen their commitment to social justice in the classroom, stimulate thought about effective and appropriate strategies for teaching ELLs in social studies classes, and provide a basis for bridging the cultural and linguistic differences they will likely encounter throughout their teaching careers. In this chapter I describe the ESOL Rounds project, and I discuss findings from my ongoing action research which seeks to understand the impact of the project and improve its effectiveness.

ESOL ROUNDS MODEL

The idea for "rounds" is based on the teaching model used in training hospitals whereby an intern works closely with a teaching physician as they visit patients and discuss their conditions and treatments on a case-by-case basis. This model has been adapted for use in pre-service and in-service teacher education (Del Prete, 1997; Elmore, 2007; Powell & Napoliello, 2005; Thompson & Cooner, 2001), and it has been implemented successfully at the University of South Carolina in our teacher education programs (Zenger, 2003).

Del Prete (1997) identified three components of a rounds approach to teacher education—orientation, observation, and reflection. The rounds group first has an orientation to a classroom activity or instructional strategy that they will observe in the host teacher's classroom. Next, the group engages in a focused observation of the activity or strategy, or the group members may participate in the activity in some clearly defined way. Finally, the rounds group meets with the host teacher and the university supervisor to reflect upon and discuss the activity or instructional strategy.

The rounds approach offers several key benefits. It provides learning experiences for participants that are embedded in the context of the classroom, and it is these shared classroom experiences that serve as the basis for reflective dialogue (Del Prete, 1997). The model brings together the diverse perspectives of university faculty, pre-service teacher candidates, and practitioners during the reflection process, which is crucial as observers will often see different things and arrive at different interpretations of the phenomena under investigation (Powell & Napoliello, 2005). By helping to bridge gaps between these multiple perspectives, the rounds approach also provides a type of superstructure that allows us to "expand the discussion of best practices across the isolation of (existing) school structures" (Thompson & Cooner, 2001, p. 87).

When implemented in educational settings, rounds typically focus attention on an instructional strategy, learning activity, or classroom management technique. However, my version of the model focused inquiry on interactions between individual students, their teachers, and classroom cultures. The cultural focus for the project meant that an ethnographic perspective had to be integrated throughout. Also, because we were interested in the transitions students make as they move from one milieu to another (e.g., classroom, hallway), my version of rounds involved focused observations of ELLs in multiple settings, including a regular content area classroom and an ESOL classroom (see Virtue 2005, 2007b).

Orientation Phase

The rounds model begins with an orientation to the observation experience (Del Prete, 1997). Because our observations would focus on cultural phenomena involving ELLs in classroom settings, my goal during this phase was to introduce my class to the concept of ethnographic observation. Together we read a selection from *Body Ritual Among the Nacirema* by Horace Miner (1956), a classic in cultural anthropology in which the author described seemingly exotic rituals of the Nacirema people. My students were surprised when they learned that "Nacirema" is "American" spelled backwards, and the strange rituals described by Miner are actually everyday activities like shaving and brushing teeth. My purpose was twofold: I wanted to provide the class with a model for ethnographic writing, and I wanted to illustrate how an ethnographic perspective brings to light cultural patterns that may be implicit, taken-for-granted, and sometimes invisible.

Next we read a selection from the book *Ethnographic Eyes: A Teacher's Guide to Classroom Observations* in which the author distinguishes between "note taking" and "note making" (Frank, 1999, pp. 9–14). Note taking is the process through which an ethnographer records what he/she sees. The observer attempts to create a narrative snapshot of the setting, events, and other classroom phenomena. In contrast, note making is the process through which the observer records his/her interpretations of what he/she sees and hears, or writes memos that raise questions about the observation or help to guide the process of thinking about the phenomena being observed.

A key issue to consider during the orientation phase is the extent to which the observation should be structured. Borich (1994) argues that observation is a systematic process that is defined by "the structure the observer brings to the observation" (p. 28). However, too much structure or too narrow a focus may restrict opportunities for discovery and may close doors to inquiry. I chose to provide a loose structure for the practice observations that included rules and guidelines for the process of conducting an ethnographic observation; specification of the settings and students under investigation; and a rigid timeframe for the observation, which was bounded by our regular class meeting time of three hours. I chose not to specify the kinds of behaviors or interactions to observe, as I wanted each intern to identify salient phenomena from her own perspective. However, I did give them a simple observation protocol (see Appendix A) to provide a structure for the practice observations, as recommended by Elmore (2007).

I asked the interns to practice their observation skills for 10 or 15 minutes in a public place, and to practice "note taking" and "note making" as we discussed in class (see Appendix A). Because our class met only once a week, I asked the interns to post the notes they "took" and the notes they "made" on our online discussion board, and to respond thoughtfully to each other's observations. This public discussion of the observations was vital, as it gave me an opportunity to assess the interns' emerging understandings of ethnographic observation and to guide or redirect the discussion as needed. It was especially important to show the interns how their biases and value judgments were affecting their "note taking."

The practice observations were conducted in diverse settings including stores, restaurants, and settings on campus. For example, two interns in the 2006 group observed a dining hall on campus and discovered a social space that may mean different things to different people—a place to be seen (or not seen), a place to meet friends, a place to study or get work done, or maybe just a place to grab a quick bite of food.

Observation Phase

The observations were planned collaboratively with an ESOL teacher, who provided schedule information and helped secure permission from the content area teachers. Because the ESOL teacher changed schools in 2006, the 2005 rounds were conducted at a different middle school than the 2006 and 2007 rounds. The ESOL rounds were a required experience for the course "Methods and Materials for Teaching Social Studies in the Middle School," so they had to be conducted within the three-hour timeframe for the regular weekly class meeting. In addition, they had to be held within a block of time on a day that was suitable for all of the interns and teachers involved. The general schedule for the ESOL rounds observations was as follows.

7:15: Meet in the middle school lobby and sign in
7:25: Proceed to the ESOL classroom
7:40–8:50: Observe the first period ESOL class
8:50–8:55: Shadow students to second period content classes
8:55–9:55: Observe the second period content classes
9:55–10:00: Return to the ESOL classroom
10:00–10:15: Debriefing in the ESOL classroom
10:15: Return to campus

On observation day we met at the school, obtained visitor passes, and then proceeded together to the ESOL classroom where we joined the teacher and her students. We observed the activities and interactions in the ESOL classroom using the same protocols we used during the practice observation (see Appendix A). After ESOL class, the interns—individually or in pairs—shadowed one of the ESOL students as he or she traveled from ESOL to a content area class. The six interns in the 2005 rounds group were put in pairs and sent to three different social studies classes, while the eight interns who participated in each of the 2006 and 2007 ESOL rounds groups observed math, science, and social studies classes.

While the interns are only expected to remain in the role of passive observer during the rounds experience, they frequently interacted with the students and teachers. In fact, several interns have recommended ways to make the ESOL rounds more interactive, which I will discuss below. My goal is to optimize the learning experience for my interns while causing minimal interruptions to the instructional environments in the ESOL and content area classrooms.

Debriefing/Reflecting Phase

An essential component of the rounds model is a debriefing phase during which the observers can ask questions that have arisen during the observations (Del Prete, 1997). After observing the students and teachers during their ESOL and content area classes, we met in the ESOL classroom for a debriefing session during which interns were able to ask the ESOL teacher questions. Later, the interns discussed their observation notes online using the class discussion board. The interns also completed a feedback form (Appendix B), which is being used throughout the College of Education to collect data on the rounds model, and they wrote journal reflections in response to the following prompt:

> Last week you engaged in an ESOL rounds observation experience. For some of you, this may have been your only chance to see English language learners in a classroom setting before you graduate. Write a thoughtful reflection (up to a page or more) in which you a) discuss the value in participating in this experience; b) suggest other kinds of classroom settings or student populations that would be worthwhile to observe, possibly before you graduate; and c) recommend ways to improve this learning experience.

The Debriefing/Reflecting Phase is the phase during which I collect data for my ongoing action research project, as comments on the discussion board, the responses to the feedback form, and the written reflections have been the main data sources. In the next section I discuss key findings from my analysis of the 2005, 2006, and 2007 data sets.

METHODOLOGY

My study is an example of action research (Arhar, Holly, & Kasten, 2001; Tomal, 2003), an approach to practitioner research that has been increasingly used in the field of middle level education (see e.g., Caskey, 2005). Suter (2006) defines action research as "research conducted by ... educational practitioners for the specific purpose of solving a local problem or gathering information so as to make better decisions" (p. 153). My action research project was designed to help improve the ESOL rounds experience and, ultimately, to help the middle level program better prepare teachers for their work in culturally and linguistically diverse classrooms.

Three questions guide this ongoing action research project:

1. What do the interns tend to see and hear during the ESOL rounds experience?
2. What do the interns learn from or value in the ESOL rounds experience?
3. In what ways can the ESOL rounds experience be improved?

Twenty-two preservice candidates have participated in ESOL rounds—six in 2005, eight in 2006, and eight in 2007. The ESOL rounds experience is a part of the course "Methods and Materials for Teaching Social Studies in the Middle School," which middle level candidates seeking certification in social studies take during their final year of study. Another culminating learning experience for all candidates in the middle level program is participation in internships; thus I refer to them as "interns" throughout this chapter. Data for my study included my field notes and copies of intern observation protocols completed during the rounds observations (see Appendix A), online discussions of the rounds observations that occurred after the rounds experience, completed rounds feedback forms (Appendix B), and journal reflections written by the interns.

Data Analysis

I employed a qualitative data analysis sequence adapted from Miles and Huberman (1994). Each of the three research questions for the study served as "sensitizing concepts" that I converted to code labels—RQ1, RQ2, and RQ3 (Patton, 1990). I engaged in two levels of coding during each iteration of the analysis procedure. During the first level of coding, the code labels were applied directly to the analytically meaningful units within the data either in the margins or on tabs or notes attached to the page (Patton, 1990). During the second level of coding I employed the technique of "pattern coding," in which I grouped units of data identified in first-level coding into subsets based on emerging themes (Miles & Huberman, 1994). Gaps, inconsistencies, and unanswered questions guided subsequent rounds of data analysis, and I repeated or reiterated this process until the conclusions were conceptually dense and additional analysis yielded no new insights (Strauss & Corbin, 1998).

My study has limitations often associated with qualitative action research. As a single researcher conducting an analysis of qualitative data, I had to ensure the trustworthiness of my interpretations (Denzin & Lincoln, 1998). To strengthen the trustworthiness of my study, I corroborated multiple forms of evidence produced by each intern and I triangulated perspectives by analyzing sets of evidence holistically across multiple interns (Creswell, 1998; Stake, 1998). As is often the case with action research, the findings cannot be generalized to other settings (Tomal, 2003). This is consistent with the purpose of my study, which is to generate local, context-specific knowledge to improve the ESOL rounds project.

RESEARCH FINDINGS AND DISCUSSION

The presentation and discussion of my findings is framed by the three guiding questions for my research:

- What do the interns tend to see and hear during the ESOL rounds experience?
- What do the interns learn from or value in the ESOL rounds experience?
- In what ways can the ESOL rounds experience be improved?

What Did the Interns Tend to See and Hear During the ESOL Rounds Experience?

Based on their comments during the debriefing session and their journal entries, some of the interns seemed to pay close attention to the extent to which the ELLs used English and the fluency with which they spoke the language:

- I found these students to have a good grasp of spoken English; however, they have issues when it comes to reading and writing in English. (T.N., 2005)
- From what I could tell [the ELL] spoke fluent English. It really did not seem as though he had a hard time with instructions or interaction with the rest of the class. (N.B., 2005)
- When they were in their regular classroom it was very hard to pick out that they were ESOL students ... they had a very light accent from what I could tell in the classroom and they also were very chatty. (K.C., 2005)
- The students seemed to speak fluently in English. (L.C., 2006)
- Very confident in speaking English. (B.H., 2006)

Given the focus on ELLs in an ESOL setting, it is not surprising that some of the interns found language use to be noteworthy. Due to scheduling constraints, the interns spent most of their time with advanced ELLs, and only the 2006 and 2007 groups spent any time with beginner-level ELLs. Thus, it is also not surprising that many interns found the ELLs to be more fluent in English than they may have expected.

Many interns made inferences about the academic ability of ELL students. In their journal entries, the interns described the ELLs as "intelligent" or "very intelligent," "bright," and "capable." Several interns also commented on the work habits they observed, referring to the ELLs as "hard workers," "eager participants," and "eager to learn." The interns appeared to recognize that ELL students may be very bright, capable students who may struggle with the English language and, as a result, academic content presented in English. As one intern asserted, "Any student that is not a native of the United States and does not speak the language will encounter problems academically, but may be very smart" (L.C., 2006).

All three rounds groups saw how the ESOL teacher built community in her classroom. Interns described the ESOL classroom environment as "vibrant and alive," "comfortable," "very relaxed," and "supportive and engaging." Student work was prominently displayed inside the room, instilling a sense of belonging and ownership for the place, and relationships between the teacher and the students seemed positive, as noted in the following comments:

- I see the [ELLs] in an environment that is very comfortable for them. (M.B., 2005)
- It is evident that there is a good relationship between the teacher and students as everyone appeared to be comfortable inside the classroom setting. (D.D., 2006)
- [The ESOL teacher] seemed to have a great relationship with every student [and] students seemed to have respect for the teacher. (M.C., 2006)
- They seemed really comfortable with the teacher. (B.H., 2006)
- [She] seemed like a great teacher who cared about her students. (A.P., 2007)

While most of the interns noted the positive relationships between the teacher and her students, several also commented on the nature of the relationships between the students in the class. For example, one wrote, "There was a comfort zone between the students" (B.H., 2006), and another similarly observed, "Students in the ESL classroom were very comfortable with each other" (L.C., 2006). One observer reflected, "[ESOL] students seemed to have respect for one another," (M.C., 2006).

Most of the interns commented on the ESOL teacher, noting her instructional approach and classroom management strategies. One 2005 intern summarized the instruction she observed in the following way:

She used many activities so that the students had little time to spend off task.... Her approach was more personal and conversational. The teacher directed the class up front. She didn't lecture though. She gave students many different activities to stay engaged. (N.A., 2005)

A key feature of instruction in the ESOL class was student talk—lots of student talk. As one intern observed, "Students were outgoing and talkative in the ESOL class" (R.B., 2007). Some interns seemed to realize the

importance of student talk in an ESOL classroom, as evident in the following journal entries.

- The teacher seems to recognize the importance of frequent speech
  and written language practice. (N.A., 2005)
- I learned the absolute imperativeness of making the classroom a
  safe place in which students can excel and ask questions. (T.C.,
  2005)

However, other interns seemed to struggle with the level of student talk in
the classroom. While they may have viewed it as something important to
ESOL instruction, they also viewed student talk as something to be controlled or "managed."

- Students were a bit talkative without any consequence. (K.C., 2005)
- [The ESOL teacher] had an interesting management style. She
  seemed to allow the students to freely communicate without being
  punished. (D.D., 2006)
- [The ESOL teacher] created a community environment where the
  students were not afraid to make comments, talk in their native language, or talk to others. (T.W., 2006)

These interns were accustomed to classrooms in which students should
be "afraid" to talk or where they could be "punished" for talking. The academic norm evident in many middle school classrooms—that students
should be silent until spoken to—did not apply in the ESOL classes we
observed.

The interns observed differences in ELL student behavior as the students transitioned from ESOL class to their content area classes. In many
cases, the interns expected to witness behavioral changes in the ELL students, and these expectations were evident in the journal entries.

- In my perception, the students would be very quiet and keep to themselves in the regular classroom, then, suddenly blossom into talkative
  and outgoing students in the ESOL classroom. (T.N., 2005)
- I expected to see a dramatic difference. I expected him to be quiet
  in the social studies class. (L.C., 2006)
- I expected the students to be conservative in the social studies class.
  (B.H., 2006)

As illustrated in the comments above, the interns expected the ELLs to
be quieter or more reserved in the content classes than in the ESOL class.

In most cases, these expectations were confirmed. In their journals entries, the interns wrote about differences they observed in both student behavior and the overall classroom environments.

- The differences in environment and student action in the ESOL class and their content class were not hard to see. The students were talkative and confident when working with others like themselves. In the content class I observed, the student was silent. There were no accommodations for this student in the content class. (T.W., 2006)
- The overall environment of the two classrooms was totally different. (D.K., 2006)
- It was interesting to see the ESOL students in two completely different settings. Several of the students were outgoing and talkative in the ESOL class, where they are obviously comfortable. In other settings, these same students were quiet. (R.B., 2007)

In some cases, interns offered hypotheses to explain the behaviors they observed. For instance, one intern observed a student who was "the life of the classroom" in the ESOL class, but "quiet" in science class. The intern surmised that, "Her comfort level with either science or the other students may not be very good at this point in the school year" (A.P., 2007). Another intern wrote:

> [The ELL] is certainly a bright girl who remains on task in class. She might be quieter due to some anxiety of speaking English in front of others. However, without further observation I think it would be hard to tell if she was naturally shy or quiet because of the setting change. She seemed willing to answer any of my questions, and was pretty descriptive as she spoke to me (she told me how she felt about her science teacher, and she explained why we had to wait outside the door of the portable.) I think it would be interesting to further investigate this girl just to see if she's quiet out of shyness or obedience/respect. (S.H., 2006)

In the latter example, the intern offers several possible explanations for the ELL's change in demeanor, including "the setting change," "shyness," or "obedience/respect." Instead of jumping to a conclusion about the girl's behavior, the intern recognizes that her interpretations of the student's behavior are tentative (e.g., "might be ... due to," "hard to tell"). This is the kind of thinking I am trying to promote through the ESOL rounds activity.

Most of the interns noted differences in student behavior across the classroom contexts observed; however, a few did not. One intern thought it was "odd that the students' personalities did not change" between the two class environments. She further noted that "many of the [ELL] students seemed to blend well with their classmates" (T.N., 2005). Another intern reported: "The student that I observed and follow was great in both classes. He fit in well and seemed just as comfortable in the classroom" (L.C., 2006).

What Do the Interns Learn From or Value in the ESOL Rounds Experience?

Every intern who participated in the ESOL rounds shared positive comments about the experience. One intern wrote: "This visit was more influential to how I view teaching than any other practicum or visit" (T.W., 2006). Another commented, "This outing really meant a lot to me and is influencing the way I view teaching" (S.H., 2006). Adjectives frequently used to describe the experience included "interesting," "valuable," "enjoyable," "inspiring," "eye-opening," "beneficial," and "great."

Many interns valued the experience because it "familiarized [them] with a setting with which [they] had no prior experience" (D.K., 2006). They either "do not ever see ESOL students at [their] internship school" (T.N., 2005), or they simply "have never seen ESOL students in ESOL class" (K.C., 2005).

Even for interns who had seen or worked with ELLs, the rounds experience was valuable because it allowed them to consider the issue in another context. One intern who had ELLs in her internship classroom commented, "It is important for us to see how different school districts handle this situation and how the ESOL students interact with each other in a separate setting" (N.B., 2005). Another intern was disappointed in the way ELLs were treated in her practicum placement, and she was concerned that her experience there might be typical. She was glad to learn that effective ESOL programs existed in the area. She wrote, "I have...since realized this issue is on the school and district level. For me, that was the greatest benefit" (N.A., 2005).

Consistent with the College of Education mission statement, the middle level program at USC strives to prepare teachers "to have a sincere understanding and appreciation of diversity as we challenge ourselves and others to work for social justice." The interns displayed dispositions related to diversity and social justice in several ways. In their journal entries, they often expressed positive attitudes toward ELL students and ESOL programs. Such attitudes were evident in the following comments:

I could not imagine being in middle school and trying to learn another language. I have nothing but respect for these students. (L.H., 2007)

- I now have more respect for the ESOL teachers. (A.P., 2007BB)
- The ESOL class gives [the ELL student] opportunities in learning not found in her regular content classes. (T.W., 2006)
- I think this student is greatly benefiting from the ESOL program. (L.C., 2006)
- This type of program is essential. (J.L., 2007)

The interns also exhibited dispositions related to diversity and social justice when they reflected upon their roles as teachers and their responsibility as teachers to teach every student, including ELLs. As one intern wrote, "We will have students...with vast cultural or language differences," and "[it] is up to us to break down those barriers and connect to our students" (E.A., 2007). Other examples of journal entries expressing this idea are as follows:

- [ESOL rounds] showed me that I, as a teacher, need to make sure that I'm trying my hardest to keep the ESOL students involved in the lesson. (K.C., 2005)
- It is the teacher's responsibility to make sure every student is learning. This includes students who are facing a language barrier. I think the resources are out there, we will just have to reach out to get the information. (RB, 2007BB)
- Working with the ESOL teachers is something that I look forward to. It's good to know there's a resource out there regarding this area of teaching. (S.H., 2007)

The comments above suggest that the interns are beginning to appreciate the importance of collaboration and relationship building among teachers in order to meet the needs of ELLs. During the debriefing session, interns always ask the ESOL teacher about her relationships with other teachers and teams of teachers in the building, and they learn that the nature of these relationships tends to vary from teacher to teacher or team to team. Importantly, these interns now recognize that the ESOL teacher can be a valuable instructional resource for other teachers in the school. As he reflected upon the debriefing session, one intern wrote, "when deliberating between job placements" he would consider "the consistent presence of ESOL instructors within the school because, as we observed, their contributions are vital" (S.W., 2007).

Several interns expressed positive dispositions toward diversity when they expressed an interest in pursuing certification in ESOL. For example, one intern reflected, "Going to see this program made me think that this may be something that I would be interested in down the road" (J.L.,

2007). Another wrote, "It made me think about maybe one day teaching an ESOL classroom" (L.H., 2007). An intern in the 2006 ESOL rounds group elaborated more deeply upon her reasons for considering ESOL certification:

> This experience meant a lot to me, because I'm considering attending graduate school to become ESOL certified. I think if I taught ESOL students I would really feel like I'm making a difference in helping students transition into their life as middle schoolers, Americans, and responsible young adults. (S.H., 2006)

In addition to enhancing their awareness of and attitudes toward ESOL students, teachers, and programs, the ESOL rounds experience also helped interns develop observation skills that may help them in the future as reflective practitioners or teacher-researchers. One intern indicated that, "It was important…to look at the [ELL] students through an unbiased perspective and to be able to understand what they are going through" (L.H., 2007). Another valued "being able to… observe people in an objective way." He continued:

> Seeing the difference between note-taking and note-making was good to give us some guide when we have to make observations in the field. I'm looking forward to when we actually get to go into the classroom and practice our observation skills. (S.H., 2007)

Another intern found value in having a purpose and clear focus for the ESOL rounds observation. She contrasted this experience with observations that were a part of her earlier practicum experiences:

> While in the education program at USC, I have been into many classrooms to observe. However, often I was placed into these classrooms with little indication of what I was observing exactly. It would have been more helpful and a more effective use of my time if we had been given certain topics to observe or been given some advice on how to take notes. Now I know what to look for when observing in a classroom. However, at the beginning of my experience as an education major, I did not know. (T.N., 2005)

In the next section, I discuss some specific recommendations for improving or expanding the use of rounds in pre-service programs.

In What Ways Can the ESOL Rounds Experience Be Improved?

The interns offered recommendations for improving the rounds experience. Feedback generally clustered around two themes: "time" and "interaction." In terms of time, many interns called for "more time spent observing the students in their ESOL classroom and in their general education classes" (N.B., 2005). Some were very specific in their comments, recommending a full day or multiple day visits.

- Time was a set back. I recommend a two day assignment. (M.C., 2006)
- Observe them the entire day. (T.W., 2006)
- Not a one day visit but a two month long or even a semester long visit … about once or twice a week. (M.B., 2005)

Other recommendations were more general, calling for "more time observing," more time going "from class to class," or more time to "shadow other groups."

Many interns wanted the ESOL rounds experience to be more interactive. They would have liked more interaction with individual students, and several suggested ways to enhance the debriefing sessions that followed the observations:

- I would also have enjoyed having more time to talk individually with the students to see how they liked their classes and life in the United States. It would have been interesting to ask questions about their educational experiences in their native countries compared to those in America. (D.K., 2006)
- Have individual interviews or a discussion panel with the students. (N.B., 2005)
- A discussion between us, the pre-service teachers, and the ESOL students would have helped make the experience more meaningful. By having this type of discussion we would have the chance to ask important questions to the students as well as gain knowledge of what they needed in the classroom to be able to learn well. (K.C., 2005)

The interns recommended numerous sites for future rounds activities. These included an alternative school, a charter school, or multiple school sites—possibly juxtaposing "a thriving school and a struggling school" (N.B., 2005). They also recommended conducting observations of effective teachers. One intern thought "it would be beneficial to take students to see a first-year teacher's classroom [because] all of the classrooms I have observed have had teachers who have been teaching for at least a few years" (T.N., 2005). Many interns recommended conducting rounds focused on various programs within schools, such as other ESOL classes, fine arts or technology-based magnet programs, and single-gender programs, which are becoming increasingly popular in South Carolina. The most frequent recommendation from all three groups of interns was to conduct rounds focused on "special education classes," "inclusion classes," or students with "special needs."

CONCLUSIONS AND IMPLICATIONS

The ESOL Rounds project has several implications for teacher education that are worth noting. First, the project illustrated how a rounds approach and ethnographic observation may be integrated with pre-service field experiences in order to help interns see beneath the surface of daily life in schools so as to better meet the needs of all students in their classrooms. While my focus has been ELLs in middle school settings, teacher educators can employ the ethnographic rounds model to give teacher candidates meaningful learning experiences with diverse students in a variety of settings.

A second set of implications involves the structure and organization of the rounds experience. I cannot overemphasize the importance of having observation protocols for my interns to use in the field and allowing them to practice using the protocols in advance. While it takes a considerable amount of time to do this, it is well worth the effort to help pre-service teachers sharpen their skills of observation and "kidwatching" (Frank, 1999; Frank & Uy, 2004; Goodman, 1985). In addition, it would be impossible to organize a project like this without support from inside the school. The teachers at the school where I conduct rounds graciously welcome my interns into their classrooms, and some of them provide logistical assistance as I arrange the schedule for the observations.

Finally, the ethnographic rounds model has implications for the continuing education of in-service teachers (see e.g., Elmore, 2007). Schools can, for example, identify exemplary teachers of ELLs in the content areas and provide release time during the day for other teachers to observe and debrief with them. This can be a cost-effective way for schools to engage teachers in meaningful staff development while also strengthening the learning community within the school.

Through the ESOL Rounds experience, my interns and I were able to witness how some middle level ELLs navigate the multilayered transitions that define their daily lives in school. We learned that students who appeared to lack confidence, motivation, and communication skills in a content area classroom might exhibit those qualities and skills in a safe ESOL learning community, and we saw how the ESOL teacher built such a community in her classroom. We also learned that ELL students who demonstrate a high level of English language fluency may have less obvious needs for support in order to help prevent them from slipping through the cracks.

This project has been a valuable learning experience for my pre-service middle level social studies candidates and for me. The feedback I receive is always positive, and candidates always have excellent suggestions about alternative settings for rounds experiences, such as self-contained special education classes and high-needs school settings. As the population of immigrant and refugee students in our schools grows, we will need to develop more and more ways to prepare our candidates to effectively teach these unique learners. ESOL rounds is one step in that direction. I hope to continue to develop this idea, to continue providing experiences that help students to sharpen and focus their "ethnographic eyes," and to develop effective and appropriate strategies for supporting English language learners in middle school classrooms.

APPENDIX A

Practice Observation

In the book *Ethnographic Eyes: A Teacher's Guide to Classroom Observations*, Carolyn Frank distinguishes between Note Taking and Note Making. Note Taking is the process through which an observer records what he/she sees. In a way, the observer attempts to create a narrative snapshot of the setting, events, and other classroom phenomena. In contrast, Note Making is the process through which the observer records his/her interpretations of what he/she sees and hears, or he/she writes memos that raise questions about the observation or help to guide the process of thinking about the phenomena being observed.

Your mission is to go to a social space where you can "hang out" for an hour and observe. You may choose from:

- Russell House dining hall
- Bookstore café in Russell House
- Cool Beans
- Thomas Cooper library
- Immaculate Consumption

Situate yourself in the place and observe. What do you see? What does it mean? What are people doing? What are they *not* doing? Why are they doing what they do? Are there observable patterns to people's behavior?

What are the "unwritten rules" that govern these behaviors? What do these places *mean* to the people who use them, and how do you know?

Record your thoughts on the EDML563 Observation Protocol™ attached to this page. Write descriptive notes in the left column and write analytical notes in the right column. Also, create a map of the physical setting on the grid provided.

When you finish your observation (after about an hour), go to a computer at home, in the library, or in Wardlaw and post a discussion of what you saw and what it meant on Blackboard.

EDML 563: ESOL Rounds Observation Protocol

Date: _____   Teacher: _____

Time: _____   School: _____

NOTE TAKING *(Description: What do I see?)*	*NOTE MAKING* *(Interpretation: What does it mean?)*

EDML 563: ESOL Rounds Observation Protocol

Date: _____   Teacher: _____

Time: _____   School: _____

Physical Setting Map:

APPENDIX B

ESOL Rounds Feedback

1. What was the topic (objective) of the lesson being taught?

    Content:

    ESOL:

2. What did you notice about classroom management and the structure of the lesson that might facilitate instruction? Was there any noticeable compensation for children that might have special needs?

3. What questions/comments/concerns do you have for the teacher regarding the lesson, classroom management and/or the teaching strategy you observed?

4. What impressed you the most during this lesson?

5. Do you think the idea of rounds is a good idea in the internship?

    a. Should rounds (or something similar) be incorporated into the internship?

    b. Please give your feedback to help us refine the use of rounds for future interns.

REFERENCES

Abrams, J., & Ferguson, J. (2005). Teaching students from many nations. *Educational Leadership, 62*(4), 64–67.

Anstrom, K. (1999, June). *Preparing secondary education teachers to work with English language learners: Social studies.* Washington, DC: Center for the Study of Language and Education at the Graduate School of Education & Human Development, George Washington University.

Arhar, J. M., Holly, M. L., & Kasten, W. C. (2001). *Action research for teachers: Traveling the yellow brick road.* Columbus, OH: Merrill.

Borich, G.D. (1994). *Observation skills for effective teaching.* New York, NY: Mac-Millan.

Brinegar, K. (2007, April). "America is confusing": The schooling experiences of young adolescent immigrant and refugee students in one small town. Paper presented at the annual meeting of the American Educational Research Association, Chicago, IL.

Brooks-Gunn, J. (1988). Transition to early adolescence. In M. Gunnar & W. A. Collins (Eds.), *Development during transition to adolescence: Minnesota symposia on child psychology* (Vol. 21, pp. 189–208). Hillsdale, NJ: Erlbaum.

Carrier, K. A. (2005). Key issues for teaching English language learners in academic classrooms. *Middle School Journal, 37*(2), 4–9.

Case, R., & Obenchain, K. M. (2006). How to assess language in the social studies classroom. *Social Studies, 97*(1), 41–48.

Caskey, M. M. (Ed.). (2005). *Making a difference: Action research in middle level education.* Charlotte, NC: Information Age.

Colton, T. (2006). *Lost in translation.* New York, NY: Center for an Urban Future.

Creswell, J. W. (1998). *Qualitative inquiry and research design: Choosing among five traditions.* Thousand Oaks, CA: Sage.

Del Prete, T. (1997). The "rounds" model of professional development. *From the Inside, Fall*(1), 72–75.

Denzin, N. K., & Lincoln, Y. S. (1998). Introduction: Entering the field of qualitative research. In N. K. Denzin & Y. S. Lincoln (Eds.), *Strategies of qualitative inquiry* (pp. 1–34). Thousand Oaks, CA: Sage.

Dryfoos, J. G. (1990). *Adolescents at risk: Prevalence and prevention.* New York, NY: Oxford University Press.

Elmore, R. (2007). Professional networks and school improvement. *School Administrator, 64*(4), 20–24.

Frank, C. (1999). *Ethnographic Eyes: A Teacher's Guide to Classroom Observation.* Portsmouth, NH: Heinemann.

Frank, C. R., & Uy, F. L. (2004). Ethnography for teacher education. *Journal of Teacher Education, 55*(3), 269–283.

Goodman, Y. (1985). Kidwatching: Observing children in the classroom. In A. Jaggar & M. T. Smith-Burke (Eds.), *Observing the language learner* (pp. 9–18). Newark, DE: International Reading Association.

Hudelson, S. (2002). 'Teaching' English through content-area activities. In V. Zamel & R. Spack (Eds.), *Enriching ESOL pedagogy: Readings and activities for engagement, reflection, and inquiry* (pp. 319–329). Mahwah, NJ: Erlbaum.

Jackson, A. W., & Davis, G. A. (2000). *Turning Points 2000: Educating adolescents in the 21st century.* New York, NY: Teacher's College Press.

Jackson, P. W. (1968). *Life in classrooms.* New York, NY: Holt, Rinehart and Winston.

Miller, P. C., & Endo, H. (2004). Understanding and meeting the needs of ESL students. *Phi Delta Kappan 85*(10), 786–791.

Miner, H. (1956). Body ritual among the Nacirema. *American Anthropologist, 58*(3). Retrieved from http://www.msu.edu/~jdowell/miner.html

Miles, M. B., & Huberman, A. M. (1994). *Qualitative data analysis: An expanded sourcebook* (2nd ed.). Thousand Oaks, CA: Sage.

National Middle School Association. (2003). *This we believe: Successful schools for young adolescents.* Westerville, OH: Author.

Olsen, L. (1997). *Made in America: Immigrant students in our public schools.* New York, NY: The New Press.

Patton, M.Q. (1990). *Qualitative evaluation and research methods.* Newbury Park, CA: Sage.

Powell, W., & Napoliello, S. (2005). Using observation to improve instruction. *Educational Leadership, 62*(5), 52–55.

Pryor, C. B. (2001). New immigrants and refugees in American schools. *Childhood Education, 77*(5), 275–283.

Reiss, J. (2005). *ESOL strategies for teaching content : facilitating instruction for English language learners.* Upper Saddle River, NJ: Pearson.

Santos, F. (2007, February 27). Demand for English lessons outstrips supply. *New York Times,* p. A1.

Santrock, J. W. (2005). *Adolescence* (10th ed.). New York, NY: McGraw-Hill.

Stake, R. E. (1998). Case studies. In N. K. Denzin & Y. S. Lincoln (Eds.), *Strategies of qualitative inquiry* (pp. 86–109). Thousand Oaks, CA: Sage.

Strauss, A., & Corbin, J. (1998). Grounded theory methodology: An overview. In N. K. Denzin & Y. S. Lincoln (Eds.), *Strategies of qualitative inquiry* (pp. 158–183). Thousand Oaks, CA: Sage.

Suter, W. N. (2006). *Introduction to educational research: A critical thinking approach.* Thousand Oaks, CA: Sage.

Thompson, S., & Cooner, D. D. (2001). Grand rounds: Not just for doctors. *Action in Teacher Education, 23*(3), 84–88.

Tomal, D. R. (2003). *Action research for educators.* Lanham, MD: Scarecrow Press.

Valdés, G. (1998). The world outside and inside schools: Language and immigrant children. *Educational Researcher, 27*(6), 4–18.

Virtue, D. C. (2005). A visit to ESOL Island: Notes on a shadowing experience with middle level English language learners in South Carolina. *South Carolina Middle School Journal, 13*(1), 42-44.

Virtue, D. C. (2007a). A glimpse into the school lives of young adolescent immigrant and refugee students: Implications for the middle level. In S. B. Mertens, V. A. Anfara, & M. M. Caskey (Eds.), *The young adolescent and the middle school* (pp. 237–254). Charlotte, NC: Information Age.

Virtue, D. C. (2007b). ESOL Rounds: An inquiry approach to preparing qualified and culturally competent teachers for South Carolina's classrooms. *Teacher*

Education Journal of South Carolina, 2006–2007 Edition, pp. 1–6. Retrieved from http://www.hehd.clemson.edu/schoolofed/scate/docs/journal/virtue.pdf

Zenger, J. F. (2003). USC "Rounds": Enhancing the clinical experience fall 2002-spring 2003. *Teacher Quality Collaborative*. Retrieved from http://tqc.ed.sc.edu/year4rounds/rounds.html

CHAPTER 2

MARGINALIZATION OR COLLABORATION

First Year ESL Teachers and the Middle School Context

Courtney George

This study emerged out of a year-long narrative ethnography that investigated the first year of ESL teachers. It describes key personal, contextual, and structural factors that influenced the teachers' professional beliefs and practices. The focus of this study centers on the conversations of three middle school ESL teachers during new teacher support group meetings that were held as part of the research design. During these meetings, the teachers articulated their understandings of the unique position they inhabited in middle schools as teachers of culturally and linguistically diverse youth. Their interest in topics such as marginalization, school relationships, and the status of ESL teachers were important narrative threads. In addition, their experiences and thoughts on collaborating with mainstream middle school teachers emerged as an important theme. In the context of this particular North Carolina school system, these ESL teachers were marginalized experts, and collaboration within mainstream classrooms illuminated the status of the ESL teachers and their students in the two middle schools

Research Supporting Middle Grades Practice,
pp. 27–53
Copyright © 2010 by Information Age Publishing
All rights of reproduction in any form reserved.

where they worked. While this study highlights the experiences of first-year ESL teachers and their students, the lessons learned apply to all middle school teachers who are working with culturally and linguistically diverse youth and their ESL teachers.

INTRODUCTION

Throughout the country, classrooms are becoming more culturally and linguistically diverse while teachers remain overwhelmingly white, middle-class, monolingual speakers of English (Bartolomé & Trueba, 2002; Gay & Kirkland, 2003; Howard, 1999). According to National Center for Educational Statistics (NCES), the population of students of color reached 42.9% in 2004–2005 while white teachers made up 83.7% of the teaching force in 2003–2004 (NCES, 2007a, 2007b). This is of particular importance in a state such as North Carolina, where the number of students officially designated as limited English proficient grew by over 600% between 1992 and 2002 (U.S. Department of Education, 2002). Demographics are shifting across the country as new migration patterns fundamentally change our schools nationwide (Suárez-Orozco, 2001; Suárez-Orozco & Páez, 2002). It is clear that we must work to diversify our teaching force to better represent students from diverse backgrounds (Howard, 1999; Suranna, 2003), but we must also better prepare all teachers to work with today's students—and increasingly, language minority students. When we consider the shifting demographics occurring in our nation's schools, both the research and teacher education agendas need to work to better understand and prepare teachers for this "new mainstream" (Gibbons, 2002; Villalva, 2008).

This year-long ethnographic study used the theoretical orientation of political and ideological clarity and care—a conceptual framework that combines Nel Noddings' (1984) notions of caring theory with political and ideological clarity (Bartolomé & Trueba, 2001)—to investigate the critical first year of ESL teachers to describe key personal, contextual, and structural factors that influenced their professional beliefs and practices. The focus of this work centers on the conversations of three middle school ESL teachers during new teacher support group meetings that were held as part of the research design. During these meetings, the teachers articulated their understandings of the unique position they inhabited in middle schools as teachers of culturally and linguistically diverse youth. Their interest in topics such as marginalization, school relationships, and the status of ESL teachers were important narrative threads. In addition, their experiences and thoughts on collaborating (or co-teaching) with mainstream middle school teachers emerged as an important theme. In the context of this particular North Carolina school system, these ESL teachers were marginalized experts, and collaboration within mainstream classrooms illuminated the status of the ESL teachers and their students in the two middle schools where they worked. While this study centers on the experiences of first-year ESL teachers and their students, the lessons learned also, in important ways, apply to all middle school teachers who are working with culturally and linguistically diverse youth and their ESL teachers.

LITERATURE REVIEW AND CONCEPTUAL FRAMEWORK

Critical multicultural education (Banks & McGee Banks, 2001, Freire, 1997; 2004; Kubota, 2004; Ladson-Billings, 2004; McLaren & Munoz, 2000; Nieto, 1994, 1995, 2004; Sleeter, 1996; Sleeter & Delgado Bernal, 2004; Sleeter & McLauren, 1995), second language acquisition theory (Baker, 2000; Cummins, 1993; Hawkins, 2004; Kubota, 2004; Minami & Ovando, 2004), and political and ideological clarity and care (Bartolomé & Trueba, 2001; Gay, 2000; Noddings, 1984; Thompson, 1998; Valenzuela, 1999) grounded the larger study from which this article emerged. These literatures and theories will be briefly addressed, but due to the focus of this article, the first-year teacher literature (Bullough, 1989, 1990; Bullough, Knowles, & Crow, 1991; Deal & Chatman, 1989; Grossman, 1990; Herbert &Worthy, 2001; Renard, 2003; Veenman, 1984), including studies on new teacher support groups (Harris, 1995; Hollingsworth, 1992; Rogers & Babinski, 2002), will be discussed in greater detail.

Critical Multicultural Education

Multicultural education grew out of the sociopolitical context of the 1960s social protest movement "as a scholarly and activist movement to transform schools and their contexts" (Sleeter & Delgado Bernal, 2004, p. 240). However, much of multicultural education as redefined and enacted today fails to address power and racism explicitly or critically. For the purpose of this chapter, I will use the work of Sleeter and McLaren (1995) to define critical multicultural education. They write that critical multicultural education links multicultural theory and critical pedagogy in a way that "seeks to construct counter hegemonic pedagogies, oppositional identity formations, and social policies that refuse, resist, and transform existing structures of domination primarily in school sites but also in other cultural sites within North American geopolitical arena" (Sleeter & McLaren, 1995, pp. 28).

This definition of critical multicultural education takes into account the criticisms of liberal and conservative multiculturalism and the work of scholars such as Nieto (1995), Ladson-Billings (2004), Kubota (2004), Banks and Banks (2004), and McLaren and Munoz (2000) that connect multicultural theory and critical pedagogy. Other authors such as Cummins (1993) and Kubota (2004) have brought a similar conceptualization of critical multicultural education to the context of second-language classrooms. Kubota (2004) argues that critical multicultural education has an important place in second-language classrooms, but she problematizes the assumption that second-language learning and second-language teachers are inherently multiculturalist. Cummins (1980, 1986, 1993, 1995) recommends that schools value the educational and personal experiences students bring with them to school, understand the process of language acquisition in order to provide effective language and content instruction, respect and continue to support students' first languages, and seek a collaborative relationship with parents and community leaders. Drawing more directly from critical pedagogy and critical multicultural education, the work of Cummins (1993) and Kubota (2004) make even more explicit the connections between second language acquisition theory (SLA) and multicultural education.

Culture and Language—Second Language Acquisition Theory

Scholars have written about the interconnected nature of culture and language, as well as identity, ideology, and critical pedagogy. Sleeter and Delgado Bernal (2004) write, "Identity, values, experiences, interpretations, and ideologies are encoded linguistically; one knows the world and oneself through language" (p. 244). As Sleeter and Delgado Bernal (2004) assert, these issues resonate with ESL and bilingual educators who are aware of the political and ideological nature of working with culturally and linguistically diverse students and families. However, SLA theory often fails to take these issues of power, identity, culture, and ideology into account. Hawkins (2004) writes about the shortcomings of traditional SLA research. She argues that the research has carried with it assumptions that have had a significant effect on how we think about language and language learning today. This narrowly focused SLA research has generally come out of the fields of formal linguistics and cognitive psychology (Chomsky, 1998; early Cummins, 1980; Hakuta, 1986; Krashen, 1994) and has focused on the mental processes of individual learning.

Recent SLA scholars (Auerbach, 1995; Baker, 2000; Corson, 1993; Cummins, 1993; Hawkins, 2004; Norton Pierce, 1995) have begun to challenge and complicate this body of literature by examining language and language acquisition by providing an analysis of identity, culture, context, politics, ideology, and power. Hawkins (2004) suggests approaching issues of language learning from a variety of perspectives and disciplines. Norton Peirce (1995) argues that SLA researchers need a more comprehensive theory that will allow research to take into account the relationship between the learner and the social world as well as relations of power. In viewing social identities as multiple, changing, co-constructed, and contested, Norton Pierce creates a new and rich way to think about language learning and the context in which such learning takes place.

Conceptualizing Political and Ideological Clarity and Care

Both critical multicultural education and recent conceptualizations of SLA theory emphasize a need for political and ideological clarity, the first part of the conceptual framework for this study. Political and ideological clarity requires that teachers acknowledge their own political and cultural assumptions by explicitly and systematically addressing issues of difference (Bartolomé & Trueba, 2001; Expósito & Favela, 2003; Howard, 1999; Rolón-Dow, 2005; Thompson, 1998; Valenzuela, 1999). This can help teachers avoid deficit ideologies and perspectives that often result in "subtractive" teaching practices that are the norm in many of our schools today (Valenzuela, 1999).

The second part of the study's theoretical framework involves political and ideological care. This part of the framework is grounded in caring theory as conceptualized by Nel Noddings (1984, 1992, 1998). Her theory of care is built upon "natural" notions of feminine nurturing and care to establish an ethic of care to be used in education (Figure 2.1) Her theory challenges the traditional "masculine" approach to educational structures that rely on hierarchy, separation, specialty, objectification, and the loss of relation in educational institutions focused on testing, sorting, labeling, and credentialing. In the era of No Child Left Behind, this caring perspective is of particular importance as even greater emphasis is placed on standardized testing (Goertz & Duffy, 2003).

Scholars such as Valenzuela (1999), Thompson (1998), Rolón-Dow (2005), and Gay (2000) have extended Noddings' caring theory to explicitly address issues of race, class, and power. These authors argue that if a teacher truly and authentically cares for her students, then she must work against the subtractive curriculum out of a genuine respect for a student's cultural integrity (Thompson, 1998). Gay (2000) writes that caring theory is one of the pillars of culturally responsive pedagogy and therefore, if a

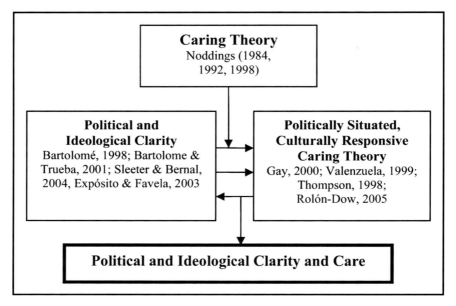

Figure 2.1.   Conceptual framework.

teacher is caring, then she must be culturally responsive. Thompson (1998), Valenzuela (1999), and Rolón-Dow (2005) argue that for teachers to care for their culturally and linguistically diverse students, they cannot pretend to be color-blind. Instead, they must attempt to learn, understand, and know their students' historical, political, and personal situations. They must reject the assimilationist and deficit ideologies that oppress students and find ways to teach students and teachers to work for social justice and societal change. This kind of caring theory is authentic, politically situated, and culturally responsive.

Political and ideological clarity and care bring all of these literatures and theories together to form a comprehensive and complex lens through which to conduct and analyze educational research. In bringing these ideas together, a theoretical orientation is created that both heightens the importance of language, culture, and power in today's schools, and grounds the work in a feminist, ideological, and caring perspective that respects the experience and perspective of teachers.

While this conceptual framework places significant importance on the individual beliefs of teachers, it is situated historically and politically, thus allowing larger, structural issues—like social, economic, and racist structures as well as institutional structures such as bureaucratic functions within schools including enrollment policies, scheduling, assignment of teachers, or disciplinary actions—to be included in the orientation to and analysis of classrooms. This ideological, caring, and politically situated view of schools listens to the voices of teachers and attempts to understand their beliefs and actions in relationship to the complex and changing environment in which they live and work (Coble, 2006; Gitlin, 1990; Hawkins, 2004). It is from this theoretical orientation and through the lens of middle school ESL teachers that the first-year teacher literature, first-year teacher support groups, and ultimately collaboration are examined in this article.

First-Year Teacher Literature

Past first-year teacher studies have rarely addressed issues of language and culture explicitly, but the first year has been well documented by researchers using a variety of theoretical perspectives (Bullough, 1989, 1990; Bullough et al, 1991; Deal & Chatman, 1989; Grossman, 1990; Harris, 1995; Herbert & Worthy, 2001; Hollingsworth, 1992; Renard, 2003; Rogers & Babinski, 2002; Veenman, 1984). In general, the first year of teaching is described in the literature as being difficult, frustrating, isolating, and disorientating for new teachers. For a variety of reasons (organizational, administrative, interpersonal), schools generally fail to support new teachers. First-year teachers often get difficult class assignments, a schedule that provides little time for planning or reflection, and little or no mentoring (Herbert & Worthy, 2001).

Studies focused on second and foreign language teachers are far less frequently documented in the first-year teacher literature (Richards, 1998). This lack of studies focusing on first-year teachers working with culturally and linguistically diverse students is obvious and problematic. There is a need to explore the first year of ESL teachers working with language minority students as well as mainstream teachers working with diverse learners—soon to be the majority in American classrooms (Kasarda & Johnson, 2006; Murdock, 2006). While there is little research to cite, first-year ESL teachers, like all teachers, must grapple with the challenges and problems described above. In addition, there are a number of other unique demands that ESL teachers must face. They must have the professional knowledge required to teach English grammar and academic English, but they are also called upon to advocate for equitable treatment of ESL students in the mainstream classroom and to serve as cultural brokers, community liaisons, and educators of mainstream teachers (Ovando, Combs, & Collier, 2006).

Due to these demands, ESL can easily become highly subtractive (Valenzuela, 1999) if new teachers, in the survival stage of development

(Veenman, 1984), can only manage to teach English language lessons at the expense of the native language and culture of their students (Valenzuela, 1999; Valdés, 1996). At the same time, there is also great potential in this first year when teachers are forming their initial identities as educators (Danielewicz, 2001). Providing support for new teachers, especially teachers working with culturally and linguistically diverse youth, is of great importance, considering the changing demographics in America's classrooms. What becomes clear is that a pre-service teacher education program could never fully prepare novice ESL teachers for the complex and demanding contexts in which they will teach. The requisite professional knowledge and self-reflection demand continued support after graduation.

More specifically, some studies have explored ways to continue the support and the professional development of new teachers in the first year. These studies include research on support groups (Harris, 1995; Hollingsworth, 1992; Rogers & Babinski, 2002), mentoring programs (Feiman-Nemser, Carver, Schwille, & Yusko, 1999; Montgomery, 1999) and administrative support (Renard, 2003). Of particular interest for this study is the research on new teacher support groups because this literature addresses the complex needs of new teachers and seeks meaningful ways for teacher educators to continue to support students after graduation. While teacher educators cannot control on-site mentors or administrative support for new teachers after graduation, they can provide opportunities for new teachers to meet with other novice teachers and supportive university mentors for collaborative conversations.

Positioning Language and Culture in Today's Classrooms

Drawing from all of these literatures and theoretical orientations and carrying these perspectives into the classroom and into a new teacher support group allowed this research to position language and culture within today's teaching context from the lived experiences of middle school ESL teachers. Classrooms are complex and changing, and therefore, our theoretical approach to educational research must reflect this diversity and respect those who work within these institutions on a daily basis. The theoretical framework for this research study attempts to consider the expertise developing in a variety of fields to find a conceptual perspective that can address the challenges in all of their complexity and through the stories of middle school teachers working with culturally, economically, and linguistically diverse students. This framework takes into account the ideological and political nature of teaching and learning and attempts to address these issues of politics and power through a politically situated, culturally responsive, and caring theory.

METHODS

This year-long qualitative research study focused on the experiences of four first-year ESL teachers (three middle school teachers and one elementary teacher) in a suburban North Carolina school system where the language minority student population is growing rapidly. While most of the data were collected between July 2005 to June of 2006, a pilot study the previous year (while the teachers were participating in their teacher training program) and follow-up during the fall of their second year of teaching also informed and provided context for the research. An important priority of the research was to use narrative inquiry and reflexive ethnography to build ethical, caring, and reciprocal research relationships in the field. In addition, the methods of this study were informed by the desire to highlight language and culture as well as the narratives and voices of teachers.

Narrative Inquiry

Narrative inquiry is grounded in Dewey's view that experience is central and continuous to learning and Vygotsky's theory that exchange and learning take place between the personal and the social (Clandinin & Connelly, 2000; Rushton, 2004). In addition, narrative inquiry pays close attention to the context in which narratives are lived out. These are the three dimensions of narrative inquiry: (1) the continuity of time (past, present, and future), (2) the interaction between the personal and the social, and (3) the context of place. Narrative inquiry allows the researcher to embrace the complexity of the teaching and learning context and to use the stories of teachers, students, and the researcher to capture, through narratives, the personal and social experiences of education.

One of the most appealing aspects of narrative inquiry is its collaborative and caring approach to research "participants." While all research is plagued by unequal power relations, the goal of narrative inquiry is to build caring, intimate, and trusting research relationships. This approach allows the researcher to become invested in the lives of the participants in a way that complicates the process but makes it richer with meaning. This caring approach to research allows a feminist ethic of collaboration and care to take priority (Hollingsworth, 1992; Noddings, 1984, 1992).

Embracing such an approach requires wakefulness and a feminist ethic of care and collaboration. While narrative inquiry does not provide a specific recipe for doing this work, it does provide an interesting set of ideas that each researcher must make their own. Of primary importance in this study were narrative inquiry's (1) ability to work within the complexity of the teaching context (taking into account time, interaction, and place) and (2) prioritization of reciprocity and a feminist ethic of research relationships.

Reflexive Ethnography

Narrative inquiry as conceptualized by Clandinin and Connelly (2000) is a reflective and an ethical approach to educational research. It does not provide a specific recipe of methodology, but instead orients a researcher to the field in a particular way. They write, "We keep in the foreground of our writing a narrative view of experience, with the participants' and researchers' narratives of experience situated and lived out on storied landscapes as our theoretical methodological frame" (2000, p. 128). However, aspects of the work closely resemble reflexive ethnography as conceptualized by Davies (1999), such as the focus on ethical research relationships and the importance of contextualizing research in time and place.

A narrative approach with reflexive ethnography as an important aspect of its methodology is a powerful and compelling lens through which to conduct educational research. Reflexive ethnography is aligned well with narrative inquiry in a number of important ways. Davies (1999) takes into account the implications of postmodernist and post-colonialist critiques. She argues that reflexivity, a process of self-reference, is a possible way to address these critiques while avoiding both self-absorption and solipsism. She writes, "I consider the implications of various postmodernist critiques for the practice of ethnographic research and suggest an epistemological perspective from which we can carry on social research while continuing to benefit from the sensitivity to issues of reflexivity and the general self-critique of the recent past" (Davies, 1999, p. 6).

Reflexive ethnography provides an important orientation to the research as well as methodological tools with which to gather and analyze data. Davies (1999) describes methods such as participant observation, formal and informal ethnographic interviews, and biography and autobiography though the lens of wakefulness and reflexivity. This methodological approach provides the tools necessary to gather the authentic and meaningful narratives of the classroom. Narrative inquiry was used to guide and shape this study in order to capture both the individual and social stories that make up the rich expressions of the teachers' beliefs and classroom practices (Clandinin & Connelly, 2000).

Positionality

As a narrative inquirer, it was important to explore my own narrative thread running through this research project. In past projects, it has been important to explore my own story because my experience was vastly different from the participants I was attempting to understand through my research. With this project, I discovered that, due to the many similarities I shared with the research participants, I had to even more thoroughly revisit my own storyline in order to better understand my reactions to and interpretations of their experiences. Like the women participating in this research project, I am a white, middle-class woman. I was an ESL teacher for four years in western North Carolina. I have known the teachers participating in this research study since July of 2004 and I have worked with them throughout their teacher education program as an instructor, teaching assistant, and student-teacher supervisor and mentor. I have had to work to understand the impact this shared history has had on the research encounter.

Research Sites and Participants

The ESL teachers were selected because of their participation in a local university's ESL teacher education program that emphasized social justice and equity in education. There were six women and one man in the ESL cohort selected, and all were invited to participate in the study (see Table 2.1). Four teachers agreed to participate and also expressed a desire to continue their education as first-year teachers through the support of a new teacher group. All of the participating teachers were white, middle-class females, and their ages ranged from early 20s to early 40s. The three middle school teachers spoke (to varying degrees) a second language. Each of the teachers happened to secure employment upon graduation in the same school system, yet each worked in unique contexts, including different grade levels, ESL program models, and student demographics. The names of all teachers and schools have been replaced with pseudonyms to protect their identities (note: Lynda was the fourth research participant who taught at the elementary level).

Data Collection

Between July of 2005 and June of 2006, ten new teacher meetings were held during the research period. These focus groups took place in a teacher's classroom or at a local coffee shop and lasted one to two hours

Table 2.1.   Sites and Focal Participants

SAUNDERS MIDDLE SCHOOL	PINE MIDDLE SCHOOL
2 full time ESL teachers	1 full time and 1 part time ESL teachers
700 students (18% Asian, 10% Latino, 17% Black, 50% White)	650 students (14% Asian, 6% Latino, 14% Black, 60% White)
SARAH • Early 20s, working knowledge of Spanish and Farsi, North Carolina native • Classes Taught: 2 ESL classes (6th grade and 8th grade); 3 collaborative Language Arts classes	**KELLY** (full time): • Early 40s, Bilingual French and English, not a North Carolina native • Classes Taught: 4 ESL classes (beginning/intermediate); 1 sheltered instruction social studies class
	REBECCA (part time): • Early 20s, working knowledge of Polish, not a North Carolina native • Classes Taught: 6th grade beginning ESL; Collaborative Science class

each. The teachers were asked to bring stories, resources, ideas, and challenges to these meetings to share with the group. In addition, a brief, semi-structured interview protocol was used at the beginning of each meeting, and the teachers were asked to write a written reflection at the end. The rest of the time the teachers directed the conversation about their most pressing needs. These conversations were tape-recorded and later transcribed. These meetings provided important data through the stories and voices of teachers. The meetings were also one important way the research attempted to reciprocate and contribute to the teachers and their students.

In addition to the monthly meetings, at least one individual formal interview (lasting between one and two hours) was conducted with each teacher. These interviews were tape-recorded and later transcribed. The interview protocol consisted of four general topics (oral history/background, decision to teach ESL, current teaching context, and feeling about participating in the research project), and the teachers took these interviews in a variety of directions due to the open-ended nature of the interview questions.

During the data collection, over 50 classroom observations and/or informal interviews were also conducted. While one day-long observation with each teacher took place, the majority of observations lasted between one or two class periods (50 minutes to two hours), with an informal interview taking place before or after the classes (10 to 30 minutes). Some of these observations were conducted from the back of the classroom while taking detailed notes, but the majority of observations included my direct participation with the teachers and students as I assisted in the classroom however the teacher requested.

When I was directly participating in the classroom, I would take a step back from time to time to record notes and tape-recorded my observations immediately after leaving the field. These recordings would then be transcribed and written into field notes. At least once per month, I spent time in each teacher's classroom, but if the teachers requested it, I would spend more time in classrooms. These classroom visits and observations were extremely important methodologically. While previous studies have used new teacher support groups to collect data (Harris, 1995; Hollingsworth, 1992; Rogers & Babinski, 2002), these studies have not followed the teachers into their classrooms to both corroborate and inform the researchers' understandings of teachers' beliefs and practice. These visits also provided important data and information about the school context and climate; teachers' perspectives on their practice; and the lives, beliefs, and actions of students.

Analysis

In terms of analysis, narrative inquiry was instrumental in informing my approach because it acknowledges the complex nature of the research encounter. Close attention was paid to the three-dimensional inquiry space by collecting past, present, and future narrative threads. The continuity of time was used as a way to organize and analyze the data and to avoid the ethnographic present (Clandinin & Connelly, 2000; Davies, 1999). Personal and social stories of the participants and the larger community were taken into account in order to tease out the multiple and interconnected nature of these narratives. Analysis relied on both micro and macro lenses in order to describe the individual and community voices and to present the personal and social experiences that impacted the teaching and learning context (Clandinin & Connelly, 2000). In addition, place played an important role not only in collecting data, but also in its analysis. Context played an important role in the narratives collected. Analysis addressed the individual classroom, the school, the community, as well as the larger political and social climate in which the research took place.

Field reports were written throughout the data collection period to systematically look at the study's progress and consider future plans for the inquiry (Glesne, 1998). Trustworthiness of this inquiry was established through a prolonged engagement in the field, persistent observation in multiple contexts, constant reflection as a researcher, and member checking (Davies, 1999; Glesne, 1998). While informal analysis was an ongoing part of this qualitative inquiry, a more formal and concentrated period of analysis began once the data collection phase ended (Davies, 1999; Glesne, 1998).

Once the data were collected, all transcriptions were finished and the data were organized chronologically, by teacher, and into an initial set of categories (beliefs, practice, context, challenges) so that relevant data were accessible and any emerging themes or theories could be tested and refined with supporting arguments and interpretations from the data (Davies, 1999). During a second pass through the data, formal coding began and new themes began to emerge. Some of these initial themes were arrived at deductively through lenses of the literature and conceptual framework to interpret and understand the narratives (care, culturally responsive teaching, family, funds of knowledge, new teacher support group, parents, planning, race, racism, school climate, teacher beliefs, time, and time management). Other categories were discovered inductively through the review and comparison of the teachers' experiences as captured in the data (collaboration, discipline, expert/expertise, immigration, Korean and Latino students, marginalization, mainstreaming, mentors, professional development, relationships, school administration, school structure, space, Spanish, student-centeredness).

As codes and themes emerged, all theories were retested for negative case examples (Glesne, 1998). During this process, the limitations of an initial focus on the individual beliefs of new teachers emerged. The role school structures and bureaucracies played—both overtly and covertly—in the lives of the teachers and their students became clear. With this new lens through which to analyze the data, a refinement of codes and themes created a more concrete understanding of the story of these teachers and their context. In addition, member checking was utilized to ensure that my assumptions, perspective, and subjectivities were countered by another's understanding and interpretation of the story.

Analysis continued throughout the writing process, and the selection of quotes to include in the manuscript was a final aspect of formal analysis. Once the initial themes were laid out and corroborated through member checking, the selection of representative quotes provided another opportunity to check and double check interpretations. Quotes were filed under each theme and this provided an opportunity to review, compare, confirm, and reject interpretations. I was able to quantify, in a sense, the strength of my analysis as I counted, charted, and selected quotes that best told the story.

While a major goal was to fill a gap in the research literature by focusing on the first year of ESL teachers, I was also committed to finding ways to reciprocate as a researcher and former teacher. One way this was accomplished was through the formation of the new teacher support group. These two aspects of the research were greatly influenced by the study's conceptual framework—political and ideological clarity and care. This conceptual and theoretical perspective helped me understand both the need to fill the language and culture gap in the first year teacher literature, and orient the research, analysis, and writing in an ethical, situated, and caring manner. In this way, political and ideological clarity and care helped conceptualize and ground every aspect of the research encounter.

MARGINALIZATION OR COLLABORATION

The major findings of this study began to emerge even during the first two or three new teacher support group meetings. The teachers' interest in topics such as marginalization, collaboration, school relationships, and the status of ESL teachers became clear and important narrative threads. These themes continued to dominate our conversations and they told important stories about the unique position of first-year ESL teachers in their schools and orientations to the field. These stories provide important information for ESL teacher educators, but they also provide insights for mainstream middle school teachers and middle grades researchers. These educators and researchers are beginning to understand the need to work effectively with both English language learners in their classrooms as well as the ESL specialists in their schools.

Teacher-Generated Themes

The Unique Perspective and Marginalized Spaces of ESL
It became clear during our conversations and interviews that the teachers positioned themselves uniquely as ESL teachers. Part of this orientation or identity as ESL teachers seemed to stem from an understanding of themselves as teachers and advocates and from their ESL-specific role in classrooms. While all of the teachers spoke to this theme frequently during the study, Sarah best articulated this point in a December interview:

> CG: Do you see ESL as being similar to or different from other teaching jobs ... or somewhere in-between?
>
> Sarah: It is hugely different.... I wish we had training in counseling because I feel like I am half counselor, half teacher, and half advocate...and there is only one of me! ESL is very different. The PARS teacher [the district hired, full-time support person

for new teachers] was saying that I see things from the side instead of from the front of the classroom and that this is why I am able to connect with students. I'm actually paying attention to what they are learning as opposed to, "What is my lesson today … you're not getting my lesson…why aren't you doing it my way?" I really appreciate that and I really am glad that I went into ESL for that reason because it is a whole different side of teaching. That makes me even more aware … even in my own teaching. I stop and make sure everyone gets it…. I see that in a lot of core classes—the teachers don't take this time. One kid is sleeping, another is writing a note, another is drawing…. It's hard for the person at the front to see any of that. [Interview, 12/14/05]

While many mainstream teachers do a lot of teaching, counseling, and advocacy work, Sarah points out how the position and perspective of an ESL teacher is unique. In seeing a classroom from the side (both literally when standing in the back of a mainstream classroom and figuratively when focusing on the individual needs of her students), the perspective is different and one's motivations and actions in the school are different as a result. I do not want to argue here that mainstream teachers do not want to have this view of their classrooms or students, but the pressures and structures of their job are different and position them at the front of the room. They must teach a large number of students a set curriculum. They do not have the built-in flexibility of an ESL teacher or the experience of watching classrooms from the side or back of the room. What became apparent in talking with the middle school ESL teachers was the fact that the mainstream teachers' status at the front of the room often marginalized not only certain students, but the ESL teachers as well. Sarah best described this occurrence in a group meeting:

As far as who feels included, that is a different thing. On the surface, you have the differentiated classes and everybody is all together…but I feel like a lot of my kids are included in a lot of things but only on the surface. Even in my collaborative classes I'm supposed to be in there and we are supposed to be working together, but I feel like I end up just working with my kids in the corner, either literally or figuratively. [Focus group, 10/24/05]

This idea of a marginalized ESL space—of being in the corner—came up a number of times. The most illustrative discussion of this issue was raised in the September group meeting when we were setting up our next meeting. We had decided to meet in Kelly's classroom at Pine Middle school and she was giving directions to her room:

Kelly: My classroom is in 025. The 0 means it's in the dungeon.
Lynda: Oh yeah, I'm in the basement too.
Sarah: Well, I'm in the closet... and I have to share it.
Kelly: And Rebecca's office is her car! [Focus group, 9/30/05]

While they all had relatively nice rooms, their descriptions of their locations say a lot. Kelly found some benefit of being tucked away in that she was able to do her work without interruption of passersby, and Rebecca found that the drive from one school to the next gave her a taste of the world outside of school. She said, "I get in my car, drink a Diet Coke, and listen to NPR or some music ... for those ten minutes, I get to be a regular person" (Focus group, 11/1/05). Sarah however, was frustrated by her small, closet-like office that she shared with five specialist teachers. The fact that the content teachers she worked with assumed she had a classroom of her own, "a home base," just made her feel even more marginalized in her school. Interestingly, her awareness of her unique perspective and marginalized space seemed to tie her even more closely to her students and to other marginalized students in the school:

It is funny because I have just become aware of how the main homeroom teacher is up in the front of the room with the "good" kids and I always go immediately to the back of the room with all the misfits...because they are the ones I see he isn't paying any attention to.... [T]hat's where the ESL kids are, the ones who get sent to the break room, the ones who are behaviorally/ emotionally disabled. I guess I always automatically gravitated toward them, but now that I'm aware of it, I do it on purpose. [Interview, 12/14/05]

This combination of the unique perspective and marginalized spaces occupied by the first year ESL teachers colored their perspective of their schools, students, and other teachers.

Relationships with Other Teachers

While the ESL teachers collaborated and got along with mainstream teachers to varying degrees, they rarely identified with those classroom teachers. Instead, they seemed to build relationships with other educators in their schools such as social workers, counselors, specialist teachers, and other ESL teachers who were not considered to be mainstream teachers. In field notes from March 23rd, I wrote:

S is not building relationships with the teachers she is collaborating with, but she is building relationships with the counselor, social worker, and special education teacher. She said those teachers can really "look at the individual student instead of grades or the whole class or the curriculum." She said that they relate because they care about these students and talk about them and see them as individuals and not just as problems. As a teacher she said she feels "totally marginalized" and that she has this status as "not a real teacher" because she works with "small groups of marginalized kids." K has also expressed some of these thoughts too. I know she has talked about becoming good friends with the counselor at her school. She initially spent a lot of time with her dealing with a situation with one particular student, but now she talks with this teacher just about every day. She also considers Rebecca's presence each day to be "a lifesaver."

This relationship building with other educators was most striking in the narratives of Sarah and Kelly, but Rebecca also struggled some with her relationships with mainstream teachers. Rebecca was most likely to go to weekly social gatherings with her teaching colleagues.

It is very important not to misrepresent these complex issues as an "us versus them" dichotomy between specialist educators and mainstream middle school teachers. While the ESL teachers were often frustrated by the treatment their students received in many of the mainstream classrooms or by their own status in those classrooms, they understood the challenges those teachers faced. My field notes and transcripts clearly show that Sarah and Kelly were very sympathetic to the demands put on mainstream teachers. Sarah stated in a February interview:

> As an outsider it is easy to say that [content teachers] are lazy or horrible people, but the more I'm in it, the more I realize that they are doing it to cope and survive. Sometimes you get to the point where you cannot handle one more email or phone call or ... one more student ruining class. At the same time, I have a lot of favorite students and I have a really hard time seeing what happens to them and I feel like I can't even say much about it because I don't want to jeopardize my relationship with that teacher. The relationships with teachers has turned out to be one of the hardest things. [Interview, 2/20/06]

She was understanding of the plight of the content teachers, but loyal to her own students at the same time. She realized that the same structures that got in the way of many mainstream teachers effectively working with her English language learners were the same structures that made it difficult for her to work effectively with the core teachers. These relationships and structures seemed to be highlighted by the school's use of collaboration.

Collaboration

Research shows that co-teaching and collaboration between mainstream classroom and special education teachers can be extremely effective models to better educate students with special needs (Bear & Proctor, 1990; Klingner, Vaughn, & Schumm, 1998; Marston, 1996; Odom et al., 2005; Patriarca & Lamb, 1994; Schulte, Osborne, & McKinney, 1990). There are a number of ways these collaborative teaching relationships are structured and negotiated. In a truly collaborative teaching situation, both teachers would share planning and instructional responsibilities equally. A more common implementation of collaborative teaching results in the specialist teacher tutoring a small group of students within the classroom context.

It is important to note that while collaboration is widely implemented for English language learners, no research has been conducted to support the assumption that these practices are beneficial for students acquiring English in the mainstream classroom. In addition, Magiera and Zigmond (2005) point out that the benefits of these co-teaching arrangements seem to be dependent upon "optimal teaching conditions" where the involved teachers have been trained in co-teaching/collaboration and when the teachers are provided co-planning time. Collaboration, as experienced by the three first-year middle school ESL teachers, corroborates this finding when applied to the ESL context.

All four of the first-year ESL teachers collaborated in some way as part of their teaching day, but the practice of collaboration rarely worked well for the ESL teachers or their students. These encounters with their mainstream counterparts seemed to exacerbate their feelings of marginalization and frustration and failed to impact the classroom teachers' practice or pedagogy. As first-year teachers, they were novices, but they also believed that they had a certain expertise to share with their colleagues. However, due to the way collaboration was set up and implemented in the schools, the ESL teachers felt like marginalized experts. The following conversation at a new teacher support group meeting highlights some of these issues:

Sarah: The 6th grade team won't tell me ahead of time when they have meetings. They'll say, "Oh it's on our team conference board, go look at it." They don't bother to tell me or include me. I've missed lots of meetings because I didn't know. These are my kids…and I'm not included in discussions about their progress…. I think really it's how the administration set that up for what I can tell…and from my experience so far. They put a mandate that we need to collaborate, but they haven't really supported it or said this is how it's going to work. They say, "You're working with her!" But they haven't said how to work together … "You're going to be doing teamwork together … you're going to be doing planning together." There hasn't been anything communicated explicitly. I mean, I wasn't even given the chance to introduce myself to the teachers I'm collaborating with. We never even got to meet each other before the first day of class. They're like, "Oh ... you're here. OK, go work with them." So I feel like that set up the year and created a pattern for the rest of the year. I'm trying to fight that but it's hard...

Rebecca: I don't think it would matter. I mean honestly, you're a second-rate citizen just by virtue of the trade. They think we're resource teachers, specialist teachers. They figure if we had the skills, we'd be classroom teachers. This is the viewpoint ... not that anyone would ever admit to this ... that we are lesser ... that if we could have been mainstream teachers we would have, but we didn't have the skills or something as opposed to just caring about ELLs [English language learners].

Sarah: Ironically we have highly specialized skills and knowledge...

Rebecca: Yeah, yeah ...

Sarah: We could probably provide a much better perspective on these particular kids ...

Lynda: And better instruction ...

Sarah: They're asking what do I do with these kids ... you know what am I doing with them? But they still see us as, "Oh, you in the back."

Rebecca: We're there because the state says we have to be there ... whereas they are there to do a job. We are not the real teachers. They are the real teachers and we are just there to help out... like a glorified TA [teaching assistant]. [Focus group, 10/24/05]

Throughout the year, all three teachers frequently expressed their frustration with collaboration stemming from a variety of structural issues such as a lack of training, no designated co-planning time, and a general misuse of their time and expertise. While the ESL teachers had been trained in collaboration and had gained some positive experience with this model during their student-teaching, they were teaching in schools where they felt like little more than "glorified TAs." Due to the ineffective implementation of collaboration and their sense of marginalization as ESL teachers, the first-year teachers came to struggle with the task of collaborating with their middle school colleagues. This was particularly pronounced in Sarah's experience. Field notes from a March 23 visit and interview make this point:

Her response to my question, "What's going well?" was that she hasn't been going to collaboration classes because she has been testing kids and that this has made life a lot easier for her. I commented that it seemed like collaboration would be easy because you don't have to plan for it. She said, "If you don't care that kids are falling behind and can't keep up with the teacher then it is easy. But if you care, it is emotionally and psychologically hard because you see how unfair and messed up it is and how much more support they need and you can't provide enough...at least how [collaboration] is currently set up."

Sarah was troubled by the treatment of her students in the school, but was always quick to point out the program's inadequacies instead of blaming the core teachers alone. She understood that the structures that got in the way of meaningful collaboration were the lack of training, zero co-planning, and insufficient time and resources. Still, she continued to try to find creative ways to get around ineffective collaboration set-up at her school. In September, she started sending "modification of the week" emails to all of the teachers of English language learners with tips and topics such as putting the agenda on the board, ways to be more aware of teacher-talk or lecture styles, and the importance of explicitly teaching key vocabulary. Within a few weeks, she began to get positive feedback from some teachers and administrators, teachers started suggesting topics for future emails, and a few teachers thanked her. This strategy made her presence, her work, and her students more visible throughout the school. The impact of this work became even more visible toward the end of the first semester when she saw the impact of her emails:

> One of the early [emails] suggested giving newcomers a buddy, I recently sent out another one saying that now it was time to incorporate them into other groups...helping them or pushing them to interact with the rest of the class more and using English more. I sent it out and didn't think anything of it, but when I went into the classrooms that week, the newcomers had been moved and were no longer clustered together... they were integrated into the classroom. That's when I realized they actually read and reacted to the emails! [Interview, 1/11/06]

In addition to these emails, she planned two workshops on differentiating instruction and collaboration for the faculty and began serving on the school's Student Support Team (SST). Her more experienced mentor teacher was not interested in helping her plan the workshops, but she was determined to contribute to the school's staff development. She recognized that she was a first-year teacher, but she wanted to be seen as a professional and she wanted to share her knowledge. After these workshops she stated, "I'm finally being seen as a professional and expert...they [the teachers she is collaborating with] are finally seeing me as an educator who has some knowledge... something to contribute" (Interview, 1/11/06). While she wasn't able to change the structure that got in the way of more meaningful collaboration on a day-to-day basis, she was able to find other ways to contribute and work with her students' core teachers.

UNIQUE PERSPECTIVE, PLACE, AND POSITION—CONCLUDING THOUGHTS

The purpose of this chapter was to explore the teacher-generated topics that these three middle school ESL teachers raised during new teacher support group meetings. Their interest in discussing the unique perspective and marginalized spaces of ESL, relationships with other teachers, and collaboration in the middle school setting allowed the research to explore narrative threads of importance to them. These discussions also provide a glimpse into their complex teaching lives and contexts. While their opinions and experiences were not uniform or static, there was a general sense of solidarity and mutual understanding communicated during the new teacher support group meetings where they found consistent support and mentoring.

I hope that these narratives can contribute to the field of teacher education and the preparation of future ESL teachers for the unique spaces occupied by teachers of culturally and linguistically diverse students. The lessons of this chapter also point out the need for mainstream teachers to be better prepared to meet the needs of their English language learners and to work collaboratively and productively with the ESL experts in their schools. The data on collaboration in this study provide new information about this common practice that is often poorly implemented and has not been adequately researched. Without training, administrative support, and thoughtful implementation, collaboration in the ESL context simply marginalizes both ESL teachers and their students instead of bringing them into an inclusive climate of learning and respect. The first-year status of the ESL teachers in the study complicated this aspect of the research and it will be important to explore the experiences of more experienced ESL teachers as well as mainstream teachers who have experience co-teaching and collaborating in other contexts. More than anything, it is imperative to prepare future ESL and mainstream teachers to work together with English language learners.

Even with the best prepared and experienced ESL teachers, the growing numbers of English language learners and diverse youth in classrooms make language and culture a priority for all future teachers and teacher educators. All educators need opportunities in their teacher education programs to gain political and ideological clarity and care. Not only do mainstream teachers need to have knowledge about second language acquisition theory, the benefits of bilingualism, and ESL teaching methods, they (like ESL teachers) need to understand the larger geopolitical landscape that receives immigrant students in society and in our schools. Finally, future mainstream and ESL teachers need experience collaborating in meaningful and productive ways to bring both ESL students and their teachers out of the marginalized corners of classrooms and into an inclusive and validating class climate.

As classrooms become more complex and diverse, it is obvious that no teacher education program can adequately provide all of the skills and knowledge necessary for every teaching context. New teachers need opportunities to reflect on their practice with other teachers and teacher educators as they grow and develop as professionals. New teacher support group meetings could take a variety of forms, but the crucial ingredient is that these teachers find their own teaching voices and share both their challenges and expertise with one another. As more mainstream teachers are responsible for the education of English language learners in their classrooms, I see an opportunity to bring ESL and mainstream teachers together to learn from and with each other. This kind of supportive collaboration and reflection could have a tremendous impact on teachers' development and potentially, teacher retention. Both the teachers and their students would benefit from this kind of dialogue occurring in the field of education. This is a worthy research agenda I plan to pursue in the future.

REFERENCES

Auerbach, E. (1995). The politics of the ESL classroom: Issues of power in pedagogical choices. In J. Tollefson (Ed.), *Power and inequality in language education* (pp. 9–33). New York, NY: Cambridge University Press.

Baker, S. (2000). What we know about effective instructional practices for English-language learners. *Exceptional Children, 66*(4), 454–470.

Banks, J., & McGee Banks, C. (2001). *Multicultural Education: Issues and Perspectives* (4th ed.). New York, NY: John Wiley and Sons.

Banks, J., & McGee Banks, C. (2004). *Handbook of research on multicultural education: Issues and perspectives* (2nd ed.). San Francisco, CA: Jossey-Bass.

Bartolomé, L., & Trueba, E. (Eds.). (2001). Beyond the politics of schools and the rhetoric of fashionable pedagogies: The significance of teacher ideology. In *Immigrant voices: In search of educational equity.* New York, NY: Rowman & Littlefield.

Bear, G., & Proctor, W. (1990). Impact of a full-time integrated program on the achievement of nonhandicapped and mildly handicapped children. *Exceptionality: A Research Journal, 1*(4), 227–238.

Bullough, R. V. (1989). *First year teacher: A case study.* New York, NY: Teachers College Press.

Bullough, R. V. (1990). Supervision, mentoring, and self discovery: A case study of a first year teacher. *Journal of Curriculum and supervision, 5*(4), 338–360.

Bullough, R. V., Knowles, J. G, & Crow, N. A. (1991). *Emerging as a teacher.* New York, NY: Routledge.

Chomsky, N. (1998). *On language.* New York, NY: The New Free Press.

Clandinin, D. J., & Connelly, F. M. (2000). *Narrative inquiry: Experience and story in qualitative research.* San Francisco, CA: Jossey-Bass.

Coble, J. (2006). *Curricular constraints, high stakes testing, and the reality of reform in high school science classrooms.* Unpublished doctoral dissertation, University of North Carolina at Chapel Hill.

Corson, D. (1993). *Language, minority education and gender: Linking social justice and power.* Philadelphia, PA: Multilingual Matters; Toronto: Ontario Institute for Studies in Education.

Cummins, J. (1980). The cross-lingual dimensions of language proficiency: Implications for bilingual education and optimal age issue. *TESOL Quarterly, 14*(2), 175–187.

Cummins, J. (1986). Empowering minority students: A framework for achievement. *Harvard Educational Review, 56,* 18–36.

Cummins, J. (1993). Empowering minority students: A framework for intervention. In L. Weis & M. Fine (Eds.), *Beyond silenced voices: Class, race and gender in the United States schools* (pp. 101–139). New York, NY: SUNY Press.

Cummins, J. (1995). Power and pedagogy in the education of culturally-diverse students. In J. Fredrickson (Ed.), *Reclaiming our voices: Bilingual education, critical pedagogy, and praxis* (pp. 139–162). Los Angeles, CA: California Association for Bilingual Education.

Danielewicz, J. (2001). *Teaching selves: Identity, pedagogy, and teacher education.* Albany, NY: State University of New York Press.

Davies, C. (1999). *Reflexive ethnography: A guide to researching selves and others.* New York, NY: Routledge.

Deal, T. & Chatman, R. (1989). Learning the ropes alone: Socializing new teachers. *Action in Teacher Education, 11,* 21–29.

Expósito, S., & Favela, A. (2003). Reflective voices: Valuing immigrant students and teaching with ideological clarity. *The Urban Review, 35*(1), 73–91.

Feiman-Nemser, S., Carver, C., Schwille, S., & Yusko, B. (1999). Beyond support: Taking new teachers seriously as learners. In M. Scherer (Ed.), *A better beginning: Supporting and mentoring new teachers* (pp. 3-12). Alexandria, VA: Association for Supervision and Curriculum Development.

Freire, P. (1997). *Pedagogy of the oppressed* (New Revised 20th Anniversary ed.). New York, NY: Continuum.

Gay, G. (2000). *Culturally responsive teaching: Theory, research, and practice.* New York, NY: Teacher's College Press.

Gay, G. & Kirkland, K. (2003). Developing cultural critical consciousness and self-reflection in preservice teacher education. *Theory into Practice, (42)*3, 181–187.

Gibbons. (2002). *Scaffolding language scaffolding learning: Teaching second language learners in the mainstream classroom.* Portsmouth, ME: Heinemann.

Gitlin, A. D. (1990). Educative research, voice and school change. *Havard Educational Review, 60*, 443–466.

Glesne, C. (1998). *Becoming qualitative researchers: An introduction* (2nd ed.). New York, NY: Longman.

Goertz, M., & Duffy, M. (2003). Mapping the landscape of high-stakes testing and accountability programs. *Theory into Practice, 42*(1), 4-11.

Grossman, P. (1990). *The making of a teacher: Teacher knowledge & teacher education.* New York, NY: Teachers College Press.

Hakuta, K. (1986). *Cognitive development of bilingual children.* Los Angeles, CA: Center for Language Education and Research, University of California.

Harris, L. R. (1995). *A journey of moments: On being and becoming a teacher.* Unpublished doctoral dissertation, University of New Mexico.

Hawkins, M. R. (2004). *Language learning and teacher education: A sociocultural approach.* Bristol, United Kingdom: Multilingual Matters.

Herbert, E., & Worthy, T. (2001). Does the first year of teaching have to be a bad one? A case study of success. *Teaching and Teacher Education, 17*, 897–911.

Hollingsworth, S. (1992). Learning to teach through collaborative conversation: A feminist approach. *American Educational Research Journal, 29*(2), 373–404.

Howard, G. (1999). *We can't teach what we don't know: White teachers, multiracial schools.* New York, NY: Teachers College Press.

Kasarda, J., & Johnson, J. (2006). *The economic impact of the Hispanic population on the state of North Carolina.* Chapel Hill, NC: University North Carolina Kenan-Flagler Business School.

Klingner, J. K., Vaughn, S., & Schumm, J. S. (1998). Collaborative strategic reading during social studies in heterogeneous fourth-grade classrooms. *The Elementary School Journal, 99*(1), 3–22

Krashen, S. (1994). The input hypothesis and its rivals. In N. Ellis (Ed.), *Implicit and explicit learning of languages* (pp.45–77). London, England: Academic Press.

Kubota, R. (2004). Critical multiculturalism and second language education. In B. Norton & K. Toohey (Eds.), *Critical pedagogies and language learning* (pp. 30–52). Cambridge, England: Cambridge University Press.

Ladson-Billings, G. (2004). New directions in multicultural education: Complexities, boundaries, and critical race theory. In J. Banks & C. McGee Banks (Eds.), *Handbook of research on multicultural education: Issues and perspectives* (2nd ed., pp. 50–66). San Francisco, CA: Jossey-Bass.

McLaren, P. & Munoz, J. S. (2000). Contesting whiteness: Critical perspectives in the struggle for social justice. In C. Ovando & P. McLaren (Eds.), *The politics of multiculturalism and bilingual education* (pp. 23–49). New York, NY: McGraw-Hill Higher Education.

Magiera, K., & Zigmond, N. (2005). Co-teaching in middle school classrooms under routine conditions: Does the instructional experience differ for students with disabilities in co-taught and solo-taught classes? *Learning Disabilities Research and Practice, 20*(2), 79–85.

Marston, D. (1996). Comparison of inclusion only, pull-out only, and combined service models for students with mild disabilities. *Journal of Special Education, 30*(2), 121–132.

Minami, M., & Ovando, C. J. (2004). Language issues in multicultural contexts. In J. Banks & C. A. MacGee Banks (Eds.), *Handbook of research on multicultural education* (pp. 567–588). San Francisco, CA: John Wiley & Sons.

Montgomery, J. (1999). Easing the way for new teachers. In M. Scherer (Ed.), *A better beginning: Supporting and mentoring new teachers* (pp. 13–18). Alexandria, VA: Association for Supervision and Curriculum Development.

Murdock, S. (2006). *Population change in the United States: Implications for human and socioeconomic resources in the 21st century.* San Antonio, TX: Institute for Demographic and Socioeconomic Research, University of Texas-San Antonio.

NCES. (2007a, June). *Characteristics of schools, districts, teachers, principals, and school libraries in the United States: 2003–04 schools and staffing survey.* Retrieved from http://nces.ed.gov/pubs2006/2006313.pdf

NCES. (2007b, June). *Public elementary and secondary school student enrollment, high school completions, and staff from the common core of data: School year 2005–06.* Retrieved from http://nces.ed.gov/pubs2007/2007352.pdf

Nieto, S. (1994). Lessons from students on creating a chance to dream. *Harvard Educational Review, 64*, 392–426.

Nieto, S. (1995). From brown heroes and holidays to assimilationist agendas: Reconsidering the critiques of multicultural education. In C. Sleeter & P. McLauren (Eds.), *Multicultural education, critical pedagogy, and the politics of difference* (pp. 191–220). New York, NY: State University of New York Press.

Nieto, S. (2004). *Affirming diversity: The sociopolitical context of multicultural education* (4th ed.). Boston : Pearson/Allyn & Bacon.

Noddings, N. (1984). *Caring: A feminine approach to ethics and moral education.* Berkeley, CA: University of California Press.

Noddings, N. (1992). *The challenge to care in schools: An alternative approach to education.* New York, NY: Teachers College Press.

Noddings, N. (1998). *Philosophy of education.* Boulder, CO: Westview Press.

Norton Pierce, B. (1995). Social identity, investment and language learning. *TESOL Quarterly, 29*(1), 9–31.

Odom, S., Brantlinger, E., Gersten, R., Horner, R., Thompson, B., & Harris, K. (2005). Research in special education: Scientific methods and evidence-based practices. *Exceptional Children, 71*, 137-148.

Ovando, C., Combs, M., & Collier, V. (2006). *Bilingual and ESL classrooms: Teaching in multicultural contexts* (4th ed.). Boston, MA: McGraw-Hill.

Patriarca, L., & Lamb, M. (1994). Collaboration, curriculum development and reflection as frameworks for exploring the integration of general and special education. *B.C. Journal of Special Education, 18*(1), 95–100.

Renard, L. (2003). Setting new teachers up for failure … or success. *Educational Leadership, 60*(8), 62-64.

Richards, J. C. (1998). *Beyond training: Perspectives on language teacher education.* Cambridge, England: Cambridge University Press.

Rogers, D., & Babinski, L. (2002). *From isolation to conversation: Supporting new teachers' development.* Albany, NY: State University of New York Press.

Rolón-Dow, R. (2005). Critical care: A color(full) analysis of care narratives in the schooling experiences of Puerto Rican girls. *American Educational Research Journal, 42*(1), 77–111.

Rushton, S. (2004). Using narrative inquiry to understand a student–teacher's practical knowledge while teaching in an inner-city school. *The Urban Review, 36*(1), 61–79.

Schulte, A. C., Osborne, S. S., & McKinney, J. D., (1990). Outcomes for students with learning disabilities in consultation and resource programs. *Exceptional Children, 57*, 162–172.

Sleeter, C. E., & Delgado Bernal, D. (2004). Critical pedagogy, critical race theory, and anti-racist education: Implications for multicultural education. In J. Banks & C. McGee Banks (Eds.), *Handbook of research on multicultural education: Issues and perspectives* (pp. 240–258). San Francisco, CA: Jossey-Bass.

Sleeter, C., & McLauren, P. (1995). *Multicultural education, critical pedagogy, and the politics of difference.* Albany, NY: State University of New York Press.

Sleeter, C. (1996). *Multicultural education as social activism.* Albany, NY: State University of New York Press.

Suranna, K. (2003). The role of preservice teacher education in serving Latino students. In V. Kloosterman (Ed.), *Latino students in American schools: Historical and contemporary views* (pp. 153–167). Westport, CT: Praeger.

Suárez-Orozco, M. (2001). Globalization, immigration, and education: The research agenda. In *Harvard Educational Review, (71*)3, 345-365.

Suárez-Orozco, M., & Páez, M. (2002). *Latinos: Remaking America.* Berkeley, CA: University of California Press.

Thompson, A. (1998). Not the color purple: Black feminist lessons for educational caring. *Harvard Educational Review, 68*(4), 523–545.

U.S. Department of Education. (2002). *North Carolina census, top language and LEP enrollment growth 2001–2002.* Washington, DC: Office of English Language Acquisition, Language Enhancement, and Academic Achievement for Limited English Proficient Students.

Valdés, G. (1996). *Con respeto: Bridging the distances between culturally diverse families and school—An ethnographic portrait.* New York, NY: Teachers College Press.

Valenzuela, A. (1999). *Subtractive schooling: U.S.–Mexican youth and the politics of caring.* Albany, NY: State University of New York Press.

Veenman, S. (1984). Perceived problems of beginning teachers. *Review of Educational Research, 54*(2), 143–178.

Villalva, K. E. (2008). *Academic English and the new mainstream.* Manuscript submitted for publication.

CHAPTER 3

THE IMPACT OF A PROFESSIONAL DEVELOPMENT PROGRAM TO IMPROVE URBAN MIDDLE-LEVEL ENGLISH LANGUAGE LEARNER ACHIEVEMENT

Jennifer Friend, Ryan Most, and Kenneth McCrary

This mixed-methodological study examined changes in perceptions of teachers ($n = 70$) engaged in a two-year professional development program designed to meet the unique needs of English Language Learners (ELL), and changes in ELL students' ($n = 235$) math and reading achievement scores. The study was conducted in two urban middle schools in Kansas with high percentages of ELLs and students from poverty backgrounds. Paired-samples t tests of 2006 and 2007 state math and reading assessments for the ELL cohort demonstrated statistically significant differences in achievement levels, and the students' growth exceeded the gains made in proficiency levels among ELL students statewide. Findings from the qualitative analysis of the teacher surveys include perceptions of the needs of urban middle-level ELLs, pedagogical strategies perceived as effective with ELLs, and recom-

Research Supporting Middle Grades Practice,
pp. 55–78
Copyright © 2010 by Information Age Publishing

mendations for strengthening relationships among ELL students, with their non-ELL peers, and with adults. Implications for improved instruction for ELLs include the value of multiculturalism, the need for first-language support, and the effectiveness of professional development on elements of the Sheltered Instruction Observation Protocol (SIOP) for all teachers.

INTRODUCTION

The United States has seen continuous growth in public school enrollment of English Language Learners (ELL) over the past decade. These students are (1) from diverse cultural backgrounds, and (2) at different levels of English language proficiency according to state and district assessments. During the 10-year period from 1995 to 2005, ELL enrollment in the U.S. increased 57.17% to nearly five million students, while total student enrollment grew by only 3.66% (NCELA, 2007). Students whose parents immigrated to the U.S. accounted for 20% of children under the age of 18 in the year 2000 and for 25% of students eligible for free or reduced lunch status (Capps et al., 2005). The Midwestern State of Kansas demonstrated growth exceeding the national average, as ELL enrollment increased during this same time period by 131.7%, while overall student enrollment in Kansas experienced a steady decline of -9.5% (NCELA, 2006).

Research over the past half-century has provided evidence of failure for many students of all backgrounds, but especially children of Latino, African American, and Native American families, as well as poor European American families, and, more recently, Asian and Pacific American immigrant students (Nieto, 2002). African American and Hispanic students are less likely than white students to receive a high school diploma (U.S. Census, 2003). A recent study by the Pew Hispanic Center (Fry, 2008) found that the achievement gap between white students and ELL students for state mathematics assessments for elementary and middle schools is quantified in double-digits.

The purpose of this mixed-methodological study was to examine changes in urban middle-level ELL students' ($n = 235$) mathematics and reading state assessment scores over a two-year period, and to explore changes in perceptions of these students' teachers ($n = 70$) who were engaged in professional development designed to improve classroom instruction for English Language Learners. The two urban middle schools in Kansas involved in this study have high percentages of ELL students and students from poverty backgrounds. Professional development to meet the unique needs of ELL students was conducted on-site as part of a three-year program for the majority of teachers.

The research questions for this study were:

1. What are teachers' perceptions of the needs of urban middle-level English language learners?
2. What are teachers' beliefs regarding effective professional development and instructional strategies that have positive or negative effects on the education of English language learners who attend middle school in an urban setting?
3. How do teachers describe relationships among ELL students, with their non-ELL peers, and among ELL students and adults in urban middle schools?
4. Were there significant gains in ELL achievement on state reading and math assessments from sixth to seventh grade and from seventh to eighth grade during the implementation of the professional development program?

YOUNG ADOLESCENT ENGLISH LANGUAGE LEARNERS

Young adolescents experience a variety of physical, intellectual, social, and emotional changes with the onset of puberty. The manner in which schools address the needs of middle-level students has great potential to help or harm the development of healthy and academically successful young adolescents. The *Task Force on Education of Young Adolescents* determined

> early adolescence to be a period of enormous opportunity for intellectual and emotional growth, yet one fraught with vulnerability and risk. The pressures facing young adolescents are indeed formidable, but so, too, is the capacity of many young adolescents to negotiate this period of intense biological, psychological, and interpersonal change successfully. (Jackson & Davis, 2000, p. 2)

English language learners have an additional layer of pressure within schools due to expectations for acculturation and language acquisition, yet these students carry with them the inherent strengths of their prior knowledge and experiences from their diverse linguistic and cultural backgrounds. Academic standards may be taught according to the diverse needs of young adolescents by differentiating instruction for students, as instruction must be at the appropriate level of difficulty for individuals so that learning outcomes are attainable for every student. With increased attention focused on improved student achievement on standardized assessments, districts across the United States have been engaged in curricular revisions and professional development to improve pedagogical knowledge and skills among teachers.

Professional development to address the needs of English Language Learners, particularly for schools with increasing numbers of ELLs, is of critical importance in the performance measures for schools, as mandated by the No Child Left Behind Act of 2001 (Public Law 107-110, 2001). Several recent research studies have examined professional development aimed at improving ELL instruction. A study of the discourse among teachers and ELL students in a California middle school found that teachers would benefit from professional development to understand how the patterns of academic language set by the teacher could either encourage or discourage growth in these students. According to Zwiers (2007):

> Many of the phrases linked to cognitive skills are figurative, embodying abstract meanings that describe complex relationships among ideas that are difficult to see, point to, touch, or act out. Teachers and academics use such phrases every day without really thinking about them....A salient feature of academic language is that it needs to be modified to meet the needs of a distant audience who do not share common background knowledge or social settings. (p. 109)

The largest percentage of ELLs in the United States and in the State of Kansas is made up of children of Hispanic heritage. Jess, Davis, and Pokorny (2004) conducted a study in nine Texas middle schools and identified elements of schools that encouraged high performance in Latino students living in low-income families. Positive school attributes included "strong leadership; a clear focus on achievement; positive climate, including supportive relationships among students and teachers; and good communications with parents" (Jess et al., 2004, p. 23). The researchers also found that the schools would benefit from strategic planning to bring the "cultural knowledge of home and community" (p. 23) into the instructional process. Schwartz (2001) addressed the importance of the educational organization for ELLs:

> The school system is one of the first institutions that immigrant children encounter in their new country. Yet, stressors related to migration and acculturation may impede the learning process for children and increase the academic gap between Latinos and other ethnic groups. (p. 2)

If Schwartz's statement is correct, schools could also be considered one of the first true tastes of American life for the children of immigrants, as well as their most valuable tool to assist in adaptation to life in the United States. In order for school systems to assist ELLs and their families, there has to be a true desire among the staff to do so, and there must be a sense of efficacy among teachers with regard to their instructional efforts.

Assessment of Middle-Level English Language Learners

In accordance with the requirements of *NCLB*, all middle-level students in Kansas participate in annual state assessments in reading and mathematics. English Language Learners enrolled in a school are considered a "sub-group" for the purposes of calculating a school's Adequate Yearly Progress (AYP) when there are at least 30 students classified as ELLs. Adequate Yearly Progress is determined by annual proficiency targets, by participation rates for state reading and mathematics assessments, and by graduation and attendance rates (Kansas State Department of Education, 2007a). Kansas Reading and Mathematics Assessments were revised in 2006, and the AYP targets for middle-level students for 2006, 2007, and 2008 included increasing expectations for the percentage of all students and sub-groups achieving at a proficient level or above (Kansas State Department of Education, 2007b).

Kansas Assessment results demonstrate significant gaps in achievement between "All Students" enrolled and students identified as "ELLs" in sixth, seventh, and eighth grades during 2006 and 2007. Kansas Reading Assessment results show trends for improvement from 2006 to 2007 annual test results for "All Students" and for "ELLs" for all grade levels. In contrast, there is a trend for the percent of "All Students" and "ELLs" who demonstrate proficiency to decline from sixth grade to eighth grade (see Table 3.1). Trends for the Kansas Math Assessment results also show

Table 3.1.   Kansas Reading Assessments Results: Percent of Students who "Meet Standards," "Exceed Standards," or Perform at the "Exemplary" Level

	2006	2007
6th grade – all students	78.0%	81.1%
7th grade - all students	79.2%	83.2%
8th grade – all students	77.4%	79.0%
6th grade – ELL	47.3%	54.3%
7th grade – ELL	44.2%	55.1%
8th grade – ELL	37.9%	41.1%

Table 3.2.   Kansas Math Assessments Results:
Percent of Students who "Meet Standards," "Exceed Standards,"
or Perform at the "Exemplary" Level

	2006	2007
6th grade – all students	74.4%	79.2%
7th grade – all students	70.1%	74.8%
8th grade – all students	66.6%	70.7%
6th grade – ELL	48.8%	59.4%
7th grade – ELL	44.7%	50.0%
8th grade – ELL	37.3%	40.3%

annual improvement from 2006 to 2007, and a decline in the percent of students who demonstrate proficiency at each grade level (see Table 3.2).

METHODOLOGY

Site Selection

Selection of the two middle school sites for this study involved seeking urban schools: (1) with large percentages of English language learners located in close proximity to the researchers, (2) whose teachers were engaged in professional development to improve instruction for ELLs, and (3) whose school and district-level administrators were willing to participate in this research. At the time of this study, the district selected served approximately 18,500 students K–12. Approximately 5,000 of those students were identified as ELLs receiving services. While the district's total enrollment has witnessed a slow decline over the years, the ELL population has steadily risen, representing an ever increasing percentage of the district's population and forestalling a rapid decline that likely would have taken place otherwise. The district includes eight middle schools, and the two schools identified for this study have led the district in ELL demographic growth.

Enrollment in Middle School A has stayed within a range of 640 to 655 over the last five years. English language learner enrollment has shown a steady increase, and was at approximately 171 students at the time of this study. Enrollment in Middle School B has ranged from a high of 708 students to a recent low of 540 students, which follows a district trend of declining enrollment. The percentage of ELL students has also increased at School B, from 25% to 34%, and most recently 47% of the school's total enrollment. Eleven languages are represented at both middle schools, with English then Spanish as the leading languages and Hmong and Laotian following.

The schools house three grade-level small learning communities (SLC) who meet weekly to discuss and plan their lessons in regards to meeting the needs of all of their students. The SLC teachers also act as a student intervention team in that they evaluate individual student needs and create and offer accommodations as needed to students not proving successful in the standard schedule of classes. These SLCs have been supported over the years by consistent, strong leadership. The previous two principals at Middle School A were promoted to central office positions, and the former principal at Middle School B is now the Executive Director of Teaching and Learning in Middle Schools in the district. The current principals at both buildings are former teachers from within the schools. Middle School B is located towards the center of the original boundaries of the school district, and projections based on the numbers in the feeder elementary schools predict a continued increase in ELL enrollment.

Professional Development Program

Due to the ever increasing number of students requiring ELL services over the years, the district has been implementing and refining ways to better prepare school staff members and teachers for meeting these needs. The most dominant option available before the current program consisted of teachers volunteering their time, money, and effort to enroll in graduate level courses through the Collaborative Intercultural and Multilingual Advocacy Center (CIMA) at Kansas State University. CIMA offers a program for any teacher wishing to enroll to earn an ESL certification to be added to their Kansas teaching certificate. The requirements include enrolling in five graduate level classes, one each semester, and the teacher must pass the associated Praxis II exam in order to add the certification to their license. The courses include videotaped lectures, reflective writing assignments, independent book studies, and practical application at work. Individuals are encouraged to enroll with others from their buildings and districts in order to foster discussion and build resources and capacity to assist ELL students. Many teachers, instructional coaches, and administrators have taken advantage of this opportunity in past years. Some were able to receive grants, scholarships, or reimbursement from the district to cover the costs and expenses related to participating in the program. This program remains available from CIMA for teachers in all of Kansas and can be completed through the mail and email. It is referred to as their CLASSIC Program.

Another program designed more specifically to the needs of two larger urban school districts in Kansas with increasing enrollment of English language learners is the APPLi + 1 ESL endorsement program. The purpose of this program is to build on the original program and make it more site-specific to not only create opportunities to increase teachers' understanding of the needs of ELLs but also to gear the professional development to more immediately and deeply impact teacher practice in their classrooms meeting the needs of their students. Rather than being based on videotaped lectures and independent book study, the courses are led by school district instructional coaches and facilitators specifically trained to deliver the content and guide the learning and implementation of best practices for ELLs in the classrooms. Both Middle School A and Middle School B have been participating in this new program since its inception along with the other two smaller middle school ESL sites, two high school sites, and numerous elementary school sites in the district selected for this study.

The new program began during the 2005–2006 school year. Administrators of these sites strongly encouraged all staff to participate. This included those who already possessed an ESL certification for middle grades. The class meetings took place during early release Wednesdays. Only one class was offered at each site each school year. This allowed for the class meetings to be spread over the course of an entire semester or even the entire school year, depending on the availability of time. Participants were required to collaborate in small groups or cohorts to dig deeper into the text and classroom experiences before completing the designated assignments.

The focus of this professional development was on better preparing content-based teachers to instruct ELLs. With this in mind, a class focusing on methods and best practices was the first class offered. Each middle school had approximately 20 teachers enrolled with additional individuals auditing the course meetings. The following year, a class focusing on assessment and gauging student understanding of concepts was offered. Again, approximately 20 teachers from each building were enrolled. The third course offered was related to working in an environment of diverse individuals with many languages, cultures, and backgrounds. During the next school year a class focusing on linguistics and second language acquisition will be offered. The fifth and final class is the practicum, where teachers create an action research project related to working with ELLs. All of the classes are paid for directly by the school district. The only out-of-pocket expense for the teachers is the Praxis exam for the subject area of English as a Second Language, and when the teachers receive documentation that they have passed the exam, the school district will reimburse them for that cost.

Research Design—Mixed Methodology

A mixed methods study involves "both numeric information as well as text information so that the final database represents both quantitative and qualitative information" (Creswell, 2007, p. 20). Multiple data sources collected for this research study include (1) school and district enrollment and demographic information for ELL students and the teachers in the two middle schools, (2) state assessment results for reading and mathematics for the ELL students over a two-year period, (3) the district coding for ELL students' English language proficiency, and (4) teacher surveys with seven open-ended questions and five Likert scale questions. All quantitative data were entered into the statistical analysis program SPSS and were examined using a paired-analysis t test to determine whether there were significant differences in the achievement of ELL students from sixth to seventh grade and from seventh to eighth grade during the implementation of the professional development program. Descriptive statistics (such as frequencies of performance levels) that examined the overall achievement on the assessments for ELLs were also analyzed for the two-year period.

The survey of teacher perceptions was conducted to determine the impact of the professional development process and experiences, including (1) the quality and effectiveness of professional development, (2) pedagogy that teachers have utilized to contribute to the academic success of ELL students, (3) stories related to the educational context that pertain to instruction and to relationships among ELL students and adults, and (4) memorable events that pertain to academic successes and failures of ELL students. Survey responses were sources of data for qualitative examination of the factors that contributed to improved achievement for ELLs, including analysis of the role of professional development for teachers, and the interaction of race/ethnicity, class, and language on attainment of academic goals for reading and math proficiency. The coding to identify themes and concepts reported in the teachers' narrative responses to survey questions was conducted independently by two researchers to provide for inter-rater reliability. The coding sequence was conducted through the use of the NVivo analysis software through processes of (1) coding the content in the narrative data, (2) organizing patterns through creation of a node system, (3) categorizing data for further analysis, and (4) adding notations and explanatory comments to describe common themes and to synthesize information.

RESULTS

Teachers' Perceptions of ELL Students' Needs

Research question one was: "What are teachers' perceptions of the needs of urban middle-level English language learners?" Teachers were prompted to share needs observed in a variety of settings, from the classroom to common areas such as hallways and the lunchroom. There were three needs identified by the highest percentages of teachers who completed the survey: (1) first-language support, (2) comprehensible input through a variety of methods, and (3) basic academic skills instruction.

Twenty-eight percent of teachers stated that ELL students need their first language supported through bilingual paraprofessionals, translators, translations, multilingual texts, and other methods of reinforcing the first language along with second language acquisition. One teacher suggested "instruction in the primary language in the form of peer tutoring." Translation services were valued for both students and families, as one teacher wrote: "Communication with parents is an element that suffers because forms sent home are not always available in all languages represented."

One fourth of respondents believed that teachers needed to use other methods of comprehensible input besides vocabulary strategies and first-language support. This included methods such as visuals, rate of speech, rate of content, and use of technology. One teacher's concern was that, "Due to pacing guidelines, ELL students are being rushed through the curriculum at the same pace as their native English-speaking peers." Several teachers also mentioned the value in increasing use of a strategy known as TPR, or Total Physical Response. Originated nearly three decades ago by Dr. James Asher at California State University, TPR as an instructional method for ELLs is grounded in the following principles:

1. Understanding the spoken language should be developed far in advance of speaking.
2. Comprehension, much of the grammatical structure, and hundreds of vocabulary items can and should be learned through movement of the teacher's and the student's body.
3. Speech is natural and developmental, and will emerge naturally in its own time.
4. Students should not be rushed into reading and writing before they have had ample listening and speaking experience (Segal, 1981, p. 1).

Of similar importance among teachers was the need for ELL students to have instruction in basic academic skills such as reading, writing, listening, and speaking in an educational setting. Other basic needs included helping ELL students to understand how to find the restroom, see the school nurse, or open a locker. One mathematics teacher stated that ELL students "usually can grasp the math content (at a slower pace).... But where they struggle is with the language or the way the test questions are worded."

Other needs for ELL students that were identified by more than 10% of teachers included improving English-language vocabulary, behavioral support to understand teachers' expectations and to acculturate to the educational setting, and multiple opportunities to interact with native speakers of English. These could include teacher models, cooperative learning groups, and structured support for oral response, scripted responses, and discussion opportunities. Teachers also stated the need for multiculturalism in the middle school program, as evidenced by having students' cultures and languages respected and accepted in the educational setting.

Professional Development & Instructional Strategies

Research question two was: "What are teachers' beliefs regarding effective professional development and instructional strategies that have positive or negative effects on the education of English language learners who attend middle school in an urban setting?" Teachers were asked to share some of the teaching strategies for ELLs that they learned during the professional development sessions. The survey also asked teachers to identify which strategies were utilized on a weekly basis, and then to gauge the effectiveness of instructional strategies in promoting learning and academic achievement for ELL students.

With regard to teaching strategies learned during professional development sessions, 42% of teachers stated that they had learned methods for comprehensible input and vocabulary strategies for ELLs. Responses referred to methods of comprehensible input other than use of visual aids and use of the students' first language. These included adjusting the rate of speech, pacing of the curriculum, role playing, use of technology, and other forms of comprehensible input. Teachers' responses related to vocabulary included some specific vocabulary strategies from the professional development activities (such as the Frayer model or use of a bilingual word wall), or referred to learning vocabulary strategies in general. Nearly 40% of teachers included use of visual aids during instruction, scaffolding (or building on students' prior knowledge), and cooperative learning as strategies learned during professional development.

Twenty percent of teachers referred to aspects of the Sheltered Instruction Observation Protocol (SIOP) other than comprehensible input. Sheltered instruction strategies include:

- use of cooperative learning activities with appropriately designed heterogeneous grouping of students
- a focus on academic language as well as key content vocabulary
- judicious use of ELLs' first language as a tool to provide comprehensibility
- use of hands-on activities using authentic materials, demonstrations, and modeling
- explicit teaching and implementation of learning strategies
- incorporating students' background knowledge into classroom lessons (Hansen-Thomas, 2008, p. 165).

The SIOP strategies mentioned by teachers included language and content objectives, building background, and guiding students to build connections and relate to prior learning. Approximately 17% of teachers referred to differentiation specifically, or making accommodations based on student needs.

Two questions on the teacher survey addressed their perceived quality of professional development using a Likert scale. The scale for responses was: 1 = Very Poor; 2 = Poor; 3 = Average; 4 = Good; 5 = Very Good. With regard to the quality of the teachers' most recent ELL professional development session, the majority of teachers rated the session Average (28.6%) or Good (42.9%). Very Poor or Poor ratings were given by 12.8% of teachers, and 7.1% of teachers rated the most recent session as Very Good. When asked to rate the overall quality of the ELL professional development program, 2.9% chose Very Good; 52.9% chose Good; 24.3% chose Average; and 8.6% chose Poor. There were no teacher ratings of Very Poor for the overall quality of the professional development program.

With regard to instructional strategies that teachers perceived to be effective with English language learners, methods of comprehensible input were the most frequently identified. Some of these methods were named specifically, such as: (1) visuals (15% of respondents), (2) cooperative learning (32% of respondents), (3) using students' first languages to support instruction (19% of respondents), (4) multiculturalism through use of texts that reflect different cultures and languages (7% of respondents), and (5) other forms such as adjusting rate of speech or content, technology, and using strategies specific to student needs (40% of respondents).

SIOP strategies besides comprehensible input were mentioned, including preparation, language/content objectives, making connections, and accessing prior knowledge or building on prior experiences. As one ELL-endorsed teacher stated, "I think that utilizing many aspects of SIOP and scaffolding the material for students are most effective because it allows the students to know what the expectations are and for the material to be comprehensible." Several teachers, especially those who were new to the school during the year of this study, were uncertain which strategies were most effective. As one teacher working toward ELL-endorsement wrote in response to this survey question, "Still trying to figure this one out."

On the Likert scale question that asked each teacher to rate the level of academic achievement for ELL students in the teacher's class(es), 50% of teachers selected Average to describe ELL achievement. Nearly 9% of teachers described ELL achievement as Poor, while 24.3% selected Good and 2.9% chose Very Good to describe ELL achievement in their classes. These perceptions suggest that the majority of teachers believe that ELL students in their classes exhibit adequate levels of academic achievement.

There was less agreement among teacher responses with regard to instructional strategies that were ineffective with English language learners. Twenty-six percent of teachers stated that independent work was not effective, including worksheets, assigned reading, or students working on their own without coaching, facilitation, or guidance. Approximately 14% of teachers believed that lecture or teacher-dominated instruction was not effective for ELLs; unstructured classroom practices were cited by 11% of teachers, and 10% stated that English as the only language used or allowed to be used in the classroom regardless of the activity had a negative impact on the achievement of ELLs.

One teacher who was not yet ELL-endorsed stated, "I will be certified next year and I hope I learn some strategies that do help. This strategy is definitely ineffective—to put an ESL in a teacher's room who is not ESL trained." Frustration was also demonstrated in this teacher's response to the prompt:

> For me, it is not teaching strategies. It is the system. I have kids that came here with no formal education and expected to be at grade level. Students are moved up to the next grade without mastering material. For real learning, students need to learn from where they are at and not move to the next grade until material is mastered.

Moving English language learners away from supportive environments was another concern expressed by teachers. Students were frequently described as being homogeneously grouped together, and then moved on to a new class as one group rather than assigned a schedule to meet the needs of the individual ELLs. According to several teachers, the placement of students within certain classes was relevant to the effectiveness of instructional strategies.

Middle-Level English Language Learners and Relationships

Research question three was: "How do teachers describe relationships among ELL students, with their non-ELL peers, and among ELL students and adults in urban middle schools?" When asked to describe the relationships that teachers observed and/or fostered among ELL students and others, the highest percentage (44%) of respondents said that students tended to socialize and choose to work with other students with the same language and culture. One teacher described efforts within the classroom to foster intercultural student friendships:

> I'm trying to get all of my students to be more considerate of other cultures. I want them to be culture pluralists and not ethnocentric. It is important to me that we're kind, caring and respectful of each other, so I demand that we focus on getting along with each other.

Another teacher stated that such efforts might work within the classroom, but that there were no lasting effects: "In my classroom we do a lot of team-building so that students get to know each other. However, at the end of the day, students return to segregated groups."

Several teachers believed that within the middle schools there was a feeling of acceptance, but not necessarily interaction among the different cultural groups present. Slightly more than 10% of teachers stated that they used cooperative learning groups to influence the interactions among students. At times teachers group students with the same culture for support of learning and content. At other times, the groups are cross-cultural to expand development of relationships and social skills.

Approximately 14% of teachers addressed the ELL–adult relationship component of the open-ended survey question, stating their attempts to reach out to students of diverse cultures and languages to make them feel more comfortable in the classroom as well as more successful. As one teacher described this process, "Relationships are developed when [teachers] show interest in their culture, demonstrate awareness of the dynamics of families, and use their 1st language." Extracurricular activities and the availability of translators were mentioned by several teachers as being helpful to ELLs building relationships with individuals outside their linguistic and cultural backgrounds.

Two questions on the teacher survey addressed their perceptions of the relationships among ELL students and others. The Likert scale for responses was: 1 = Very Poor; 2 = Poor; 3 = Average; 4 = Good; 5 = Very Good. Teachers viewed the relationships between ELLs and adults favorably, with ratings of 18.6% Very Good; 54.3% Good; 17.1% Average; 2.9% Poor, and 1.4% Very Poor. With regard to ELLs and their non-ELL peers, the majority of teachers perceived the relationships to be Good (41.4%) or Average (38.6%), with 7.1% rating them Very Good and 7.2% rating relationships Poor. These findings suggest that teachers view the ELL–adult relationships in the school as being more positive than the relationships among ELLs and their non-ELL peers.

Statistical Analysis of Academic Achievement

Research question four was : "Were there significant gains in ELL achievement on state reading and math assessments from sixth to seventh grade and from seventh to eighth grade during the implementation of the professional development program?" This involved analysis of 235 English language learners' achievement data in two urban middle schools. Criteria for students selected for this sample included all English language learners enrolled in the two middle schools who remained at the same school for the two years of this study and who completed the 2006 and 2007 Kansas Reading and Math Assessments. Demographics for this student sample according to gender included 53.7% male ($n = 126$) and 46.3% female ($n = 109$). Students began this study as sixth-grade or seventh-grade students, and their achievement on state assessments was collected over a two-year period. There were 53.6% ($n = 126$) of students in the sample who began in the sixth-grade cohort and completed seventh grade in the same school, and 46.4% ($n = 109$) of students who began in the seventh-grade cohort and completed eighth grade in the same school. Racial categories according to the Kansas Assessment criteria included a majority of Hispanic students at both schools (95.8% of the overall sample). The majority of students (95.7%) qualified for free or reduced lunch ($n = 225$). See Table 3.3 for the number and percentages of English language learner participants by school, gender, grade level, race, and socioeconomic status.

Performance levels for Kansas Reading and Mathematics Assessments include: (1) Academic Warning, (2) Approaches Standard, (3) Meets Standard, (4) Exceeds Standard, and (5) Exemplary. Students who score at a level three or above are considered to meet proficiency in that subject area according to the definitions for Adequate Yearly Progress outlined in the No Child Left Behind Act (2001). The means of performance levels

Table 3.3.   Urban English Language Learner Participants by School, Gender, Grade Level, Race, and Socioeconomic Status

	Middle School A (n = 114)		Middle School B (n = 121)	
	n	p	n	p
Gender				
Female	49	20.8	60	25.5
Male	65	27.7	61	26.0
Grade Level				
Grade 6 (in 2006)	60	25.5	66	28.1
Grade 7 (in 2006)	54	23.0	55	23.4
Race				
American Indian	0	0	0	0
Asian/Pacific Islander	2	.8	3	1.3
Black	2	.8	3	1.3
Hispanic	110	46.8	115	49.0
White	0	0	0	0
Socioeconomic Status				
Not free/reduced lunch	4	1.7	6	2.6
Reduced lunch	103	43.8	104	44.2
Free lunch	7	3.0	11	4.7

for all students ($n = 235$) on the reading and math assessments demonstrated growth from the 2006 to the 2007 testing period for both middle schools. When compared to the state-wide performance of middle-level English language learners on the reading and math assessments, the percentage of ELLs at the two middle schools who performed at or above the proficient level demonstrated lower levels of performance on each assessment; however, there were greater gains over the two-year period when compared to ELL performance at the state level (see Figure 3.1 and Figure 3.2).

The means for the performance levels (1 through 5) and the raw scores on the state reading and math assessments increased from 2006 to 2007 for the ELL students in this study. Paired-samples t tests were conducted using the SPSS program, and significant differences ($p < .01$) were evident for both the math and reading assessments. The ELLs' achievement on the Kansas Mathematics Assessment $t (234) = -3.629, p = .000$ demonstrates that the mean performance levels after the two-year period that the ELL students were instructed by teachers engaged in the professional development program ($M = 2.37$) was significantly higher than the mean performance level at the beginning of the ELLs' sixth- or seventh-grade year ($M = 2.17$). Similarly, the Kansas Reading Assessment ELL achieve-

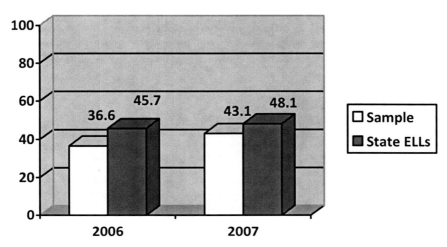

Figure 3.1. Kansas reading assessments results: Percent of middle-level English language learners who "meet standards," "exceed standards," or perform at the "exemplary" level.

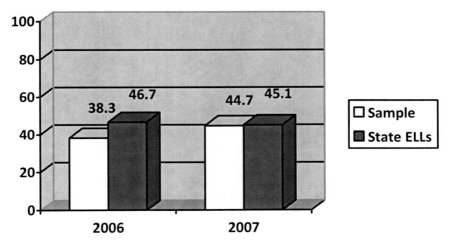

Figure 3.2.   Kansas math assessments results: percent of middle-level English language learners who "meet standards," "exceed standards," or perform at the "exemplary" level.

ment t (234) = -3.085, p = .002 indicated a significant increase in the means of ELLs' performance levels from 2006 (M = 2.26) to 2007 (M = 2.08). The data were analyzed according to All Students in the sample

**Table 3.4.   Kansas Math and Reading Assessment Levels:
Means, Standard Deviations and Percent of Students who "Meet
Standards," "Exceed Standards," or Perform at the "Exemplary" Level**

	2006 Math	2007 Math	2006 Reading	2007 Reading
All Students *Mean*	2.40	2.59	2.63	2.75
N	602	602	602	602
SD	1.147	1.176	1.216	1.192
% Proficient	47.8	53.9	55.8	61.2
ELL Students				
Mean	2.17	2.37	2.08	2.26
N	235	235	235	235
SD	1.084	1.130	1.065	1.145
% Proficient	38.3	44.7	36.6	43.1
School A *Mean*	2.11	2.35	2.16	2.31
ELL *N*	114	114	114	114
SD	1.111	1.105	1.027	1.138
% Proficient	36.0	43.9	38.6	41.2
School B *Mean*	2.22	2.40	2.01	2.21
ELL *N*	121	121	121	121
SD	1.061	1.158	1.099	1.154
% Proficient	40.6	45.5	34.7	44.6
Free or Reduced Lunch				
ELL *Mean*	2.16	2.37	2.09	2.25
N	225	225	225	225
SD	1.092	1.131	1.074	1.154
% Proficient	38.2	44.0	36.9	42.7
Full-Pay Lunch				
ELL *Mean*	2.30	2.50	1.90	2.40
N	10	10	10	10
SD	.949	1.179	.876	.966
% Proficient	40.0	60.0	30.0	50.0

and according to disaggregation of student demographic variables (see
Table 3.4).

Limitations of This Study

The research conducted in this study was limited by several factors.
The sample size for analysis was relatively small, comprised of two middle
schools in one urban school district in the Midwest. Measurement of ELL
student achievement over the two-year period was based on instruments
administered annually in the spring, the Kansas Reading Assessment and

the Kansas Mathematics Assessment; however, the paired-samples t test did enable a value-added analysis for cohort groups of students. The analysis of student achievement did not include a control group of ELLs in Kansas whose teachers were not engaged in a professional development program designed to improve pedagogical techniques for ELLs; however, the means of middle grades ELL performance levels in the State were reported as part of the comparative findings with the ELL participants in this study.

DISCUSSION

Implications and recommendations for improved instruction for ELLs include the value of multiculturalism, the impact of teacher attitudes and expectations, the need for first-language support, and the effectiveness of a professional development program for teachers of ELLs that includes elements of the Sheltered Instruction Observation Protocol (SIOP), such as differentiation of instruction. The opportunity for teachers to engage in professional development through the weekly early-release of students and the district-funded opportunity to add an ESL-endorsement to state teaching certification were features of the program in these schools that encouraged wide participation in the voluntary sessions. Teacher responses on the open-ended survey questions provided insight into their perceptions of the needs of urban middle-level ELLs both instructionally and socio-culturally within the school.

Multicultural Paradigms

Throughout the teacher responses to the open-ended questions in the survey, the theme of multiculturalism was indicated as important to meeting the academic and social needs of ELLs in the school. In response to the teacher survey question on ineffective instructional strategies, one teacher stated that "[t]rying to make them assimilate to the American culture without respect to their native cultures" was detrimental to ELL growth. The ideology of assimilation and related concepts such as the American "melting pot" or "colorblindness" toward diverse students encourages educators to approach instruction of ELLs or minority students from a paradigm of uniformity or a dominant-culture orientation.

Howard (1999) stated that, "the declaration of colorblindness assumes that we can erase our racial categories, ignore differences, and thereby achieve an illusory state of sameness or equality" (p. 53). This ideology is evidenced in ways such as the "Americanization" of the names of students, which one teacher in this study understood quickly to be an oversight: "It was during my first year at my school that I realized how important it was for me to pronounce names correctly." It is important for educators to examine conscious and unconscious beliefs regarding linguistic and cultural diversity, which may impact instructional practice and expectations for ELLs when teachers approach students, "from a cultural 'deficit' framework in which the perceived emotional, social, or psychological needs of students of color can overrun their academic competencies," thus impacting student achievement (Atwater, 2008, p. 252).

Value for cultural experiences outside the school and classroom settings was also expressed in the teacher surveys. One teacher described a field trip to the city's museum of art:

> My first year as a teacher at this building we took a group of students to Nelson-Atkins museum and to see the looks on their faces as they wandered and made their way through the museum was wonderful to see. Many of our students, especially the ELL students never get to witness anything outside of [the neighborhood] and to be able to take them somewhere to learn, touch, and see art, sculptures, tools, and other artifacts was a learning experience for them as it was for me.

Another teacher described the school's music program and enjoying the cultural diversity of the selections of instrumental music for the band, and Spanish-language songs performed by the choir. One of the eighth-grade teachers described the value of adapting curriculum to address cultural diversity after having a difficult time "getting through" to a class of students with a high percentage of ELLs:

> I could never present material that grabbed their attention until I presented a unit on the Toltec, Olmec, Inca, Aztec and Maya. These kids just tore into it and produced a great deal of work. They had finally found material that interested them.

The professional development program in this study included outcomes related to the value of cultural pluralism in the school setting and activities designed to raise teachers' cultural awareness and understanding. A culminating student autobiography project was described by one teacher as being very "enlightening" to learn about ELLs through a non-academic lens. Another teacher stated the significance of listening to the students' stories: "By hearing the experiences of my students being new in the U.S. allowed me to see through a different light and to understand behavior more easily." Shuman's (2005) description of storytelling as "an aspect of the ordinary ... touted as a healing art ... a means for transforming oppressive conditions by creating opportunity for suppressed voices to be heard or for creating opportunities to listen to those voices" (p. 5) provides a connection to the value of teachers' openness to diverse multi-cultural perspectives and a willingness to listen to the voices of English language learners as they share their backgrounds and experiences.

Teacher Attitudes and Expectations

Students who are culturally, racially, and linguistically diverse are often viewed as having a lower likelihood of academic success than nonminor-ity, English-speaking students. When conducting interviews concerning issues experienced by Hispanic immigrant students in public education, Suarez-Orozco and Suarez-Orozco (2001) found many teachers tended to view minority immigrant students as less intelligent and lazy. They felt these students were more likely to get into trouble and less likely to assim-ilate into the mainstream. These teachers were very verbal about their feelings. One teacher predicted that one of her Hispanic boys would probably end up in prison. She also voiced doubt about the likelihood of any of her Hispanic girls going to college. She stated, "They just don't have the IQ's" (Suarez-Orozco & Suarez-Orozco, 2001, p.127). A superin-tendent in this study said his biggest educational problem was convincing his principals and teachers that minority and immigrant children were teachable. These students are less likely to be enrolled in competitive classes or classes designed for college-bound students. In addition, these lower expectations may translate into instructional practice.

Landsman (2004) found that during her study, "Students in one St. Paul, Minnesota high school talked about a teacher who asked the white kids in an advanced placement class the tough questions, but turned to the few black or Latino students when she had an easy question that [any-one could answer]" (p. 29). When confronted, the teacher admitted to this practice, claiming, "I just assumed you didn't know the answers and I didn't want to embarrass you" (p. 29). These views can lead teachers and policy makers to ignore what they know to be best practices because they feel there is little likelihood that these will make much difference anyway.

At the urban middle schools in this study, one of the first acts of the small learning communities (SLCs) each year is to review the scheduling of students, especially in regards to the ELLs and placement in the appro-priate classes. Priority is given to those students needing the most support and to ensuring that they are scheduled with as many teachers as possible that have or are working towards an ESL teaching endorsement. One teacher leads a classroom that continues to fill the role of a newcomer's center. Those students scheduled with that teacher remain with her throughout the day. Only those students who have been in the country for less than a year are placed in that class. Another teacher facilitates a literacy pullout class that takes the place of a student's language arts credit. Two bilingual aides, both speaking Spanish and English, are also present in the building, and their schedules are based on the greatest amount of contact and need with the ELL students in the general education classrooms, usually with core subject teachers.

Teachers need to be educated as to how to build a cultural context in their classroom. They must understand that for students from poverty and minority backgrounds, the expectations cannot be lowered. Students must be expected to perform regardless of their environmental conditions. Blankenstein (2004) states, "High-performing schools realize that (1) what they do matters to the learning of each of their students, and (2) all children can indeed perform at high levels" (p.101).

First-Language Support and Sheltered Instruction Observation Protocol

Throughout the open-ended survey question responses from the teachers in this study, the concepts of providing first-language support and utilizing Sheltered Instruction Observation Protocol (SIOP) strategies were evident. Teachers identified effective first-language support structures from sources such as peer tutoring during classroom activities, bilingual paraprofessionals, and translators provided by the district. Instructional materials and information communicated to parents were often translated, or multilingual texts were used to reinforce first language along with second language acquisition. One teacher described a memorable story related to the opportunity for bilingual instruction in a language arts class for Spanish-speaking ELLs:

> The best experience I had with my ELL kiddos was when I had a para in my classroom that was able to work in bilingual groups. Because of her assistance my kiddos could get the English content from me, Spanish from her, and then when possible [they were] able to complete assignments in Spanish. My students grew more academically that year than any other with that group. It was awesome to be part of it!

Teachers were provided with SIOP strategies throughout the first year of the professional development program, and these were referenced by teachers in the open-ended survey questions related to effective instructional practices for ELLs. Specific mention of the effectiveness of creating language and content objectives to share with the students, building background knowledge, planning differentiated lessons, and guiding students to build connections and relate to prior learning were evident throughout teacher responses. Teachers also described scaffolding practices and use of visual aids and manipulatives as being effective instructional methods.

CONCLUSION

Teachers who participated in the professional development program shared their perceptions of the needs of urban middle-level ELLs and their recommendations for effective instructional techniques and methods to build positive relationships between ELLs and non-ELL peers, and between ELLs and adults. A statistical analysis of the achievement of ELLs during a two-year period demonstrated significant growth in reading and mathematics, and teacher comments on the survey echoed positive achievement. As one teacher stated:

> It has been neat to see how the students have grown and become successful at school since they arrived during 6th grade. I've seen several students who started in the Newcomers center in 6th grade become top students this year as an 8th grader. Each of these students has blossomed and will have a very bright future ahead of them.

Recommendations for further research include investigations to examine the relationship between professional development designed to improve instruction for ELLs, and ELL academic achievement with larger sample sizes of ELLs in diverse regions in the United States.

REFERENCES

Atwater, S. A. C. (2008). Waking up to difference: Teachers, color-blindness, and the effects on students of color. *Journal of Instructional Psychology, 35*(3), 246–253.

Blankenstein, A. M. (2004). *Failure is not an option.* Thousand Oaks, CA: Corwin Press.

Capps, R., Fix, M. E., Murray, J., Ost, J., Passel, J. S., & Herwantoro, S. (2005). *The new demography of America's schools: Immigration and the No Child Left Behind Act.* Washington, DC: Urban Institute.

Creswell, J. W. (2007). *Qualitative inquiry & research design: Choosing among the five approaches* (2nd ed.). Thousand Oaks, CA: Sage.

Fry, R. (2008). *The role of schools in the English language learner achievement gap.* Washington, DC: Pew Hispanic Center.

Hansen-Thomas, H. (2008). Sheltered instruction: Best practices for ELLs in the mainstream. *Kappa Delta Pi Record, 44*(4), 165–169.

Howard, G. R. (1999). *We can't teach what we don't know: White teachers, multiracial schools.* New York, NY: Teachers College Press.

Jackson, A., & Davis, G., with Abeel, M., & Bordonaro, A. (2000). *Turning points 2000: Educating adolescents in the 21st century*. New York, NY: Teachers College Press.

Jess, D., Davis, A., & Pokorny, N. (2004). High-achieving middle schools for Latino students in poverty. *Journal of Education for Students Placed at Risk, 9*(1), 23–45.

Kansas State Department of Education. (2007a, December). *Education in Kansas: 2006–2007accountability report*. Retrieved from http://www.ksde.org/LinkClick .aspx?fileticket=rBsrOtUuP4o%3d&tabid=228&mid=5038

Kansas State Department of Education. (2007b). *Report card 2006–2007*. Retrieved from http://online.ksde.org/rcard/state.aspx?org_no=D%

Landsman, J. (2004). Confronting the racism of low expectations. *Education Leadership, 62*(3), 28–32.

National Clearinghouse for English Language Acquisition. (2006). *Kansas rate of LEP growth 1994/1995–2004/2005*. Retrieved from http://www.ncela.gwu.edu/ policy/states/reports/statedata/2004LEP/Kansas-G-05.pdf

National Clearinghouse for English Language Acquisition. (2007). *The growing number of Limited English Proficient students 1995/96–2005/06*. Retrieved from http://www.ncela.gwu.edu/policy/states/reports/statedata/2005LEP/ GrowingLEP_0506.pdf

Nieto, S. (2002). *Language, culture, and teaching: Critical perspectives for a new century*. Mahwah, NJ: Erlbaum.

Public Law 107-110 (2001). *The No Child Left Behind Act of 2001*. Retrieved from http://www.ed.gov/policy/elsec/leg/esea02/index.html.

Schwartz, W. (2001). *Strategies for improving the educational outcomes of Latinas*. ERIC Digest. [www.ed.gov/databases/ERIC_Digests/ed458344.html]

Segal, B. (1981). *Teaching English through action*. (ERIC Document Reproduction Service No. ED224291)

Shuman, A. (2005). *Other people's stories: Entitlement claims and critiques of empathy*. Champaign, IL: University of Illinois Press.

Suarez-Orozco, C., & Suarez-Orozco, M. M. (2001). *Children of immigration*. Cambridge, MA: Harvard University Press.

U.S. Bureau of the Census. (2003). *Educational attainment in the United States: 2003*. Washington, DC. Retrieved from http://www.census.gov/population/www /socdemo/educ-attn.html

Zwiers, J. (2007). Teacher practices and perspectives for developing academic language. *International Journal of Applied Linguistics, 17*(1), 93–116.

CHAPTER 4

QUANTITATIVE REPORTING PRACTICES IN MIDDLE-GRADES RESEARCH JOURNALS

Lessons to Learn

Robert M. Capraro and Mary Margaret Capraro

This study examines two journals specific to the middle grades where original quantitative empirical articles are published—*Research in Middle Level Education* and *Middle Grades Research Journal*—to determine what quantitative statistics are used, how they are used, and what study designs are used. It is important for those who write for the middle-grades community to make a cognizant effort to adhere to recommendations that will improve the quality of what we know and how we can best situate our research findings to provide maximum information for the reader.

INTRODUCTION

There are many research paradigms and traditions that comprise middle grades research; this report does not in any way attempt to diminish or

Research Supporting Middle Grades Practice,
pp. 79–89

exalt any particular one. Several professional organizations have developed standards for quantitative reporting practices, and as of yet, there has been limited interest in attempting to establish reporting practices for the numerous rich traditions that comprise qualitative research.

It is important to examine and contextualize the strengths and weaknesses in quantitative reporting for middle-grades researchers. One important reason is that advocacy for the middle grades is often upheld by stakeholders (i.e., teachers, principals, parents, and the organizations that support these groups) and not researchers. If researchers are to make a lasting impact, likely to influence those who primarily advocate for the middle grades, they must provide authentic empirical research that is interpretable by those who will apply it. Therefore, the research published for this group must be written with attention to delivering the message to a two-tiered audience. This chapter carefully examines the journals specific to the middles grades where original quantitative empirical articles are published—*Research in Middle Level Education* and *Middle Grades Research Journal*—to examine what quantitative statistics are used, how they are used, and what study designs are used.

Rationale

Educational research yields its greatest potential contribution to middle-grades practices when recommended reporting practices are followed (American Educational Research Association [AERA], 2006; Natriello, 2006; Wilkinson & American Psychological Association [APA] Task Force on Statistical Inference, 1999). AERA adopted standards for assisting the research community in producing high quality empirical research reports. These standards provide guidance to editors, reviewers, and educational researchers alike, in vetting manuscripts submitted for publication (AERA).

Why Examine Reporting Practices

The middle-grades community relies on empirical reports of research to deal with recurring questions such as which grade configuration (5–8, 6–8, or 7–9, possibly others) is more likely to yield improved achievement, or are self-contained classes taught by generalists preferable to rotating students among teachers who are content area specialists. These are in addition to issues of emerging research topics such as socialization, affect and bonding, identity, technology, and cognition. To interpret results from these studies, reporting practices are important for communicating findings that will be used to influence middle-level education. In middle-grades research, we expect our findings will precipitate educational innovation and side-step known issues with the intellectual and emotional development of middle graders. While there is a need to produce middle-grades research for consumption by researchers, it is important to carefully report the findings accurately and with attention to the fact that some applied readers will have insufficient background knowledge to know if there are inherent flaws in either the design or analytic aspects (Stipek, 2005)—that is, in the reporting of the research it is important to build the skills of the reader who has to interpret it. Therefore, it is essential to educate those who make important middle-grades decisions within schools and districts (Wolk, 2007). To attain this goal, published research must include both the necessary and sufficient information for readers to evaluate claims.

The Lens for Examining Research

Reporting standards facilitate research quality by articulating a set of expectations by which informed editors, their boards and reviewers, and manuscript authors can have agreed upon dialog about the appropriateness of any particular manuscript for publication. In addition to having an unbiased set of criteria by which to judge a manuscript, it is important to provide a clear understanding of how scientific claims are warranted. While the APA and the AERA have developed a generic set of standards in general for social science researchers to follow, the American Statistical Association and the American Mathematics Association have developed sets of specific standards for their disciplines. Therefore, it is incumbent upon each discipline to develop and engender its own set of standards to ensure quality (Feuer, Towne, & Shavelson, 2002) and middle-grades research should not be left out.

There are important considerations in attaining the goal of providing useful and interpretable middle-grades research. First and foremost, our research questions should be clear. From these questions one can decide upon the design (e.g., experimental, quasi-experimental, or convenience). Then, from this design determine the research paradigm (Raudenbush, 2005). The analyses should be thoughtful and appropriately applied. It is important not to reduce primarily humanistic research endeavors of middle-grades research into a set of preprogrammed algorithms in an attempt to claim scientific rigor. All social science research, whether for middle grades or not, is about the iterative process of contemplation, reflection, and then employment of good judgment (Thompson, 2006) in making design and analytic choices. In the careful consideration of the methods we choose, our focus should deemphasize the technicalities of conducting statistical procedures, in favor of understanding their appropriate use and interpretation (Quilici & Mayer, 1996).

Thus, the lens through which middle-grades research in this study will be examined is (1) score reliability as reported for the data in hand (Capraro & Capraro, 2003; Henson, Capraro, & Capraro, 2004; Thompson, 2003); (2) null hypothesis statistical testing methods that are clear; (3) reported effect sizes (Capraro, 2004; Thompson 2007), and (4) confidence intervals (AERA, 2006; Capraro & Capraro, 2002).

METHODS

For the purposes of this chapter, three journals were considered that specifically report middle-grades research: *Middle Grades Research Journal*, *Research in Middle Level Education*, and *The Middle School Journal*. While *The Middle School Journal* deals mainly with the middle grades, it does not contain original reports of empirical research and was eliminated from further consideration. Therefore, the remaining two journals met the criteria of (1) dealing specifically with middle-grades research without limitation to any particular content area of developmental or structural aspects of middle grades, and (2) primarily containing reports of original empirical research. The inception of the *Middle Grades Research Journal* in spring 2006 expanded opportunities for publishing middle-grades research, presumably increasing the vitality of research in the area and providing additional signature space for the field. Therefore, for purposes of this study, the period from which articles were selected was from spring 2006 through May 2009.

Article selection was done by reviewing each article in each issue for the given time period. For an article to be selected for coding it had to contain reports of quantitative analyses and sufficient details about the sample to make generalizability claims clear. Too few articles provided sufficient detail to classify articles by design.

Coding

The coding criteria were based on recommendations contained in the guidelines established by the AERA Task Force (2006) and Wilkinson et al. (1999), but only a subset of those criteria were chosen for coding. The following categories were used: (1) descriptive statistics, (2) null hypothesis statistical significance testing (NHSST)/inferential statistics, (3) score reliability, (4) effect sizes, (5) confidence intervals (CI), and (6) types of statistical analyses. Each category contained additional indicators scored dichotomously as present or not present in each quantitative study. Among the indicators were types and quantity of descriptive statistics, NHSST, inferential statistics, types of score reliability and reliability induction, types and interpretation of effect sizes or contextualized effect, quantity and interpretation for CI, quantity and types of statistical analyses and if an alpha correction was employed when numerous univariate techniques were used, and finally quantity and types of graphical representations of the data. Of the 34 articles in *MGRJ* and the 32 articles in *RMLE*, 47 were quantitative, yielding 465 separate statistical analyses.

RESULTS

The findings were reported as a composite of the two journals by coding criteria.

Descriptive Statistics

Of the 38 studies reporting descriptive statistics (58% of the articles), many included standard deviations along with means. In five cases, insufficient descriptive statistics were provided, or some component, means, standard deviations, or a referent to what the reported descriptives were referring to was omitted. Descriptive statistics were less likely to be reported for the sample (58%) than for the variables of interest (73%). For example, it was common to calculate a mean for some measure but it was rarely disaggregated by subpopulation even in cases where the analyses focused on subsamples such as males and females within treatment or control, or ethnicity. Descriptive statistics were exclusively reported in the form of means and standard deviations, but several studies did not include standard deviations for the means (25%). For those 25% of the studies, effect sizes for tests of differences between means were also not reported. Therefore, another researcher who may be interested in meta-analytically using those findings would have difficulty calculating the effect sizes because the exact p-value does not contain information about the obtained effect (see Thompson, 2009; Zhang, 2009).

Null Hypothesis Statistical Significance Testing (NHSST)/ Inferential Statistics

The NHSST and inferential statistics generally included at least one exact p-value (68%), but in five manuscripts authors who reported exact p-values also reported $p = 0.00$. This error results from rounding within statistical packages. If the researcher were to double click the value in SPSS or PASW, it would reveal a very small value represented in scientific notation. It should have been reported as less than .001 if indeed it was. Additionally, authors who reported exact p-values for p-calculated when it was less than .05 tended to not report exact p-values (80%) when it was greater. The inferential statistics were often underreported. It was common to invoke tests without examining the assumptions underlying their use. The three most abused were the failure to examine normality or departure from normality before choosing parametric or nonparametric statistics (93%), failure to discuss independence of observation before using ANOVA (100%), and using multiple univariate analyses without experiment-wise Type I error correction. It is important to note that the data are univariate normal supporting parametric statistics; however, when they are not univariate normal, nonparametric statistics should be invoked. Independence of observation is not about the data but about the study design. When the design is fully nested—such as students within teacher or teacher within school—one fails to meet this assumption. Just under 25% of the studies used any correction even though this is a very simple process that can be applied to alpha or p-critical. The formula for a Bonferroni correction is $1 - (1 - \alpha)^{1/n}$, where α equals the a priori alpha level, .05 in most cases, and n equals the number of comparisons. Therefore, in the study that reported 70 t tests, a critical value of .00073 should have been used. This is a safeguard against multiple tests of statistical significance on the same data falsely giving the appearance of significance, because at $\alpha = .05$, 1 out of every 20 hypothesis-tests is expected to be statistically significant purely due to chance. The problem is that we do not know which one. Therefore, each test must be set to a substantially more stringent alpha level. A simpler correction is to divide the a priori alpha level by the number of tests; therefore, .05/70 would equal an alpha level of .00071, essentially the same as the previous estimate. For the three studies reporting the most number of univariate tests, there would have been no statistically significant results to talk about. Additionally, for the next four highest, nearly half the results reported as statistically significant would not have been if they had used a corrected p-critical.

In addition, nearly 28% of the articles contained arbitrary p-critical values; for example, in some places $p < .70$ was reported, on occasion within the same paragraph and set of analyses a $p < .031$ and $p < .003$, were used without a rationale. It is important to set the p-critical value before one begins analysis of the data, and criteria should be stated in the article along with reporting the exact p-calculated value to three places.

Score Reliability

It is important to report the reliability for the data in hand because it attenuates the obtained effects (cf. Reinhardt, 1996). Twenty of the studies reported a Cronbach's alpha reliability and one reported Cohen's Kappa for the data in hand. Unfortunately, 14 reported a reliability coefficient from a test manual or source other than their study or reliability induction. The obtained reliability may be very different from that reported by other researchers or from the test manual. Because researchers often perform statistical analyses that consider subsamples of the dataset, reliability should be reported for all subsamples of interest because it is likely that the reliability for a subgroup can vary greatly from the entire sample. Only two studies considered all the reliabilities for the subsamples of interest that were used in their analyses. Only two articles included all the items for all the instruments used in the study. It is difficult to accumulate knowledge when a researcher-designed instrument is used once and not provided for subsequent authors to use in subsequent studies. While it is acceptable practice for authors to say the instrument is available by request, academia affords a great deal of mobility, and tracking down authors can be daunting. Additionally, it is possible that a particular line of research would not achieve a following until an author is no longer in academia and the instrument would be lost to future generations of researchers attempting to further that particular line of inquiry.

Effect Size

Nearly 70% of the studies reported some estimate of effects. The most common metric was percent change (48%) of measured variables followed by eta^2 and ANOVA; however, eta^2 was not reported for all ANOVAs. A phi coefficient, reported with nonparametric methods, was only reported 6% of the time while nonparametric methods were represented quite heavily. Typically, regression results include an R^2 effect; however, in these two journals it was only reported 21% of the time. Cohen's d was used 15% percent of the time but almost never with t tests. The Cohen's d is among a class of effect sizes that can be easily computed. The formula is $d = \dfrac{\bar{X}_E - \bar{X}_C}{\sigma}$, the difference in the means divided by the standard deviation for the whole sample. Even though this formula is straightforward, it was underused given t tests were so heavily represented in the articles.

Confidence Intervals

Thinking meta-analytically is important and CIs function to provide more information than a single point estimate (cf. Skidmore, 2009). CIs can provide a graphical representation of the preciseness of the estimate as well comparative estimates when considering other similar studies. Only one article reported and graphed CIs.

Types of Statistical Analyses

The most common analytic choice by number of times it was used was the t test ($n = 212$; range of 1–70 times per article), followed by χ^2 ($n = 120$; range 1–102), ANOVA ($n = 65$; range 1–10), regression ($n = 19$; range 1–3), and correlations ($n = 15$). If each correlation had been counted individually, it would have been the most widely used analytic choice. In some articles, correlation coefficients were computed for all variables and latent variables by subgroups, even though none of the coefficients were interpreted. Some complex analyses were also reported, albeit to a much lesser extent. Hierarchical regression was used 10 times but in only two articles. Exploratory and confirmatory factor analyses were used a total of six times in three articles. MANOVA represented about 3% of the analyses across the articles. Using MANOVA reduces the number of univariate analyses, thus managing Type I error.

FOR THE MIDDLE-GRADES RESEARCHER, CONSUMER, AND REVIEWERS

The important messages for those who write for the middle-grades community is to make a cognizant effort to adhere to recommendations that will improve the quality of what we know and how we can best situate our research reports to provide maximum information for the reader. The typical quantitative research article should provide the psychometrics for the instruments being used, minimally the reliability for the data in hand, plus (if applicable) a copy of the instrument in the appendix or provide availability from the author. Next, it is important to inform the reader of how null hypothesis testing will be evaluated, making use of corrected p-values when planning to use multiple univariate tests. It is also important to make explicit how implicit assumptions for each analytic choice are met. Because small sample sizes limit the power to reject the null hypothesis, it is always a good idea to report the effect size for every hypothesis test. Some may hold that unless the results are statistically significant, one does not need to consider the magnitude of the effect or that a statistically significant result automatically makes the obtained effect practically important. Both of these are false conceptions. First, a small sample size can mask a practically important effect, and this information may have real implications for theory development and should not be brushed aside because it was masked by a small sample size. Secondly, if one has a sample of 2000 participants, a very small difference will be statistically significant even when that difference is not practically important. Therefore, obtaining statistically significant results do not assure practically important differences.

One option for reducing the reliance on *t* test and chi square analyses is to use multivariate methods that are more effective. Using MANOVA allows two or more dependent variables to be compared to several independent variables, which can provide a much more parsimonious model and a better portrayal of reality.

Confidence intervals provide insights into the precision of the estimate as well as a metric for comparing variables. Additionally, it helps to conceptualize that the point estimate obtained in every study is just an estimate, and many other estimates are equally plausible.

We offer a set of guidelines for middle-grades researchers who engage in quantitative research, rooted in an evaluation of practice for consideration when writing reports of original research to maximize the transportability of their work and to facilitate its usefulness. These topics are no less important, but the What Works Clearing House has already emphasized issues related to design and participant selection, so reemphasizing them here would limit the message rooted in the reporting practice of middle-grades researchers. We applaud the tireless work of those who participate in the peer-review process. Without their efforts and the dedication of editors, reviewers, and authors, this manuscript would not have been possible, nor would the field have the opportunity for reflecting and reexamining its cumulative work.

The four-part lens of score reliability, null hypothesis statistical significance testing, effect sizes, and confidence intervals, through which middle-grades research was examined, yielded recommendations that these authors hope middle-grades journals, editors, reviewers, and authors will embrace when using quantitative methods:

1. requiring the instrument in initial publications and psychometrics each time it is used

2.   reporting alpha a priori and any requisite corrections when using multiple univariate tests
3.   reporting exact p-values to three decimal places and less than .001 when smaller, thus never reporting a calculated p-value as .000
4.   reporting and discussing effect size estimates and making explicit comparisons to those reported in other similar studies
5.   limiting the use of multiple univariate tests and increasing the use of multivariate tests

REFERENCES

American Educational Research Association. (2006). Standards for reporting on empirical social science research in AERA publications. *Educational Researcher, 35*(6), 33–40.

Capraro, R. M. (2004). Statistical significance, effect size reporting, and confidence intervals: Best reporting strategies. *Journal for Research in Mathematics Education, 35*, 57–62.

Capraro, R. M., & Capraro, M. M. (2002). Treatments of effect sizes and statistical significance tests in textbooks. *Educational and Psychological Measurement, 62*, 771-782.

Capraro, M. M., & Capraro, R. M. (2003). Exploring the impact of the new APA 5th Edition Publication Manual on the preferences of journal board members. *Educational and Psychological Measurement, 63*, 554–565.

Feuer, M. J., Towne, L., & Shavelson, R. J. (2002). Scientific culture and educational research. *Educational Researcher, 31*(8), 4–14.

Henson, R., Capraro, R. M., & Capraro, M. M. (2004). Reporting practice and use of exploratory factor analysis in educational research journals. *Research in the Schools, 11*(2), 61–72.

Natriello, G. (2006). Research and educational policy (Part 1): The relationship between research and policy. *Teachers College Record.* Retrieved from http://www.tcrecord.org, ID No. 10636

Quilici, J. L., & Mayer, R. E. (1996). Role of examples in how students learn to categorize statistics word problems. *Journal of Educational Psychology, 88*, 144–161.

Raudenbush, S. W. (2005). Learning from attempts to improve schooling: The contribution of methodological diversity. *Educational Researcher, 34*(5), 25–31.

Reinhardt, B. M. (1996). Factors affecting coefficient alpha: A mini Monte Carlo study. In B. Thompson (Ed.), *Advances in social science methodology* (Vol. 4, pp. 3–20). Greenwich, CT: JAI Press.

Skidmore, S. T. (2009). What confidence intervals really do and why they are so important for middle grades educational research. *Middle Grades Research Journal, 4*, 35-56.

Stipek, D. (2005). 'Scientifically based practice': It's about more than improving the quality of research. *Education Week, 24*(28), 34–35.

Thompson, B. (Ed.) (2003). *Score reliability: Contemporary thinking on reliability issues*. Thousand Oaks, CA: Sage.

Thompson, B. (2006). *Foundations of behavioral statistics: An insight-based approach*. New York, NY: Guilford.

Thompson, B. (2007). Effect sizes, confidence intervals, and confidence intervals for effect sizes. *Psychology in the Schools, 44*, 423–432.

Thompson, B. (2009). Computing & interpreting effect sizes in educational research. *Middle Grades Research Journal, 4*, 11-24.

Wilkinson, L., & APA Task Force on Statistical Inference. (1999). Statistical methods in psychology journals: Guidelines and explanations. *American Psychologist, 54*, 594–604.

Wolk, R. A. (2007). Education research could improve schools, but probably won't. *Education Week, 26*(24), 38–39.

Zhang, G. (2009). *t*-Test: The good, the bad, the ugly & the remedy. *Middle Grades Research Journal, 4*, 25-34.

CHAPTER 5

t TEST

The Good, the Bad, the Ugly, and the Remedy

Guili Zhang

The *t* test is one of the most commonly used significance tests to assess whether the means of two groups are statistically significantly different from each other. The use of *t* test has become a natural choice, and rarely do practitioners question its appropriateness. This chapter reviews and discusses *t* test's value in providing a rough comparison of two means (the good), its inability to provide the amount or magnitude of the difference in means (the bad), and its deficiency in that its outcome essentially depends completely on the sample size (the ugly). The *t* test's failure to provide the amount of difference offers no basis for us to judge practical significance. Furthermore, it makes meta-analysis impossible or ineffective and, therefore, seriously hinders the advancement of educational research. Its direct dependency on sample size makes a *t* test virtually useless in providing reliable information. Effect size (ES) and confidence interval (CI) for ES are recommended to address *t* test's inadequacies by serving as a supplement to or replacement of the *t* test. The commonly used effect size indices are reviewed and discussed in regard to their performance and robustness.

Research Supporting Middle Grades Practice,
pp. 91–100

INTRODUCTION

Middle-grades researchers often use t tests to determine if two means are statistically significantly different from each other. Researchers are happy when the t test informs them that group A's mean is bigger than group B's or vice versa. Researchers rarely ask themselves: Is this all I can know? Do I not want to know how much bigger group A's mean is than group B's? Furthermore, they often fail to realize that the statistical significance of the difference between the two groups' means directly depends on the sample size. In fact, given big enough sample sizes, the two means will almost always be statistically significantly different from each other!

It has been nearly 15 years since the publication of Cohen's wakeup call article (Cohen, 1994) titled "The Earth is Round ($p < .05$)," in which he discussed four decades of severe criticism of significance testing and rigorously criticized this practice, including the use of the t test. Yet, significance testing, the mechanical dichotomous decision around a sacred .05 criterion, still persists, despite the great deal of mischief that has been associated with the test of significance (Bakan, 1966).

Using an ES in addition to or in place of a hypothesis test such as a t test has been recommended by some statistical methodologists since as early as the 1960s because ESs are recognized as being more appropriate and more informative (Cohen, 1965, 1994; Cumming & Finch, 2005; Finch, Thomason, & Cumming, 2002; Hays, 1963; Meehl, 1967; Nickerson, 2000; Steiger & Fouladi, 1997; Zhang & Algina, in press). Further, a CI for ES contains all the information found in the significance test as well as vital information not provided by the significance test about the magnitude of effects and precision of estimates (Cohen, 1994; Cumming & Finch, 2001, 2005). A CI indicates the range of population ESs with which the data are consistent. By contrast, a hypothesis test merely indicates whether the data are consistent with a population ES of zero or not.

PERSPECTIVE AND METHODOLOGY

t Test—The Good: It Tells the Direction

The t test is often used to test a hypothesis regarding the equality of two means. The process is as follows (Fraenkel & Wallen, 2008):

1. Specify the research hypothesis, which is the predicted outcome of a study (e.g., There is a difference between the population mean of students using method A and that of students using method B).

2. State the null hypothesis (H_0) (e.g., There is no difference between the population means of students using method A and students using method B).

3. Find the sample statistics pertinent to the hypothesis.

4. Find the p value—that is, the probability of obtaining the observed results in the samples if the null hypothesis is true. This is done by comparing the observed t statistic with the t distribution. The shape of the t distribution is directly tied to the sample size, or more precisely the degree of freedom, df, which is the number of *independent* observations.

5. Reject H_0 and accept the research hypothesis if the p value is smaller than the pre-specified type I error rate α, usually .05.

6. Do not reject H_0 if the p value is greater or equal to α.

As such, the t test serves as an administratively convenient method through which researchers obtain crude information about the comparison of two means (see Figure 5.1). Specifically, with a nondirectional hypothesis, the t test answers the question, "are the two population means different?", and in a directional hypothesis, it answers the question regarding the direction of the difference: "is the mean of population A bigger or smaller than that of population B?" Such information, although rudimentary, can be useful in some situations.

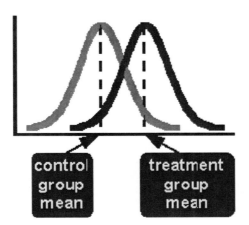

Figure 5.1.   Idealized distributions for two groups' scores.

t Test—The Bad: It Does Not Tell Us the Magnitude of Difference

Significance testing has not only failed to support the advance of psychology (social science) as a science, but also has seriously impeded it (Cohen, 1994). What it tells researchers is very elementary and crude. It tells the direction (i.e., which one is bigger?), not the amount—that is, how much group A's mean is bigger than group B's. Tukey (1991) discounted the value of what a *t* test can offer researchers by stating, "It is foolish to ask 'are the effects of A and B different?' They are always different—for some decimal place" (p. 100).

The ritual dichotomous reject–accept decision is not the way any science is done (Cohen, 1994). Cohen's opinion echoed Rozeboom's assertion in as early as 1960: "The primary aim of a scientific experiment is not to precipitate decisions, but to make an appropriate adjustment in the degree to which one ... believes the hypothesis ... being tested" (Rozeboom, 1960, p. 420). Physical scientists have learned much by storing up the amounts, not just directions. Measuring things on a communicable scale lets researchers stockpile information about amounts, which serves as foundation for meta-analysis.

t Test—The Ugly: It Completely Depends on Sample Size

The ugly side of the *t* test is, given big enough sample size, the null hypothesis is always false (Cohen, 1994). This shortcoming very much discredits the value of *t* test entirely. As Cohen (1990) stated,

> It can only be true in the bowels of a computer processor running a Monte Carlo study (and even then a stray electron may make it false). If it is false, even to a tiny degree, it must be the case that a large enough sample will produce a significant result and lead to its rejection. So, if the null hypothesis is always false, what's the big deal about rejecting it? (p. 1308)

In fact, Berkson expressed a similar view in as early as 1938, "It would be agreed by statistician that a large sample is always better than a small sample.... But since the result of the former [large sample] test is known, it is no test at all" (p. 526f). Thompson (1992) made the same point even more piercingly:

> Statistical significance testing can involve a tautological logic in which tired researchers, having collected data on hundreds of subjects, then conduct a statistical test to evaluate whether there were a lot of subjects, which the researchers already know, because they collected the data and know they are

tired. This tautology has created considerable damage as regards the accumulation of knowledge. (p. 436)

t Test: The Remedy

An important caveat when overusing *t* tests (see Capraro & Capraro, 2009) as a first option for avoiding multiple univariate tests is to use a multivariate method like canonical correlation analysis (see Yetkiner, 2009). However, when considering *t* tests, effect sizes are recognized as being more appropriate and more informative than *t* tests (Cohen, 1965, 1994; Cumming & Finch, 2005; Finch et al., 2002; Hays, 1963; Meehl, 1967; Nickerson, 2000; Steiger & Fouladi, 1997; Zhang & Algina, in press). In the last two decades, reporting an ES has become mandatory in some editorial policies (Murphy, 1997; Thompson, 1994) and is strongly recommended for *American Psychological Association* (*APA*) journals. *The Publication Manual of the American Psychological Association* (APA, 2001) stated that it is almost always necessary to include some index of ES or strength of relationship in the results section of a research paper. In fact, the manual cites the failure to report effect sizes as a defect in reporting research. The APA Task Force on Statistical Inference (Wilkinson & the Task Force on Statistical Inference, 1999) also supported this position. A CI for an ES is recommended as a superior replacement for significance testing because this CI contains all the information found in the significance tests and vital information not provided by the significance tests about the magnitude of effects and precision of estimates (Cohen, 1994; Cumming & Finch, 2001, 2005).

The merit of providing magnitude of effects and precision of estimation is clearly shown in the following example. Suppose a researcher conducted two experiments to test whether there was a significant difference between the treatment group and the control group. Recall that Cohen (1969) suggested .20, .50, and .80 as small, medium, and large ESs in experiments comparing two treatments. There were 400 participants in experiment A, resulting in 200 participants in each group. The researcher found a small ES of .20, which was significantly different than zero ($t = 2$, $p < .05$) and indicated statistical support for a treatment effect. For experiment B, the researcher was only able to find 16 participants, resulting in 8 participants in each group, and found a large ES of .80, which was not significantly different from zero ($t = 1.6$, $p > .05$) and did not indicate support for a treatment effect. Given hypothesis testing and effect sizes, one apparent contradiction is that a small ES results in statistically significant evidence of a treatment effect (experiment A), while a large ES results in nonsignificant evidence of a treatment effect (experiment B).

The apparent contradiction can be resolved by setting a CI for the ES in each experiment. In experiment A, the CI is [.003, .396]. The CI tells us that the data in experiment A are consistent with a population ES between .003 and .396, and thus indicates a population ES that is larger than zero but may be extremely small or may approach a medium ES. In experiment B, the CI is [−.236, 1.810], indicating the data are consistent with a population ES anywhere between −.236 and 1.810 and thus indicates that the population ES may be anywhere from a small ES in favor of the control treatment to a very large ES in favor of the experimental treatment. Clearly the CIs provide more complete information than the ES and the hypothesis test. The CIs also explain why the hypothesis tests indicated that a small ES was significantly different from zero in experiment A, while a large ES was not significantly different from zero in experiment B. In Experiment A, the population ES was much more precisely estimated than the population ES in experiment B.

EFFECT SIZE INDICES

A large number of ES indices have been developed and proposed (Algina, Keselman, & Penfield, 2005). There are a variety of commonly used ESs measuring separation of two independent samples. Among them are Cohen's d (Cohen, 1965) (for more information about Cohen's d, see Thompson, 2009), Glass's d, Hedges' g (Hedges & Olkin, 1985), two versions of Cohen's d based on trimmed means and Winsorized variances (d_R suggested by Hogarty and Kromrey, 2001 and d_R suggested by Algina et al., 2005), eta squared, omega squared, McGraw and Wong's (1992) common language ES (CL), Cliff's dominance statistic (1993, 1996), Kraemer and Andrews γ_1^* (1982), Wilcox and Muska's W (1999), and Vargha and Delaney's A (2000).

Hedges' g is a variation of Cohen's d that provides some adjustment to reduce small sample bias. Eta squared and omega squared are similar in that both are proportion-of-variance measures conveying the proportion of the total variance that is due to the groups. McGraw and Wong's (1992) CL provides an estimate of the probability that a score for a member in a population is greater than a score for a member in another population under the assumption of independence, normality, and equal variances. Denoting this probability as $p_{2 > 1}$, Cliff's dominance statistic estimates the value of $p_{2 > 1} - p_{1 > 2}$. In other words, Cliff's d is used to estimate the degree to which the probability that a score in the second treatment exceeds a score in the first treatment is different from the probability that a score in the first treatment exceeds a score in the second treatment, the property that Cliff referred to as "dominance." Kraemer and Andrews' γ_1^* (1982) is a nonparametric index of effect size that is based on the degree of overlap between samples. Wilcox and Muska's W is a nonparametric analogue of omega squared that estimates the degree of certainty with which an observation can be associated with one population rather than the other. Vargha and Delaney's A is a measure of stochastic superiority that applies to distributions that are at least ordinally scaled (Hogarty & Kromrey, 2001).

Performance of the Effect Size Indices

Research investigating the performance of the various ES measures is fairly limited. Hedges and Olkin (1985) suggested that Cohen's d evidences a small sample bias. Hogarty and Kromrey (2001) compared the performance of nine effect size indices when they are used in the context of populations with various levels of nonnormality and variance heterogeneity. The nine indices include Cohen's d, Cliff's dominance statistic, g, γ_1^*, CL, A, $d_R^\dagger$, a naïve estimator of W, and a .632 bootstrap estimator of W. They evaluated the performance of these nine indices in terms of their statistical bias and standard error by using Monte Carlo methods. The results indicate that Cohen's d and Hedges' g, the two most frequently used effect size estimates, showed nontrivial sensitivity to violations of normality and homogeneity of variance, which confirms the concerns raised about the appropriateness of using these indices as indicators of effects in such populations (Kraemer & Andrews, 1982; Wilcox & Muska, 1999). In addition, $d_R^\dagger$ evidenced severe bias under small sample conditions. Indices CL, γ_1^* and the naïve estimator of W only appeared to be slightly less sensitive than Cohen's d and Hedges' g, but showed pronounced bias under small sample size condition or nontrivial sensitivity to violations of normality and homogeneity of variance. Cliff's dominance statistic and Vargha and Delaney's A showed better performances in producing relatively unbiased estimates and consistent standard errors.

Hess and Kromrey (2004) investigated the performance of the CIs for Cohen's d and Cliff's dominance statistic constructed by using seven CI construction methods. The CI construction methods included the normal theory Z band, the percentile bootstrap, the bias corrected bootstrap, the bias corrected and accelerated bootstrap (BCa), pivotal, Studentized pivotal, and the Steiger and Fouladi interval inversion band. (For a description of these methods, see Hess & Kromrey, 2004.) Monte Carlo methods were used to compare confidence interval estimates using random samples generated from populations under known and controlled conditions. There were four design factors: (1) sample size ranging from 5 to 200 including balanced and unbalanced designs; (2) population effect sizes .00, .20, .50, and .80; (3) population distribution shape (population skewness and kurtosis of 0,0 and 2,6; and (4) variance in the two populations: 1:1, 1:2, 1:4, and 1:8. Across all of the conditions, all of the CI construction methods provided slightly better coverage probabilities for Cliff's dominance statistic than for Cohen's d, with the exception of the Pivotal Bootstrap method.

Reporting a CI for the effect size is important as was well put by Wilkinson et al. (1999) (for more information on CI's consider Capraro & Capraro, 2009; Thompson, 2009). Steiger and Fouladi (1997) asserted that it is much more informative to state a confidence interval on $\mu_2 - \mu_1$ than it is to give the p level for the t test of the hypothesis that $\mu_2 - \mu_1 = 0$. Interests in the accuracy and usefulness of the ESs have motivated explorations of the usefulness and effectiveness of CIs for ESs (cf. Algina & Keselman, 2003a, 2003b; Cumming & Fitch, 2001; Zhang & Algina, in press). For more information on CI's consider Skidmore's recent work (2009).

RESULTS AND DISCUSSION

It is recognized that t test is not an effective method for comparing two means. The t test only informs us whether "A is different from B." Moreover, this only piece of information that t test provides us is virtually worthless because given big enough sample size, A is always different from B. Therefore, we cannot learn much from a t test. It is clear that amount, as well as direction, is vital.

Confidence intervals for effect size are strongly recommended to be used as a useful supplement to and maybe even a superior replacement for the t test. Effect size indices such as Cohen's δ are able to provide all information that is provided by the t test as well as vital information not provided by the t test such as the magnitude of the effects and precision of estimates.

The use of adequate effect size index and confidence intervals to supplement or take the place of t test will make studies on two group comparisons more informative and useful as a basis for judging practical significance. Quantifying the differences between the means on a commutable scale also makes meta-analysis possible and the replication and comparisons of research studies achievable, which can serve as the cornerstone for the advancement of quantitative educational research.

REFERENCES

Algina, J., & Keselman, H. J. (2003a). Approximate confidence intervals for effect sizes. *Educational and Psychological Measurement, 63*, 537–553.

Algina, J., & Keselman, H. J. (2003b, May). *Confidence intervals for effect sizes*. Paper presented at a conference in honor of H. Swaminathan, Amherst, MA.

Algina, J., Keselman, H. J., & Penfield, R. D. (2005). Effect sizes and their intervals: The two-level repeated measures case. *Educational and Psychological Measurement, 65*, 241–258.

American Psychological Association. (2001). *Publication manual of the American Psychological Association* (5th ed.). Washington, DC: Author.

Bakan, D. (1966). The test of significance in psychological research. *Psychological Bulletin, 66*, 1–29.

Berkson, J. (1938). Some difficulties of interpretation encountered in the application of the chi-square test. *Journal of the American Statistical Association, 33*, 526–542.

Cliff, N. (1993). Dominance statistics: Ordinal analyses to answer ordinal questions. *Psychological Bulletin, 114*, 494–509.

Cliff, N. (1996). Answering ordinal questions with ordinal data using ordinal statistics. *Multivariate Behavioral Research, 31*, 331–350.

Cohen, J. (1965). Some statistical issues in psychological research. In B.B. Wolman (Ed.), *Handbook of clinical psychology* (pp. 95–121). New York, NY: Academic Press.

Cohen, J. (1969). *Statistical power analyses for the behavioral sciences*. New York, NY: Academic Press.

Cohen, J. (1990). Things I have learned (so far). *American Psychologist, 45*, 1304–1302.

Cohen, J. (1994). The earth is round (*p* < .05). *American Psychologists, 49*, 997–1003.

Cumming, G., & Finch. S. (2001). A primer on the understanding, use, and calculation of confidence intervals that are based on central and noncentral distributions. *Educational and Psychological Measurement, 61*, 532–574.

Cumming, G., & Finch, S. (2005). Inference by eye: Confidence intervals and how to read pictures of data. *American Psychologist, 60*, 178–180.

Finch, S., Thomason, N., & Cumming, G. (2002). Past and future American Psychological Association guidelines for statistical practice. *Theory and Psychology, 36*, 312–324.

Fraenkel, J. R., & Wallen, N. E. (2008). *How to design and evaluate research in education*. San Francisco, CA: McGraw-Hill.

Hays, W. L. (1963). *Statistics*. New York, NY: Holt, Rinehart & Winston.

Hedges, L. V., & Olkin, I. (1985). *Statistical methods for meta-analysis*. Orlando, FL: Academic Press.

Hess, M. R., & Kromrey, J. D. (2004, April). *Robust confidence intervals for effect sizes: A comparative study of Cohen's d and Cliff's delta under non-normality and heterogeneous variances*. Paper presented at the annual meeting of the American Educational Research Association, San Diego, CA.

Hogarty, K. Y., & Kromrey, J. D. (2001, April). *We've been reporting some effect sizes: Can you guess what they mean?* Paper presented at the annual meeting of the American Educational Research Association, Seattle, WA.

Kraemer, H. C., & Andrews, G. A. (1982). A nonparametric technique for meta-analysis effect size calculation. *Psychological Bulletin, 91*, 404–412.

McGraw, K. O., & Wong, S. P. (1992). A common language effect size statistic. *Psychological Bulletin, 111*, 361–365.

Meehl, P. E. (1967). Theory testing in psychology and physics: A methodological paradox. *Philosophy of Science, 34*, 103–115.

Murphy, K. R. (1997). Editorial. *Journal of Applied Psychology, 82*, 3–5.

Nickerson, R. (2000). Null hypothesis significance testing: A review of an old and continuing controversy. *Psychological Methods, 5*, 241–301.

Rozeboom, W. W. (1960). The fallacy of the null hypothesis significance test. *Psychological Bulletin, 57*, 416–428.

Skidmore, S. T. (2009). What confidence intervals really do and why they are so important for middle grades educational research. *Middle Grades Research Journal, 4*(2), 35-55.

Steiger, J. H., & Fouladi, R. T. (1997). Noncentrality interval estimation and the evaluation of statistical models. In L. Harlow, S. Mulaik, & J. H. Steiger (Eds.), *What if there were no significance tests?* (pp. 221-257). Hillsdale, NJ: Erlbaum.

Thompson, B. (1992). Two and one-half decades of leadership in measurement and evaluation. *Journal of Counseling and Development, 70*, 434–438.

Thompson, B. (1994). Guidelines for authors. *Educational and Psychological Measurement, 54*, 837–847.

Thompson, B. (2009). Computing & interpreting Effect Sizes in educational research. *Middle Grades Research Journal, 4*(2), 11-24.

Tukey, J. W. (1991). The philosophy of multiple comparisons. *Statistical Science, 6*, 100–116.

Vargha, A., & Delaney, H. D. (2000). A critique and improvement of the CL Common Language effect size statistics of McGraw and Wong. *Journal of Educational and Behavioral Statistics, 25*, 101–132.

Wilcox, R. R., & Muska, J. (1999). Measuring effect size: A non-parametric analogue of ω^2. *British Journal of Mathematical and Statistical Psychology, 52*, 93–110.

Wilkinson, L., & The Task force on Statistical Inference (1999). Statistical methods in psychology journals. *American Psychologist, 54*, 594–604.

Zhang, G., & Algina, J. (2008). Coverage performance of the non-central F-based and percentile bootstrap confidence intervals for Root Mean Square Standardized Effect Size in one-way fixed-effects ANOVA. *Journal of Modern Applied Statistical Methods, 7*(1), 56-76.

Zhang, G., & Algina, J. (in press). A robust root mean square standardized effect size and its confidence intervals in one-way fixed-effects ANOVA. *Journal of Modern Applied Statistical Methods*.

CHAPTER 6

EFFECTIVE ALTERNATIVE
URBAN MIDDLE SCHOOLS

Findings From Research
on NativityMiguel Schools

L. Mickey Fenzel

The purpose of the present study is to summarize the research to date and
report additional findings on a successful alternative model for urban middle level education that is incorporated in NativityMiguel schools. These
schools, designed particularly to meet the educational and social developmental needs of young adolescents at risk because of social and economic
disadvantage, incorporate much of what is known about effective urban
middle level education. Previous research has shown that students in these
schools demonstrate exceptional academic gains while they develop skills of
leadership and effective coping and problem solving. The present study
examines particular aspects of the NativityMiguel model that are employed
in a number of the schools and takes a closer look at the program at one
NativityMiguel school that educates a diverse group of students, most of
whom are chosen by lottery from among applicants from low-income families. Implications for a wider implementation of the model in urban schools
are also discussed.

Research Supporting Middle Grades Practice,
pp. 101–118
Copyright © 2010 by Information Age Publishing
All rights of reproduction in any form reserved.

101

INTRODUCTION

The chorus has grown in size and volume. Its song laments the condition of urban public schools for children of color placed at risk because of economic and social forces that deprive them and their families of access to a high-quality education. A number of alternative approaches to educating these children have appeared with mixed success. One model of middle level education that has provided consistent and impressive results is the NativityMiguel model. This article will provide evidence of the levels of success achieved by NativityMiguel schools and identify the qualities of these alternative schools that contribute to the enviable levels of success they have in educating children from high-poverty urban communities.

Noguera (2003) and others have declared that urban schools have failed to provide urban children and adolescents with an education that can prepare them for successful educational and professional lives. As researchers (Joftus, 2002; Thernstrom & Thernstrom, 2003) have noted, urban school failure has had particularly detrimental effects on African American and Latino children and adolescents, for whom dropout rates are exceptionally high and prose and quantitative literacy skills more deficient than those of whites. With respect to middle level education, the Carnegie Council on Adolescent Development (1989) reported over 20 years ago in its *Turning Points* document that far too many young adolescents were seriously deficient in critical reasoning skills and at high risk for school failure. The Council declared that a serious mismatch existed between the ways middle school students were taught and their developmental needs and that the difficulties and risks faced by young adolescents were greater for those who are economically poor and members of minority groups. Efforts to improve poorly performing middle schools for students placed at risk have been slow coming.

Among the successful schools for these students, however, are the NativityMiguel schools, which educate over 4,000 students in 64 schools across the U.S. each year. In this study, I address the characteristics of these schools that contribute to the success of urban students placed at risk because of economic and social disadvantage. In addition, a more thorough analysis of the program at one school that employs the NativityMiguel model is presented.

NATIVITYMIGUEL SCHOOLS

The first NativityMiguel model middle school opened in 1971 to meet the academic needs of the children of economically poor Puerto Rican immigrant families on the lower East side of Manhattan that were not being addressed in the public schools they were attending. Having tutored the middle school boys from the neighborhood for several years at the Nativity Mission Center in order to advance their academic skills to the point of gaining admittance to high-quality Catholic high schools in the borough, a group of concerned educators, led by the Jesuit order of Catholic priests, decided to take the step of transforming the Center into a middle school. One impetus behind the move to establish the middle school, a new venture for the Jesuits who operated many high schools, colleges, and universities in the United States and other countries, was the desire to put more than a bandage on the problem of economic poverty and to take steps toward systemic change.

The limited square footage in the narrow four-story building that housed the school restricted the size of the student population to approximately 60 boys in grades six through eight, and the experience of the founders in tutoring the students who came to them with limited academic skills helped them to see the importance of keeping class sizes small. In addition, the lack of student academic skills, the dangerous nature of the students' neighborhoods, and the availability of volunteers from local high schools and colleges led the school to continue late afternoon and evening tutoring in order to help the students "catch up" academically. A gift from a supporter enabled the school to continue the students' social, character, spiritual, and academic education during the summer at a camp in upstate New York (see Fenzel, 2009). The small school size and summer camp program became two of the defining features of what was to become the Nativity model of middle level education.

It took nearly 20 years for educators affiliated with the original Nativity Mission Center middle school to take the model north to Harlem and to Boston, both Jesuit initiatives that bore fruit in 1991, and 1993 saw the opening of seven new schools modeled after the Nativity Mission Center program. One of these schools, founded by the Lasallian Christian Brothers in Providence, RI, became the first of several Lasallian San Miguel schools that operated under its own umbrella organization until it merged with the Nativity school network in 2006. By that year, over 60 schools that employed the Nativity Mission model had been in operation under the auspices of the NativityMiguel Network of Schools (see Fenzel, 2009; NativityMiguel Network of Schools, 2008).

Today, 52% of the NativityMiguel schools educate children in single-sex environments, the majority of which educate boys, and academic classes in coeducational schools segregate boys and girls for instruction for most of the school day. The 64 schools, which educate students in grades 5 through 8 or 6 through 8, cater mostly to children of color, with African American (51%) and Latino (39%) children making up the vast majority of enrolled students. In addition, because having a family income that is at or near the poverty line is one criterion for admission to the schools, 87% of the students qualify for the federal free and reduced price meal program. The majority of the schools included in the network are operated by Catholic communities of religious men or women, although other groups, including the Episcopal church and groups of lay individuals, also operate NativityMiguel schools (Fenzel, 2009; NativityMiguel Network of Schools, 2008).

The characteristics of NativityMiguel school programs are consistent with what researchers over the years have identified as essential characteristics of effective middle schools (George & Alexander, 2003; Lipsitz, 1984; Trimble, 2004). Among these characteristics are small class sizes for instruction, small group advisories led by teachers, interdisciplinary team teaching, a common planning time and ongoing professional development for teachers, a curriculum that is engaging and challenging, an environment that values mutual respect and care and that also holds students and teachers to high standards of conduct, and the meaningful involvement of parents. In addition, the academic day in NativityMiguel schools extends into the late afternoon and evening to accommodate co-curricular activities and tutoring or homework assistance for its students, most of whom enter the schools considerably below grade level on standardized tests of reading and mathematics achievement. Also included in the NativityMiguel schools is a summer program, varying in length from two to seven weeks, that addresses continued academic development, along with social, character, leadership, physical, and spiritual development and the development of a close-knit community of students and teachers (Fenzel, 2009). In addition, two features of NativityMiguel schools that are truly distinctive are the widespread use of uncertified volunteer teachers in instructional and support roles and the graduate support programs. The role that these features play in student success is examined below.

Academic Achievement in NativityMiguel Schools

Research to date has shown that students in NativityMiguel schools, or what were known as Nativity schools prior to the joining together of the Nativity and San Miguel schools into a single network in 2006, have demonstrated outstanding levels of academic achievement and attainment. For example, Podsiadlo and Philliber (2003) reported that students at the original Nativity Mission Center school demonstrated gains in standardized test scores and achieved high school graduation rates and college matriculation and success far beyond that of Latino students in New York and U. S. public schools. Findings from a study of another NativityMiguel school for boys in Baltimore (Fenzel & Hessler, 2002) also showed impressive student gains on standardized test scores in reading and math over their three years of attendance that exceeded the equivalent of one grade level per year. This study also showed that the NativityMiguel education the boys received contributed to high levels of confidence to achieve academic success in challenging independent high schools and the skills needed to succeed socially as well in selective schools where the vast majority of students were Caucasian from middle and upper class families.

More recent research (Fenzel, 2009; Fenzel & Domingues, 2009; Fenzel & Monteith, 2008) has shown that NativityMiguel students perform at higher levels on standardized tests of reading and mathematics than do students from similar socioeconomic backgrounds who attend parochial or public schools. In addition, the gains in standardized test scores during the years of attendance at their particular schools favor NativityMiguel students as well, as 70% of students gain the equivalent of one grade level or more per year in math and 77% do so in reading. This research also showed high rates of high school completion (87% in four years) and college matriculation (92% among high school completers) for NativityMiguel school graduates (Fenzel, 2009).

In this recent work (Fenzel, 2009; Fenzel & Domingues, 2009; Fenzel & Monteith, 2008), eleven schools in the NativityMiguel network and two comparison urban parochial schools were examined using a multimethod approach. These methods included the collection of several years of standardized test score data, core subject report card grades, and official attendance data, the administration of surveys to students, teachers, and principals, the observation of classes and activities at the schools, and interviews with students, teachers, administrators, and, in many cases, alumni and parents. (See Fenzel, 2009, for a complete description of these methods.)

In addition to the higher levels of achievement on standardized tests, NativityMiguel students perceived the quality of the environments of their schools and classes somewhat differently than did students in comparison parochial schools (Fenzel & Monteith, 2008). For example, on written surveys, NativityMiguel students indicated that they perceived the quality of the peer social climate and learning climate of their classes to be higher and their school experience to be more enjoyable with rules that were more fair. More specifically, they felt that their teachers were more supportive of students' efforts and more focused on learning in their math and language arts classes and employed learning activities that were more engaging. With respect to the peer social climate, NativityMiguel students, when compared to students in successful comparison urban parochial schools, indicated that their schoolmates were more respectful, they made more good friends, and they enjoyed participating in school projects and activities with their schoolmates more. Also, with respect to the school climate, NativityMiguel students indicated that their teachers and principals were more caring and fair and set and communicated clear expectations to a greater extent. This research also showed that NativityMiguel students perceived their parents to be more involved in their schools.

School Characteristics

What then is it that distinguishes NativityMiguel schools as successful alternative institutions for urban middle school students placed at risk? My research over the past several years has responded to that very question. The answer can be found in the structure of the NativityMiguel model, as well as in the ways in which teachers and administrators carry out the elements of the model and the mission associated with the model.

First, with respect to structural components, all NativityMiguel middle schools educate fewer than 100 students, with most educating fewer than 65. In addition, a recent study of eleven schools in seven cities (Fenzel, 2009) showed a mean of 18 students per grade, a class size that ranged from 1 to 16 for academic instruction, and a student–teacher ratio that averaged 5.8 to 1. The two largest schools in the study were those that educated both boys and girls. When asked whether he saw the possibility of school size increasing, one principal indicated that similar levels of academic success could be achieved with a larger enrollment of students, but what the school accomplishes with respect to students' character and leadership development would be compromised. Findings from interviews with NativityMiguel alumni showed that graduates appreciated how the small size of their schools and classes enabled them to form strong, positive relationships with teachers and remain more focused on their studies.

Students interviewed for this study (Fenzel, 2009) consistently described their schools as caring places because of the respectful and supportive relationships students reported having with their schoolmates and teachers, whom students reported as extending themselves to help them learn and help them with family and other social struggles. Small faculty-led advisories also contributed to the strong community experience at these schools. In these cross-grade advisory groups, students could address issues of leadership, interpersonal, and character development and challenges they wished to discuss in small groups with people they trusted.

Another characteristic of the NativityMiguel model that contributes substantially to student academic achievement is the extended day, week, and year, all of which are necessary to help students build the academic and social skills they need to succeed academically and professionally. A typical day at one of these schools begins with a 7:30 a.m. breakfast and ends with late afternoon or evening tutorial, homework help, and study sessions. In some schools, students remain at the school until 7:30 p.m. or later up to four days a week, with students also having their evening meal at the school. These homework and study sessions are often supervised by teachers and staffed by volunteers from local high schools and colleges, as well as other adults from nearby churches or other community organizations.

The academic part of the day is packed with active classroom learning that usually includes a double period each day devoted to language arts that focuses on skill development in reading and writing and a longer period each day for mathematics as well. Most classes are enjoyable but task-oriented, with very little time wasted on correcting student misbehavior. At one school for girls, for example, I observed a sixth-grade language arts class (80 minutes long) that focused first on noun–verb agreement and then C. S. Lewis's, *The Lion, the Witch, and the Wardrobe*. Selecting at random from her hand a Popsicle stick on which was written the name of a student, the teacher led a discussion on the book asking a number of questions that began, "Why do you think...?" In the lesson, the teacher made use of a text book, the novel, students' homework papers, and worksheets and moved the students from one activity to the next with excellent transitions and a caring manner. At another school for girls, the fifth-grade language arts teacher, a second-year intern, started the period with 20 minutes of silent reading after which she asked students to write five "very important points" or VIPs about what they had read. She, too, moved the students from one activity and location in the room to another very quickly and continued to engage the students in a vocabulary building activity and cooperative group tasks like a seasoned professional. Students are also assigned a substantial amount of homework, most of which is actually completed during late afternoon and evening study periods.

Graduate Support

Likely the most unique feature of the NativityMiguel schools is the graduate support program. As the Nativity Mission Center school began to send its graduates off to high schools, administrators saw that they continued to require academic and social support. As one teacher and alumnus of Nativity Mission Center reported, the world after Nativity is much bigger and more challenging, particularly with respect to the social adjustment to a highly selective high school. In addition, the negative neighborhood influences and family struggles continue to challenge students throughout their high school years. As the number of graduating classes grew and more students headed off to high school, what began as an informal support program for graduates became more organized. Most schools allocate nearly a full-time position to the director of graduate support, and school officials make it clear to new students and their parents that the NativityMiguel school program extends for four years beyond middle school graduation.

The role of the director of graduate support at Nativity Mission Center, a graduate of the school whom I interviewed during a school visit, provides a good example of how someone in that position contributes to continued student success. His work schedule usually began at noon and lasted until 8:00 p.m. during the week and included many Saturdays. He, as do most graduate support directors, taught one class to eighth graders and began working with them in seventh grade to prepare them for high school entrance exams. He also worked with each eighth grader individually to provide counseling about high schools that might provide a good fit for him and helped the students and parents understand the application process and complete application forms for admission and financial aid. He also supervised a weekly study hall for graduates in high school, with each night of the week (Monday through Thursday) set aside for a particular graduating class, and Friday activities at the school. As the graduates' junior year rolled around, he would begin the process of helping them investigate colleges that included accompanying them on college visits on Saturdays. He also arranged review courses for college entrance exams and guided the students and parents through the process of admission and financial aid applications that was not familiar to parents who had never attended college. I found that these support services were provided by graduate support directors at the other network schools as well.

The investment of resources into the graduate support program represents a clear indication that NativityMiguel school leaders are truly committed to the long-term success of their students and recognize that helping students succeed in and graduate from a high quality middle school program does not remove all obstacles to an adolescent's continued engagement and success in school. Graduate support directors are most effective when they get to know the families as they are sometimes called upon to mediate difficulties that their graduates have with their parents and guardians who may not understand the importance of continued education and try to draw their children back into the kinds of lives that they have come to accept. The effectiveness of the graduate support directors is increased, too, when they understand the ways in which neighborhood peer influences involving drugs, violence, sexual activity, and early pregnancy contribute to adolescent struggles.

Volunteer Teachers

Similar to corps members who serve with Teach for America, intern or volunteer teachers in NativityMiguel schools commit two years of service teaching and serving other support functions. Provided with a small but adequate living allowance, health care, housing, and an AmeriCorps education award, NativityMiguel volunteer teachers, the vast majority of whom do not possess a teaching certificate or much if any teaching experience, are selected from among a number of applicants and receive some training prior to the start of the school year and mentoring and other professional development throughout the course of their service.

NativityMiguel schools vary in the extent to which they employ volunteer teachers. One school for boys has a staff of eleven volunteer teachers along with three experienced master teachers, while two schools I visited employed just one or two volunteer teachers, preferring instead to staff its classrooms with experienced, certified teachers and making use of high school and college student volunteers for afternoon and evening study and homework help. The AmeriCorps volunteer at one school did teach a nearly full load of classes and one at another school taught art classes and provided academic tutoring during the school day. A curious finding from my study of eleven NativityMiguel schools (Fenzel, 2009) showed that the greater the percentage of teaching positions held by volunteer teachers in the schools, the greater the gain in students' standardized test scores in reading and mathematics. This finding does not suggest, however, that the inexperienced volunteer teachers are more effective than are experienced teachers. Rather, volunteer teachers contribute considerably to student achievement because of the important roles they play as classroom teachers, tutors, coaches, advisors, and playground and cafeteria supervisors and because of the quality of classroom instruction provided by the experienced teachers and the mentoring the volunteers receive from them. The classroom assignments for first-year volunteer teachers range from ten to twenty classes per week and, in some cases, their teaching is conducted in partnership with a more experienced instructor until they are able to handle effectively a classroom on their own. Second-year volunteers are usually assigned a bit more teaching responsibility and they provide higher quality instruction (see Fenzel & Flippen, 2006). Their professional development is enhanced at nearly every NativityMiguel school by the regular formal and informal mentoring they receive; in some cases teacher offices are located in one large space that facilitates teacher interaction and sharing.

Despite the controversy over the effectiveness of employing inexperienced teachers in the classrooms of children placed at risk, including that associated with the use of Teach for America corps members (Decker, Mayer, & Glazerman, 2004; Laczko-Kerr & Berliner, 2002; Raymond, Fletcher, & Luque, 2001), the success of the NativityMiguel schools shows that, when used strategically and carefully, volunteer teachers can contribute substantially to the education and development of urban middle school students. Of the more than fifteen volunteer teachers I observed in classroom teaching roles, there were three first-year teachers who struggled to manage their classes well and one science teacher who was not as vigilant as an experienced teacher would be with respect to monitoring the proper implementation of a lab activity by one of the student working groups I observed. In such cases, then, the quality of the learning experience of some of the students was compromised by the poor quality of the teaching. Fortunately, even in these few cases, there were processes in place at the schools to ensure that beginning teachers would become quite effective within that first year of teaching. All of the second-year volunteer teachers I observed were very effective instructors.

SCHOOL CASE STUDY

Among the many exemplary middle schools in the NativityMiguel network is one school in Massachusetts with a student body of approximately 85 boys and girls in grades 5 through 8. The Head of School had taught in another NativityMiguel school for a few years and, with the support of the Episcopal diocese, was able to implement the model in the new school. In this rather diverse school there are children whose ethnic/racial backgrounds are African American, Cape Verdean, West Indian, Haitian, Latino, Caucasian, and Asian. While nearly all NativityMiguel schools engage in a selection process in which they observe student applicants in academic settings on Saturdays or during the summer before deciding if they demonstrate adequate commitment to the school program, this school takes a unique approach by selecting its students by lottery among the applicants who qualify for the federal free and reduced meal program. Among the selected students each year are four children from the foster care system. The only exception to the lottery policy is the selection of siblings of students already enrolled in the school, as long as the family continues to meet qualifying income levels. According to the principal, students tend to test between one and two grade levels behind on standardized tests when they first enter. Opened in 1997, the school prides itself on its commitment to see to it that all children who enter the school, regardless of the extent of their social and academic difficulties, succeed. It provides a full-service program that takes care of students' health and psychological needs, in addition to their academic needs, as well as social services required by their families. The school charges no tuition—only a small book deposit for the year that seems to help children take good care of their books.

As with other NativityMiguel schools that educate both girls and boys, students at this school are segregated by sex for academic classes. The academic day begins at 7:50 A.M. with homeroom, with students arriving at 7:30 A.M. for breakfast. Following an afternoon activity period and early evening dinner, students participate in evening study until 7:15 P.M. Monday through Thursday. Students are dismissed at 3:15 P.M. on Fridays, although students who need to complete assignments remain somewhat longer. Students compete in sports such as soccer, basketball, baseball, and softball during activity periods and the school is open on Saturday mornings for sports, dance, computer time, and other activities. The schools simply could not afford to provide these study and activity periods unless they employed sufficient numbers of volunteer or intern teachers.

Its summer program, as is the case for a number of NativityMiguel schools, is a sleep-away camp experience for rising 7th and 8th graders that lasts for the month of July; younger students participate in their summer experience on school grounds during the same time period. Academic skill development is the focus of the morning at the summer camp, and the afternoon is devoted to the development of skills in technology, oral communication, and the arts, in addition to sports and outdoor activities (e.g., hiking and canoeing) that build a sense of community and enable children to develop athletic skills while having fun. Students and graduates have remarked how the summer program helps them get closer to one another, contributes to their academic skill development, and provides them with a respite from the sometimes violent neighborhoods where they live. Students at this and other NativityMiguel schools have reported that the relaxing summer approach to academics has contributed also to their growing love of independent reading and confidence in their reading and other abilities.

The extent of the program with its long days and extended year requires a relatively large, active, and committed teaching staff. In no way can a teacher just "go through the motions" at the school. Consistent with the NativityMiguel model, the school employs nine experienced master teachers, along with nine volunteer or intern teachers, all of whom have very busy days. The latter group consists of young college graduates with an interest and some degree of experience in working with urban children; the vast majority of them are not certified to teach and have majored in something other than education. In addition to teaching small language arts "skills" or, in their second year, regular academic classes, interns coach a sport or supervise another afternoon activity; serve on a school-wide committee; supervise evening study sessions, meals, and recess; and assume other nonacademic duties. The intern teachers live in community with other interns and receive a small living allowance and an AmeriCorps educational benefit in exchange for their two-year commitment to the school. Administrators at this and other NativityMiguel schools view the intern program as an essential contributor to student and school success, despite interns' limited experience and commitment to just two years of service. Interestingly enough, I encountered several master teachers and administrators who had their first experiences as volunteer teachers in their own or another NativityMiguel school. Many noncertified NativityMiguel teachers pursue graduate study in education and initial teacher certification while teaching. As with other network schools, the Massachusetts school works in partnership with a local university to provide this education.

Although the use of noncertified, inexperienced classroom teachers flies in the face of what is regarded as essential and effective practice for improving the academic competencies of urban children placed at risk, the NativityMiguel model incorporates practices that ensure the best use of every staff person in the school. The interns help NativityMiguel schools maintain an incredibly small student–teacher ratio (4.4-to-1 at this particular school—one of the smallest ratios in the network) that enables the schools to operate as caring communities where every member of the staff is committed to the optimum development of the students—academically, socially, morally, emotionally, and athletically. The interns also perform necessary supervisory and administrative duties that would simply put too much on the plates of the full-time experienced teachers.

Professional development for intern teachers at this school seems to be adequate for preparing most of them for the challenges they face in the classroom. It begins with an eight-day orientation to the mission and characteristics of the educational model the school follows and a crash course on lesson planning and preparation, pedagogy, assessment, classroom management, and effective communication approaches with students and parents led by school personnel and educational consultants, some of whom are board members of the school. Intern teachers also attend weekly follow-up sessions with the principal that continue to address these competencies and the particular needs of their urban students.

I found the classes taught at the school to be task-oriented and engaging and to challenge students to think critically. In a pre-Algebra class of ten 7th-grade girls, the teacher opened the class with a sample problem involving the addition of positive and negative numbers (–20 + 10) and asked students to predict the answer. After selecting a few students to provide their predictions, this first-year intern related the problem to a football game when a team loses 20 yards on one play and then gains 10 on the next play. He asked for predictions on a second problem (–12 + 6) and then set out to teach the concept and process of conducting such computations. At the end of the class he called on a student to stand and summarize what she learned in class that day. In a 6th-grade social studies class with eleven girls, the teacher opened the class with a question: "Why would homo erectus need to cut wood?" With each student response, the teacher would thank the student or acknowledge the student in some positive way. She then engaged the students in the reading of selections from the text book, never failing to acknowledge their participation and interjecting questions to check for students' understanding. Moving adeptly from one activity to another, the teacher, a first-year master teacher who had taught as an intern at the school for two years, asked students to summarize the two most important things they learned in the book chapter they had just read and then directed students to work with their "heart partner" to answer four questions from the text while she walked around the room checking on students' progress. As the class time drew to a close, she spoke positively about what she liked about the students' work and effort that day and directed students to write in their journals responses to some guiding questions and a summary of what they learned or struggled with in class that day.

As was the case in nearly every NativityMiguel school I visited, the girls in a 6th-grade focus group at this school complained about the strict behavioral expectations at the school while they praised how much the teachers cared about them and were interested in speaking with them about problems they might be having. They used the term *family* to describe their perceptions of the quality of togetherness they felt with their classmates and teachers. They also recognized that their academic skills, specifically writing and reading, had improved and that they had come to learn to listen and focus on their studies better than they had in elementary school. They seemed to enjoy working to receive recognition and recognized that they had learned how to get along better with their schoolmates and solve interpersonal problems without fighting.

I also interviewed a graduate of the school who was present one evening tutoring a 7th-grade girl as part of her high school community service requirement. She expressed the view that the long days students spend at the school, along with the summer programs, help to build a strong sense of community among the students and teachers. She reflected how she came to the school quiet and distrusting of others and, from the extent to which teachers reached out to her, was able to learn to trust others to help and listen to her and grow more self-confident in her abilities to succeed as a result. This alumna also spoke of the teachers' high expectations for academic progress and behavior and of how teachers push students academically beyond their comfort zone but then also provide meaningful feedback and support that gives the students the confidence to succeed. She indicated that she returned to her NativityMiguel school on occasion to discuss the books she was reading in high school with her middle school language arts teacher and was confident to take on leadership roles in her highly selective high school as a result of her NativityMiguel experience.

The administration and faculty at the school have outlined both academic and behavioral benchmarks for students at each grade level that form the basis for periodic evaluations of their progress. Benchmarks with respect to conduct, academic performance, and effort are rated quarterly and discussed with students' parents or guardians and must be met in order for a child to advance to the next grade level. Some of the behaviors that are rated for frequency of occurrence include: *Follows teacher directions, Encourages and supports peers, Accepts correction, Is respectful of teacher* (Conduct); *Work is complete & accurate, Demonstrates comprehension of material presented by teacher, Formulates opinion based on material* (Academic Performance); *Uses notebook appropriately, Completes homework, Makes an effort to do all work, Participates in class* (Effort). A summary grade is also given for each of the three domains on the progress report.

DISCUSSION

NativityMiguel schools face sizable challenges in creating a school community where teachers and students are actively committed to forming and maintaining a culture of respect and achievement in large part because most students and parents or guardians have not been exposed to schools in which such a culture has been established successfully. Children who are two grade levels behind in academic achievement face a school environment that insists on respectful conduct and well-managed and academically challenging classes in which students are held responsible for completing assignments and taking steps to improve their academic skills. Master and intern (or volunteer) teachers must be selected carefully because the jobs they are asked to perform are incredibly challenging, and administrators and teachers, along with the older students, must put forth a great deal of consistent and effective effort to socialize new students into the respectful, supportive, and achievement-oriented community at the school.

Summer programs at NativityMiguel schools play a big part in socializing new and continuing students to the behavioral expectations of the school and helping students with behavioral challenges to learn respectful alternatives to addressing conflicts and effective ways of coping with stress. At the summer experience for Nativity Mission Center students, which consists of a seven-week stay in the Adirondack Mountains, boys also participate in spiritual activities and academic learning activities that are enjoyable. One alumnus of the Nativity Mission Center school expressed a great deal of praise for what is accomplished at camp. In addition to helping new students understand the mission of the school and get to know other students and teachers before the school year began, camp also reinforces the concept of brotherhood. By this he meant that students learn and internalize the value of working for the development of oneself as well as one's schoolmates. Students also come to commit themselves to honesty and respect in their interactions with others and take these lessons with them when they leave the school. The school meant so much to this alumnus that he wanted to return to the school to teach part time and invest himself in the development of the students who were attending the school years after he graduated.

A principal of one of the schools for girls spoke about how remarkable it is to see the girls arrive in fifth grade with a rough persona and often carrying a great deal of anger brought on by life circumstances and then transform into respectful, caring, and confident people in the course of a year or two. Lacking confidence in their academic abilities and fearful of reading out loud in class when they first come to the school, the students become confident leaders and models for the younger students. She indicated that several aspects of the school program help this type of transformation to occur. At the top of the list is the personal and caring touch exhibited by every teacher and administrator toward every student that eventually breaks through the girls' tough exteriors and convinces them of their inherent value. Small classes and cross-grade advisories facilitate this personal approach, and older girls who have seen themselves grow and develop high levels of self-esteem serve as important models for the younger students. The school also does an excellent job of involving the parents; most schools require parents to commit to several hours of service each month to support clerical or cleaning functions or participate in tutoring. I also found it remarkable that some of the graduates actually move far from home to attend boarding schools that represent a culture that would be very foreign to them and their families.

Many aspects of the NativityMiguel programs can be applied effectively in public and charter schools that serve urban students placed at risk. These schools show that effective and caring instruction in small classes and extended day and year programs that increase the number of hours that students engage in academic skill development can accelerate the academic development of students during the middle school years to the point of preparing them for success in strong high school programs. A number of initiatives, such as KIPP (Knowledge is Power Program) schools, have adopted many of the NativityMiguel features with good success. However, one initiative that has not been adopted by other alternative school programs for urban students, and which should be considered, is the graduate support program. NativityMiguel schools show how important it is to have a system in place that continues to provide support to students when they leave middle school and continue to face the stressors and challenges that come with living in high-poverty urban environments.

One concern raised by several NativityMiguel administrators is the profound lack of academic skills they observe among children from urban elementary schools who apply for admission and are subsequently selected. Rather than expand the size of each class, some administrators and school boards have considered accommodating more students by adding a fourth or fifth grade to start children on a sound academic path before it becomes too difficult to help them improve their skills. One school in Washington, DC, for example, has added a fourth grade to their program recently in response to this concern, and a school in the Boston area runs a tutoring and academic skill development program for fourth graders, many of whom then seek admission to the school program that begins in fifth grade.

NativityMiguel schools have also shown that making strategic use of a corps of volunteer teachers can make a difference with respect to helping urban students improve their academic skills and their commitment to higher educational attainment. Although students and administrators alike are disappointed that most of these volunteers leave the schools after 2 years to pursue other professional and educational goals, I find that the presence of these committed young adults contributes a great deal to students' development across several domains. Learning to use such resources as these men and women can benefit high-poverty public and parochial schools alike and should be pursued.

Having a substantial effect on reducing the achievement gap and reducing the cycle of economic poverty that profoundly affects many urban families will require a greater commitment to establishing and maintaining schools similar to those that follow the NativityMiguel model. Operating NativityMiguel schools is expensive, and the school featured in this chapter is probably the most expensive of the schools in the network because of its full-service model devoted to addressing unmet health and other needs of its students. However, these schools and others like them are needed to reverse the downward spiral that so many urban children encounter because of the poorly performing elementary schools they attend. Large urban public school districts need to embrace more independently operated alternative school initiatives with strong track records of accelerating the academic skill development in order to make substantive headway in reducing the achievement gap and providing a better future for more of their children placed at risk.

REFERENCES

Carnegie Council on Adolescent Development. (1989). *Turning points: Preparing American youth for the 21st century.* New York, NY: Carnegie Corporation of New York.

Decker, P. T., Mayer, D. P., & Glazerman, S. (2004). *The effects of Teach for America on students: Findings from a national evaluation.* Princeton, NJ: Mathematica Policy Research. Retrieved from http://www.teachforamerica.org/documents/mathematica_results_6.9.04.pdf.

Fenzel, L. M. (2009). *Improving urban middle schools: Lessons from the Nativity schools.* Albany, NY: State University of New York Press.

Fenzel, L. M., & Domingues, J. (2009). Educating urban African American students placed at risk: A comparison of two types of Catholic schools. *Catholic Education: A Journal of Inquiry and Practice, 13,* 30–52.

Fenzel, L. M., & Flippen, G. (2006, April). *Student engagement and the use of volunteer teachers in alternative urban middle schools.* Paper presented at the annual meeting of the American Educational Research Association, San Francisco, CA.

Fenzel, L. M., & Hessler, S. P. (2002, April). *Nativity schools: Follow-up evaluation of the success of an alternative middle school for urban minority boys.* Paper presented at the annual meeting of the American Educational Research Association, New Orleans, LA.

Fenzel, L. M., & Monteith, R. H. (2008). Successful alternative middle schools for urban minority children: A study of Nativity schools. *Journal of Education for Students Placed At Risk, 13*(4), 381–401.

George, P. S., & Alexander, W. M. (2003). *The exemplary middle school* (3rd ed.). Belmont, CA: Wadsworth.

Joftus, S. (2002, September). *Every child a graduate: A framework for an excellent education for all middle and high school students.* Washington, DC: Alliance for Excellent Education.

Laczko-Kerr, I., & Berliner, D. C. (2002, September 6). The effectiveness of "Teach for America" and other under-certified teachers on student academic achievement: A case of harmful public policy. *Education Policy Analysis Archives, 10*(37). Retrieved from http://epaa.asu.edu/epaa/v10n37/

Lipsitz, J. (1984). *Successful schools for young adolescents.* New Brunswick, NJ: Transaction Books.

NativityMiguel Network of Schools (2008). *Overview.* Retrieved from http://www.nativitymiguelschools.org

Noguera, P. A. (2003). *City schools and the American dream: Reclaiming the promise of public education.* New York, NY: Teachers College Press.

Podsiadlo, J. J., & Philliber, W. W. (2003). The Nativity Mission Center: A successful approach to the education of Latino boys. *Journal of Education for Students Placed at Risk, 8,* 419–428.

Raymond, M., Fletcher, S. H., & Luque, J. (2001, August). *Teach for America: An evaluation of teacher differences and student outcomes in Houston, Texas.* Stanford, CA: Center for Research on Educational Outcomes, the Hoover Institution, Stanford University.

Thernstrom, A., & Thernstrom, S. (2003). *No excuses: Closing the racial gap in learning.* New York, NY: Simon & Schuster.

Trimble, S. (2004). *What works to improve student achievement.* NMSA Research Summary #20. Retrieved from http://www.nmsa.org/research/summary/student-achievement.htm

CHAPTER 7

REACHING THE
HARD TO REACH

A Comparison of Two Reading Interventions
With Incarcerated Youth

**Cynthia Calderone, Susan V. Bennett, Susan Homan,
Robert F. Dedrick, and Anne Chatfield**

The purpose of this quantitative study, funded by the Florida Department of Education (FLDOE) through Just Read, Florida!, was to investigate the use of Tune in to Reading, an innovative reading intervention, with struggling adolescent readers in the juvenile justice system. One hundred and three students who exhibited issues ranging from behavioral problems to substance abuse and sexual offenses, from 6 residential sites, participated in this study. All participants were male with 52% African American, 31% Caucasian, and 13% Hispanic. Sixty percent of the students were in Grades 8 and 9 and 44% of the students were identified as students with disabilities. At each site, students were randomized to the reading intervention, Tune in to Reading (TIR), or to a control condition (typically FCAT Explorer). A Cloze assessment was administered to students in both treatment and control groups before and after the 9-week study period. Results across the 6 sites were mixed with TIR showing more positive

Research Supporting Middle Grades Practice,
pp. 119–139

effects compared to the control in two schools, and similar effects compared to the control condition in four schools. Larger treatment effects (TIR) compared to the control condition were observed for certain subgroups of students, including Hispanic, African American, and students with disabilities.

INTRODUCTION

Children and adolescents who struggle to learn to read require access to more innovative and effective reading approaches to improve their fluency and achievement in reading (Baines, 2008; Homan, Calderone, & Dedrick, 2009; National Reading Panel, 2001; Rasinski, Padak, & Fawcett, 2010). Typically, struggling readers have problems meeting federal, state, and district benchmarks as they navigate their literacy learning experiences within the context of reading and writing. The implementation of benchmarks and standards was intended to promote equal treatment of all students. Educators who are trying to help their students meet those standards are customarily advised, or required, to utilize traditional teaching methods, which are often narrow in scope and do not consider, or allow for, diversity in students (Chatfield, 2003; English, 2004; Larson & Murtadha, 2002; Russo, 2007; Shields, 2004).

The need for innovative instructional methods in reading is especially true of many children and adolescents within the juvenile justice system, a group that tends to underperform in school. They usually have poor attendance and perform below grade level (McCord, Spatz Widom, & Crowell, 2001; Russo, 2007). In addition to performing below their peers academically, there also is a strong tendency among most incarcerated youth for greater rates of absenteeism, retention, suspensions, and expulsions (National Center on Education, Disability and Juvenile Justice, 2001). Russo's (2007) study confirms previous research by Fox and Lyons (2003), who reported that the average reading level for ninth graders who enter incarceration facilities is only at the fourth-grade level. Clearly, these students have special needs that require serious, careful consideration.

Although reading interventions have been utilized with struggling readers in public schools to improve reading achievement, there is no evidence to show reading interventions have been used with struggling readers in the juvenile justice system. It is difficult to conduct research studies involving incarcerated youth, which might be why there is a lack of research with this particular student population. Despite the recognized need for reading curricula and interventions to improve reading achievement of children and adolescents in the juvenile justice system, scientific studies of innovative interventions with incarcerated youth are rare (Chatfield, 2003; Russo, 2007).

Some strategies, reported as effective with adolescents who experience reading difficulties, also may prove effective with students in the juvenile justice system. Muse (1998) found that providing a wide variety of reading materials, adaptive materials, individual assignments, and high expectations for work led to gains in literacy skills. Another successful strategy involved the use of multimedia and hypermedia (Bewley, 1999) with low-achieving students. Students who utilized computers demonstrated an increase in positive attitudes, motivation, and participation. Students who were able to actively engage in relevant activities, as opposed to passively drill on skills, were better equipped to control their learning and thus showed greater learner independence.

The major difference between incarcerated and nonincarcerated youth is the disparity in their social functioning. Many incarcerated youth are antisocial and experience a loss of freedom and control over their lives (Chatfield, 2003). The strategies recommended for low-achieving students might also work for low-achieving students in the juvenile justice system because they would provide incarcerated youth with choices and give them opportunities to control their learning, which might shift the locus of control back to them and motivate them to take responsibility for their learning and ultimately for their lives.

Results of a study conducted on the effectiveness of the Boys Town Reading Program (Longo, Chmelka, & Curtis, 1997) indicated significant growth in reading achievement for students in the juvenile justice system. One reason for this success was believed to be the differentiated approach to instruction. Students were placed at their appropriate reading instructional levels and were continuously challenged by material that allowed them to progress to increasing levels of difficulty, giving the students a sense of control over their learning.

Students on the lower end of the achievement spectrum in schools often lack literacy skills. Hayes (2006) has suggested that many juvenile offenders were poor performers in schools before their incarceration and did not have access to effective educational programs. When schools must play catch-up with their lower-achieving students, opportunities for teaching and learning are diminished (Cochran-Smith, 2004; Furman & Gruenewald, 2004). According to legislative mandates, these students must be brought up to the reading level of their peers in order to meet the appropriate benchmarks. It is extremely important for educators to make every effort to ensure juvenile offenders have equitable educational opportunities to encourage their smooth and successful transition back to the public school system and to society in general (Chatfield, 2003).

Tune in to Reading (TIR), a computer program that engages students with its alternative format and its unique approach to reading through a musical medium, has been used with struggling elementary, middle school, and high school readers (Baines, 2008). Preliminary research supports TIR as a successful intervention that provides both motivation and enhanced fluency to support instructional level gains in comprehension (Biggs, Homan, Dedrick, Minick, & Rasinski, 2008; Rasinski, Homan, & Biggs, 2009). Struggling readers who experienced failure in reading experienced engagement with this program (Rasinski, Padak, & Fawcett, 2010).

Tune in to Reading (TIR) has been studied as a reading intervention since its initial development in 2005. Over 1,000 struggling readers in grades 3 through 12 have been involved in studies predominately funded by the Florida Department of Education through Just Read, Florida! The results have been consistent. After using TIR, the mean instructional reading level for more than 1,000 struggling readers increased by more than one year at the end of a nine-week study (Homan, Calderone, & Dedrick, 2009).

The purpose of this study, funded by Florida Department of Education (FLDOE) through Just Read, Florida!, was to investigate the use of *Tune in to Reading* with struggling adolescent readers in the juvenile justice system. *Tune in to Reading* was compared to FCAT Explorer, a program linked to the Florida Comprehensive Assessment Test (www.fcrr.org), at six nontraditional school sites for incarcerated youth. TIR and FCAT Explorer are described in the next section. Specific questions examined in this study included:

1. What is the effect of *Tune in to Reading* (TIR) compared to FCAT Explorer on 6th–12th grade student reading achievement scores as measured by the TIR Cloze Assessment?

2. Is the effect of *Tune in to Reading* (TIR), compared to FCAT Explorer, on 6th–12th grade student reading achievement scores (i.e., TIR Cloze) similar or different for groups of students defined by the following demographic variables: ethnicity and exceptional student education (ESE) status?

METHODS

Participants

The six nontraditional schools were located in a large school district (one of 10 largest) in the southern United States. The district mirrors the

Table 7.1.   Description of School Sites

School	Sample	Length of Stay	Enrollment	Grade
1	24	12-18 months	50	7th-11th
2	13	7-12 months	100	8th-10th
3	10	9-15 months	25	6th-12th
4	12	6-9 months	165	7th-12th
5	27	6-9 months	28	6th-10th
6	17	6-9 months	33	7th-10th

Note: All schools were located in urban settings except for school 6, which was located in a rural setting; all schools were for students deemed a moderate risk to public safety except for school 3, which was deemed high risk.

nation with significant numbers of students representing high, middle, and low SES, as well as diverse and linguistic minority groups. The schools served a male population of moderate- to high-risk juvenile offenders who were housed in residential facilities.

The year-round residential sites in this study provided specialized treatment for youth who exhibited issues ranging from behavioral problems to substance abuse and sexual offenses. The residential programs were designed for a length of stay between 6 and 18 months. Educational services included vocational programs as well as academic programs. Table 7.1 provides a description of the school sites in this study.

Locked doors secured all residential facilities, and visitors were required to turn in their keys before entering the secure areas. The classrooms and dorms were also locked. In addition, four of the six facilities were located within barbed-wire fencing. The students were supervised 24 hours per day. Officers accompanied the students to their classes. All students were expected to wear blue jumpsuits or uniforms during their incarceration. The officers and school personnel strictly enforced rules and expectations for behavior. Serious consequences were administered for misbehavior, including an extension of student time in a facility. When this occurred, students were given a different colored jumpsuit to wear to alert staff members to diligently watch and protect these students from harming themselves or others.

Most of the facilities were for students deemed a moderate risk to public safety, but one facility in the study sample provided services to students considered to be a high risk. The goal of the educational services at the juvenile justice school sites was for students to earn either a GED or high school diploma.

As our knowledge of the juvenile justice system grew, the site-to-site differences became obvious. Because of this, the design of the studies varied for each site, and the decision was made to conduct separate analyses for each school site when possible. One hundred and thirty eight students from the six sites were enrolled in the study (52 in the control condition and 86 in the *Tune in to Reading* condition). Thirty five students were eliminated from the analyses because of incomplete posttest data. The overall attrition rate of 25.3% was similar for the control (25%) and treatment condition (25.6%). Attrition rates ranged from 0% at school 1 to 56.7% at school 2. Attrition rates were similar for students with disabilities (28.6%) and without disabilities (22.7%). Attrition rates were greatest for African American students (29.9%), followed by Caucasian (22.0%), and Hispanic students (13.3%). Comparison of the pretest Cloze measure for students with complete data ($n = 103$, $M = 5.46$, $SD = 2.89$) and those who were missing posttest data ($n = 35$, $M = 5.44$, $SD = 2.40$) indicated no statistically significant differences on the pretest Cloze measure, t (136) = 0.03, $p > .05$.

A total of 103 students from the six schools participated in the study. The number of students participating from each school ranged from 10 (school 3) to 27 (school 5). All participants were male with 52% African American, 31% Caucasian, and 13% Hispanic (4% were missing data on race/ethnicity). Eighteen percent of the students were in grades 3 to 7; 20% were in grade 8; 40% were in grade 9; and 20% were in grades 10 to 12. Forty-four percent of the students were identified as students with disabilities (e.g., learning disabilities).

Research Design

The unit of analysis for this study was the individual student. Teachers at each of the six sites were asked to rank order their students by reading ability from most proficient to least proficient. For each pair of students, starting with the highest ability pair and moving to the lowest ability pair, a coin was tossed and students were randomly assigned to either the treatment (*Tune in to Reading*) or control (FCAT Explorer) condition (these conditions are described in the next section).

To evaluate the equivalence of the treatment and control conditions on the demographic variables of ethnicity, disability status, and grade level, chi-square tests were conducted at each school. Tables 7.2 to 7.4 present the ethnicity, disability status, and grade level, respectively, of the sample by school and condition.

Overall, the ethnic composition of the treatment and control conditions at the schools was similar with the exception of schools 1 and 5 (Table 7.2). The distribution of students with disabilities also was similar for treatment and control conditions (Table 7.3), while for schools 2 and

**Table 7.2.   Race/Ethnic Characteristics
of the Sample by School and Condition**

School	Group Ethnicity	Control	Treatment	χ^2
		Condition		
1		($n = 9$)	($n = 12$)	4.77*
	White	33.3%	58.3%	
	African American	33.3%	41.7%	
	Hispanic	33.3%	0.0%	
2		($n = 4$)	($n = 9$)	3.34 ns
	White	75.0%	22.2%	
	African American	25.0%	66.7%	
	Hispanic	0.0%	11.1%	
3		($n = 5$)	($n = 5$)	2.50 ns
	White	0.0%	40.0%	
	African American	100.0%	60.0%	
	Hispanic	0.0%	0.0%	
4		($n = 4$)	($n = 7$)	2.93 ns
	White	75.0%	28.6%	
	African American	25.0%	28.6%	
	Hispanic	0.0%	42.9%	
5		($n = 9$)	($n = 18$)	5.91*
	White	44.4%	27.8%	
	African American	22.2%	66.7%	
	Hispanic	33.3%	5.6%	
6		($n = 7$)	($n = 10$)	2.55 ns
	White	0.0%	10.0%	
	African American	100.0%	70.0%	
	Hispanic	0.0%	20.0%	

Note: *$p < .10$. ns = not statistically significant ($p > .10$).

3, the grade level distribution differed for the treatment and control conditions (Table 7.4).

Materials

The two reading programs (TIR and FCAT Explorer) investigated in this study were programs already used in schools to improve student reading achievement. Although both programs target reading practice, their approaches differ. TIR is an innovative reading program developed to improve reading through singing on pitch. This program is holistic in

Table 7.3.   Disability Status of the Sample by School and Condition

	Condition		
	Control	Treatment	
School	% with Disability	% with Disability	χ^2
1	(n = 10)	(n = 14)	0.05 ns
	60.0%	64.3%	
2	(n = 4)	(n = 9)	1.05 ns
	0%	22.2%	
3	(n = 5)	(n = 5)	0.40 ns
	40%	60%	
4	(n = 4)	(n = 8)	0.30 ns
	25%	12.5%	
5	(n = 9)	(n = 18)	1.19 ns
	33.3%	55.6%	
6	(n = 7)	(n = 10)	0.49 ns
	57.1%	40.0%	

Note: ns = not statistically significant ($p > .10$).

nature and is used to increase reading fluency and comprehension. FCAT Explorer is a skill-based program specifically designed to improve student scores on the Florida Comprehensive Assessment Test (FCAT), which is a battery of criterion-referenced subtests administered in schools in the state of Florida.

Tune in to Reading

Sometimes serendipitous events initiate cascading positive results. As a reading researcher, Dr. Susan Homan was asked to evaluate a software program called *Carry-A-Tune* (Electronic Learning Products, 2004). It was originally developed for home use to improve singing for children and adults. After the success of an initial pilot study of 48 struggling middle school readers, the company changed the product name to *SingingCoach*. *SingingCoach* was used in the second pilot study involving elementary, middle, and high school students (Homan & Biggs, 2007).

Based on the success of the struggling readers in the second pilot study, the developers made changes in the software to make it a teacher- and student-friendly product. The new product, called *Tune in to Reading* (TIR), reflects the revised purpose of the program. The software is purported to increase the user's ability to sing on pitch, but more importantly, the users, without realizing it, will continuously work on increasing their fluency and prosody. Using the "hook" of an alternative format far removed from traditional text, student engagement increases. It keeps the singing focus, but the changes were designed to facilitate school use.

Table 7.4.   Grade Level of the Sample by School and Condition

School	Group Grade	Condition		χ^2
		Control	*Treatment*	
1		(n = 10)	(n = 14)	1.89 ns
	3-7	30.0%	14.3%	
	8	10.0%	28.6%	
	9	30.0%	35.7%	
	10-12	30.0%	21.4%	
2		(n = 4)	(n = 9)	5.46*
	3-7	0%	0%	
	8	25.0%	66.7%	
	9	50.0%	0%	
	10-12	25.0%	33.3%	
3		(n = 3)	(n = 5)	8.00**
	3-7	0%	100%	
	8	33.3%	0%	
	9	0%	0%	
	10-12	66.7%	0%	
4		(n = 4)	(n = 8)	3.00 ns
	3-7	0%	37.5%	
	8	0%	12.5%	
	9	100%	50.0%	
	10-12	0%	0%	
5		(n = 9)	(n = 18)	4.50 ns
	3-7	11.1%	0%	
	8	0%	22.2%	
	9	66.7%	66.7%	
	10-12	22.2%	11.1%	
6		(n = 7)	(n = 10)	2.96 ns
	3-7	28.6%	20.0%	
	8	0%	30.0%	
	9	28.6%	30.0%	
	10-12	42.9%	20.0%	

Note: *$p < .10$. **$p < .05$. ns = not statistically significant ($p > .10$) .

Tune in to Reading (TIR) has several unique features. For example, it provides real-time pitch recognition and feedback to the user. The inclusion of pitch recognition is important because Lamb and Gregory (1993) found that pitch discrimination is significantly correlated with reading ability. The scoring mechanism, which is part of the *Tune in to Reading* software, accommodates each individual's vocal range. It contains a portfolio sign-in menu that aligns to the particular vocal range of each participant. Each student uses an individual soundproof microphone headset for listening, singing, and recording. TIR contains over 600 songs analyzed for readability level. The song reading levels range from 2nd to 12th grade. Students sing songs progressing from lower to higher readability levels. Students read and reread the lyrics while attempting to improve their singing. In this way, repeated reading is integrated into the singing program.

Two different formats of textual presentations are utilized in the software program. The first format, linear sheet music, allows students to read the lyrics silently three times while listening to the background music and tempo. This practice aligns with the recommended number of repetitions suggested by Samuels (1979). The next step is a graphic textual view. This alternative text format provides a visual display of words broken into syllables without the accompanying musical staff. The software automatically places each syllable accented at the appropriate pitch within each student's personal vocal range.

Along with visual tracking of the words, the software provides a guideline for accurate pitch and tone, with a real-time track line of the students' voices while they are singing and recording a song. Students can actually see what they are singing in terms of pitch. The instant feedback provides a fundamentally interactive experience that promotes visual tracking, which encourages the student to improve pitch throughout the song and during additional repeated singings (readings). After singing each time, the student receives a score. These scores, ranging from 0–100, represent the accuracy of the student's pitch and tone.

Tune in to Reading appears to be a successful intervention for struggling readers (Biggs & Homan, 2006; Rasinski, Homan, & Biggs, 2009). The idea that music can help improve reading skills is not new. Eastlund (1980) studied links between the use of music and the increase in literacy skills. More recent research (Anvari, Trainor, Woodside, & Levy, 2002; Douglas & Willatts, 1994; Patel, 1998) concurs that there is indeed a link between the use of music and an increase in reading abilities. Although the TIR program was not specifically developed for use with students performing below proficiency in reading, previous research has shown TIR to be effective with struggling readers in elementary, middle, and high school (Rasinski, Homan, & Biggs, 2009). Our research team was interested in examining the effectiveness of TIR with incarcerated youth who performed below grade level in reading.

FCAT Explorer

FCAT Explorer is an innovative, Web-based, instructional support tool derived from Florida's Sunshine State Standards (www.fldoe.org). FCAT

Explorer programs provide students with practice and guidance for the benchmarks tested on the Florida Comprehensive Assessment Test (FCAT), the state's criterion-referenced test. The student programs are designed to improve proficiency for students at all performance levels. The programs provide challenging work to students to help them master the skills they need to improve and ultimately succeed in school. FCAT Explorer provides instructional feedback for both correct and incorrect answers, with an engaging, colorful interface. The Florida Department of Education offers FCAT Explorer to public schools, free of charge (Martindale, Pearson, Curda, & Pilcher, 2005). Educational specialists, instructional designers, teachers, and testing professionals collaborated with the Florida Department of Education, and FCAT Explorer was then produced by Infinity Software, Inc. (http://www.fcatexplorer.com/home.asp; Martindale, Pearson, Curda, & Pilcher, 2005).

The FCAT Explorer website (http://www.fcatexplorer.com/) and the Florida Department of Education (http://www.fldoe.org/) offer little information with regard to rationale or theory of effectiveness for the use of FCAT Explorer. Limited research and literature exist on the effects of student use of FCAT Explorer on FCAT test scores (Martindale, Pearson, Curda, & Pilcher, 2005). The lack of research with FCAT Explorer in both high school and elementary schools leaves a plethora of unanswered questions to its effectiveness. As Martindale, Pearson, Curda, and Pilcher (2005) suggest, researchers need to continue to critically evaluate not only the program but teachers' use of the application, beliefs of the program, and other instructional considerations. For the present study, students in classes assigned to the FCAT Explorer condition used the reading programs for their individual instructional levels and worked on the state benchmarks for their levels.

Measures

The measure employed in this research study was the *Tune in to Reading* (TIR) Cloze assessment. The TIR Cloze assessment is an informal reading assessment developed by Arleen Mariotti (Shearer, 1982; Mariotti & Homan, 2005) from the University of South Florida (USF). The assessments are generated by the TIR software program on the computer for individual students. Teachers designate the appropriate reading level for each student in the computer database before the students use the TIR program. When students log on to the program for the first time, they receive a folder with a pretest for their individual reading level.

The Cloze assessments (pretests and posttests) consist of a reading passage for each grade level. Words are omitted from the passage and replaced with a blank space. Word choices are listed for the students next to the passage. Students must monitor the meaning of the passage to select the correct word to type in each blank space. After a student has completed the first passage and clicked the "finish" button, a percentage is calculated based on the percentage of correct answers on the assessment. If the assessment is too hard for a student, the computer will produce a passage on a lower grade level. If the passage is too easy, the computer will generate a passage on a higher grade level. The computer will continue to provide Cloze passages until the student has reached his or her instructional reading level.

A preliminary study was conducted in 2006–2007 to evaluate the concurrent validity of the TIR Cloze assessment scores. The *Qualitative Reading Inventory* was administered to 62 4th and 5th grade struggling readers from three Title I elementary schools. The Cloze assessment scores were correlated .70 with the *Qualitative Reading Inventory,* supporting the concurrent validity of the Cloze scores. In the current study, posttest Cloze scores were correlated .56 (n = 87) with the criterion-referenced component of the Florida Comprehensive Assessment Reading Test (part of Florida's statewide assessment plan) providing additional validity evidence. Pretest and posttest Cloze scores for the control and treatment conditions were correlated .82 (n = 39) and .89 (n = 64), respectively.

Procedures

The randomly assigned students used the appropriate software (TIR or FCAT Explorer) in their reading classes with their teachers for 90 minutes per week. Since the classes were grouped by period, each of the classes used the appropriate software for 45 minutes two times per week. The students used the designated software for a minimum of nine weeks. The students who were assigned to the control condition used either FCAT Explorer in their reading class for 45 minutes two times per week for a minimum of nine weeks, or received their regularly scheduled reading instruction if FCAT Explorer was not available at a site. Although attempts were made by school personnel to obtain FCAT Explorer, three of the sites were unable to do so. Therefore the students at those sites who were assigned to the control condition simply did not use TIR. They used specific skill work from the Florida Sunshine State Standards. The students at each of the school sites used the assigned programs during the same time of the day in the same classroom and were monitored by their classroom teacher.

The students at each of the six sites (both in the treatment and control groups) completed the TIR Cloze assessment before the study period to obtain an instructional reading level pretest score. Upon the completion of the pretest, the students in each group used the appropriate software (TIR or FCAT Explorer) for at least nine weeks. At the end of the nine-week study period, all of the students in the study completed the TIR Cloze assessment once more to determine their individual instructional reading level posttest score. These data were then analyzed and comparisons were made between the treatment and control conditions.

RESULTS

The focus of this project was on the effects of TIR (compared to FCAT Explorer) on reading achievement for subgroups of struggling readers in nontraditional school sites for incarcerated youth. The results presented in this section address the research questions.

Descriptive Statistics

Table 7.5 summarizes the descriptive statistics for the Cloze pretest and posttest scores by treatment conditions. Pretest scores were approximately normally distributed for both control and treatment conditions and ranged from 0 to 9.5 for the control group ($M = 4.97$, $SD = 3.16$) and 0 to 11.5 for the TIR condition ($M = 5.75$, $SD = 2.70$). Mean posttest scores for the control group ($M = 5.90$, $SD = 3.75$) increased 0.93 points from the pretest, while mean posttest scores for the TIR group ($M = 7.27$, $SD = 2.85$) increased 1.52 points from the pretest.

**Table 7.5.   Descriptive Statistics
for Cloze Measures by Time and Condition**

Statistics	Control (n = 39)		Treatment (n = 64)	
	Pretest	Posttest	Pretest	Posttest
M	4.97	5.90	5.75	7.27
SD	3.16	3.75	2.70	2.85
Skewness	0.20	0.08	0.19	−0.05
Kurtosis	−1.19	−1.21	−0.98	−0.62

Analysis of Variance of Cloze Scores

Comparisons of the treatment and control conditions across the six schools were conducted using a 6 (School) by 2 (Condition) by 2 (Time) repeated measures ANOVA of the Cloze scores. School and Condition were between-group factors, while time was a within-group factor. In view of the small sample sizes that diminish statistical power, effect sizes were calculated for the repeated measures (posttest–pretest) by treatment condition and school using the formula, presented by Dunlap, Cortina, Vaslow and Burke (1996). In this formula: $tc * \sqrt{2*(1-r)/n}$, tc is the t-statistic from the dependent or correlated t test and r is the correlation between the pretest and posttest measures. N is the number of pairs of scores for the group. Effect sizes of 0.2, 0.5, and 0.8 were interpreted as small, moderate, and large effects (Cohen, 1992).

The Condition (control vs. treatment) by Time interaction from the repeated measures ANOVA was not statistically significant, $F(1, 91) = 1.82$, $p > .10$, indicating that there was no evidence that the pattern of change in pretest–posttest Cloze scores was significantly different for the control and treatment conditions. The patterns of change in pretest–posttest Cloze scores, however, were significantly different across the six schools, $F(5, 91) = 3.72$, $p < .01$.

Follow-up analyses of the Cloze change scores using the effect sizes calculated at each school for the control and treatment conditions revealed mixed results (see Table 7.6). At schools 2 and 6, the TIR groups exhibited moderate levels of change (effect sizes = 0.66 and 0.69), while the control conditions at the corresponding schools exhibited little change (effect sizes = -0.16 and 0.04). In contrast, at schools 3 and 4, the control conditions showed greater change (effect sizes = 0.43 and 0.76) compared to the TIR groups (effect sizes = 0.25 and 0.63).

Finally, at school 1 each condition produced little change (effect size for TIR = 0.35 vs. 0.05 for the control), while at school 5, each condition produced moderate to large changes (effect size for TIR = 0.91 vs. 0.71 for the control). Table 7.6 summarizes the mean pretest, posttest, and change scores for the Cloze measure.

Analysis of the Cloze Change Scores by Student Group

Additional analyses were conducted to examine the pattern of change on the Cloze test for different subgroups of students defined by race/ethnicity and ESE status (disability present, disability not present).

**Table 7.6. Cloze Mean Scores (*SD* in Parentheses)
Across Time for Treatment and Control by School**

School	Group	n	Pretest	Posttest	Mean Change	Effect Size
1	Control	10	4.10	4.25	0.15 *ns*	0.04
			(4.08)	(3.94)	(0.58)	
	Treatment	14	6.00	7.00	1.00****	0.35
			(2.82)	(2.90)	(0.88)	
2	Control	4	7.88	7.50	−0.38 *ns*	−0.16
			(1.97)	(2.31)	(0.75)	
	Treatment	9	6.61	7.78	1.17**	0.66
			(1.76)	(1.75)	(1.46)	
3	Control	5	2.50	3.70	1.20 *ns*	0.43
			(1.41)	(2.39)	(1.30)	
	Treatment	5	5.10	5.90	0.80*	0.25
			(3.21)	(3.07)	(0.76)	
4	Control	4	6.50	9.63	3.13*	0.76
			(3.49)	(4.25)	(2.25)	
	Treatment	8	7.06	9.31	2.25***	0.63
			(3.09)	(3.58)	(1.34)	
5	Control	9	5.28	7.06	1.78 *ns*	0.71
			(1.84)	(3.05)	(3.55)	
	Treatment	18	4.06	5.75	1.69****	0.91
			(1.83)	(1.90)	(1.16)	
6	Control	7	5.07	5.29	0.21 *ns*	0.04
			(3.25)	(3.97)	(1.04)	
	Treatment	10	6.95	8.95	2.00***	0.69
			(2.93)	(2.88)	(1.90)	

Notes: *p < .10. **p < .05. *** p < .01. **** p < .001. *ns* = not statistically significant (p > .10)

Mean change was tested for statistical significance using the dependent t test. Effect size = $tc * \sqrt{2} * (1-r)/n$, where tc is the t-statistic from the dependent or correlated t test and r is the correlation between the pretest and posttest measures. N is the number of pairs of scores for the group.

Race/Ethnicity

Comparisons of the treatment and control conditions across the three racial/ethnic groups (Caucasian, African American, Hispanic) were conducted using a 3 (Race/Ethnicity) by 2 (Condition: treatment vs. control) by 2 (Time) repeated measures ANOVA of the Cloze scores (see Table 7.7). The ANOVA results indicated a statistically significant Condition by Race/Ethnicity interaction, F (2, 93) = 4.59, p < .05. Examination of the effect sizes for the change in pretest–posttest Cloze scores for each group

Table 7.7.   Cloze Mean Scores Across Time (*SD* in Parentheses) for Treatment and Control by Race/Ethnicity

Ethnicity/Race	Group	n	Pretest	Posttest	Mean Change	Effect Size
Caucasian	Control	13	6.00 (2.84)	7.38 (3.49)	1.38** (1.97)	0.42
	Treatment	19	5.97 (2.86)	7.55 (2.37)	1.58**** (1.69)	0.58
African American	Control	19	5.00 (3.33)	5.58 (3.61)	0.58 (1.80)	0.16
	Treatment	35	5.17 (2.32)	6.51 (2.45)	1.34**** (1.12)	0.56
Hispanic	Control	6	3.50 (2.49)	4.67 (3.93)	1.17 (3.61)	0.34
	Treatment	7	8.36 (2.27)	10.29 (2.66)	1.93**** (0.89)	0.70

Note: **$p < .05$. ****$p < .001$. ns = not statistically significant ($p > .10$).
Mean change was tested for statistical significance using the dependent t test. Effect size = $tc * \sqrt{2} * (1-r)/n$, where tc is the t-statistic from the dependent or correlated t test and r is the correlation between the pretest and posttest measures. N is the number of pairs of scores for the group.

revealed that for Hispanic students the TIR condition produced the largest effect (effect size = 0.70) compared to the control condition (effect size = 0.34).

For African American students the effect of TIR was stronger than the effect of the control condition (effect sizes = 0.56 and 0.16, respectively) but not as pronounced as for the Hispanic students. Finally, for Caucasian students, the effect of TIR was greater than the effect of the control condition, but the difference in effect sizes was small (effect sizes = 0.58 and 0.42, respectively). Table 7.7 presents the Cloze mean scores for each condition by Race/Ethnicity.

Exceptional Student Education (ESE)

Comparisons of the treatment and control conditions across ESE status (no disability, disability reported) were conducted using a 2 (Exceptional Student Education) by 2 (Condition: treatment vs. control) by 2 (Time) repeated measures ANOVA of the Cloze scores. The ANOVA results indicated statistically significant main effects for Condition, $F(1, 99) = 4.10$, $p < .05$ and for Exceptional Student Education status, $F(1, 99) = 4.68$, $p < .05$. Examination of the effect sizes for the change in pretest–posttest Cloze scores for each group revealed that for students with disabilities, the

Table 7.8.   Cloze Mean Scores Across Time (SD in Parentheses) for Treatment & Control by Exceptional Student Education Status

ESE	Group	n	Pretest	Posttest	Mean Change	Effect
No	Control	23	5.65	6.74	1.09**	0.36
			(2.82)	(3.15)	(2.36)	
	Treatment	35	6.07	7.60	1.53****	0.52
			(2.79)	(3.03)	(1.34)	
Yes	Control	16	4.00	4.69	0.69	0.16
			(3.44)	(4.28)	(1.87)	
	Treatment	29	5.36	6.86	1.50****	0.58
			(2.59)	(2.62)	(1.34)	

Note: **$p < .05$. ****$p < .001$. ns = not statistically significant ($p > .10$).
Mean change was tested for statistical significance using the dependent t test. Effect size = $tc * \sqrt{2} * (1 - r)/n$, where tc is the t-statistic from the dependent or correlated t test and r is the correlation between the pretest and posttest measures. N is the number of pairs of scores for the group.

TIR condition produced the largest effect (effect size = 0.58) compared to the control condition (effect size = 0.16). For students without disabilities, the change for the treatment group was moderate (ES = 0.52) while the change for the control group was small to moderate (ES=0.36). Table 7.8 presents the Cloze mean scores for each condition by Exceptional Student Education Status.

DISCUSSION

The American Correctional Association recommends that educational facilities for juvenile justice education programs assess the educational status of each incarcerated youth and develop individualized educational plans. While this implies an expectation of quality instruction, there is a recognized disparity between the established standards and the quality of educational programs in juvenile justice facilities across the United States (Chatfield, 2003; Russo, 2007).

Not surprisingly, it is typical for adolescents in the juvenile justice system to have performed poorly in school and to have significant educational needs (McCord, Spatz Widom, & Crowell, 2001). Many educators in the juvenile justice correctional facilities recognize the need for innovative approaches to literacy improvement (Chatfield, 2003) to address the students' individual educational needs. Studies of successful literacy innovations for this marginalized student population would be helpful to determine what innovations might work best to improve the reading achievement of students in the juvenile justice system.

The Boys Town study (Longo, Chmelka, & Curtis, 1997) provided a strong model of a successful innovative approach to literacy. It was suggested that the differentiated instruction, autonomy, and measure of self-selection contributed to the program's success. Similarly, the *Tune in to Reading* program promoted student reading improvement through the same instructional means. Students were placed at appropriate instruction reading levels and monitored for their individual singing and reading progress.

Many challenges existed while conducting a research study at the Department of Juvenile Justice school sites. The six incarcerated youth sites were not on a regular school calendar, but were (by need and purpose), year-round. Students were typically assessed when they entered the program and when they left the site. Among other variables, students needing to return to their home counties to stand trial for their offenses affected the attrition rate. Following the trials, they may or may not have returned to the same site. Because of this attrition, it was difficult to obtain pretest and posttest scores on the Cloze assessment for all of the students. While there were missing data, the pretest and posttest measures still demonstrated student instructional reading level improvement for those students who were able to use the TIR program and the control program as prescribed. While all groups experienced gains in instructional reading level, the treatment group gains, especially for Hispanic students and students with disabilities, were greater than the control group's instructional level gains. These results should be viewed with caution, however, due to the difficulty with monitoring the implementation at these sites.

CONCLUSIONS

While there has been a growing awareness at both the state and national levels of literacy problems of struggling adolescent readers, scientific studies of innovative interventions are rare. Research of reading interventions with students in the juvenile justice system is even more rare (Chatfield, 2003). One reason might be the lack of either a standard reading curriculum or innovative reading interventions designed for juvenile correctional facilities (Russo, 2007). A more likely reason, however, is the difficulty in obtaining permission to study this particular student population. Researchers wishing to study programs used in correctional facilities for juvenile offenders must obtain permission not only from their own Institutional Review Boards, but also from the Department of

Juvenile Justice's Institutional Review Board. Although it is certainly understandable why juvenile offenders should be protected, it is unfortunate that the protection often prevents conducting research on programs used in the facilities. Consequently, a great need exists for studies that can lead to curricular change for incarcerated youth in the Department of Juvenile Justice.

Evidence from this study supports further investigation of *Tune in to Reading* as a reading intervention for struggling readers in the juvenile justice system. TIR Cloze instructional level gains demonstrated improvement for the treatment students. Further investigation of comprehension would help determine if the comprehension gains supported by TIR Cloze results are sustainable.

The study of the juvenile justice population offered a true learning experience. On the one hand, the researchers found a great need for innovative literacy support for students in the juvenile justice system. On the other hand, the Department of Juvenile Justice made it very difficult to provide that support to their students because of the restrictions placed upon educators wishing to work directly with the students.

As with most projects, we have many thoughts on different ways to conduct a similar study in the future. The phrase "if we knew then what we know now" perfectly sums up our current situation. While it may not always be clear in the statistical context, we did see change, we did see interest, and we did see students make the decision to choose literacy.

REFERENCES

Anvari, S. H., Trainor, L. J., Woodside, J., & Levy, B. A. (2002). Relations among musical skills, phonological processing, and early reading ability in preschool. *Journal of Experimental Psychology, 83*(2), 111–130.

Baines, L. (2008). A teacher's guide to multisensory learning: Improving literacy by engaging the senses. Alexandria, VA: Association for Supervision and Curriculum Development.

Bewley, R. J. (1999). The use of multimedia and hypermedia presentation for instruction of juvenile offenders. *Journal of Correctional Education, 50*, 130–139.

Biggs, M., & Homan, S. (2006). *Using interactive singing program with struggling readers in grades 4–12: What happens to fluency and comprehension?* Paper presented at Just Read, Florida! Annual Conference, Orlando, Florida.

Biggs, M., Homan, S., Dedrick, R., Minick, V., & Rasinski, T.V. (2008). Using an interactive singing software program: A comparative study of struggling middle school readers. *Journal of Reading Psychology, 29*(3), 195–213.

Chatfield, A. (2003). *Literacy standards in juvenile justice education: An integration of case study and literature synthesis methodology.* Unpublished doctoral dissertation, University of South Florida, Tampa, Florida.

Cochran-Smith, M. (2004). *Walking the road: Race, diversity, and social justice in teacher education.* New York, NY: Teachers College Press.

Cohen, J. (1992). A power primer. *Psychological Bulletin, 112*, 155–159.

Douglas, S., & Willatts, P. (1994). The relationship between musical ability and literacy skills. *Journal of Research in Reading, 17*(2), 99–107.

Dunlap, W. P., Cortina, J. M., Vaslow, J. B., & Burke, M. J. (1996). Meta-analysis of experiments with matched groups or repeated measures designs. *Psychological Methods, 1,* 170–177.

Eastlund, J. (1980). Integrating music and reading. *Music Educators Journal, 67*(3), 60–63.

English, F. (2004). Undoing the "done deal": Reductionism, ahistoricity, and pseudoscience in the knowledge base and standards for educational administration. *UCEA Review, 46*(2), 6–7.

Fox, K., & Lyons, D. (2003). Juvenile confinement conditions and services. *National Conference of State Legislatures, Legislative Briefings, 11*(5).

Furman, G. C., & Gruenewald, D. A. (2004). Expanding the landscape of social justice: A critical ecological analysis. *Educational Administration Quarterly, 40*(1), 47–76.

Hayes, K. (2006). *Constructing a prison to school pipeline: An examination of the educational experiences of incarcerated youth.* City University of New York. Unpublished doctoral dissertation: AAT 3213169.

Homan, S., & Biggs, M. (2007, April). *Using an interactive singing program with elementary struggling readers: A comparison of reading progress.* Paper presented by 21st Century Schools Conference, Daytona Beach, FL.

Homan, S., Calderone, C., & Dedrick, R. (2009). *Using Tune in to Reading with struggling readers in the juvenile justice system.* Research Report: Just Read, Florida!

Lamb, S. J., & Gregory, A. H. (1993). The relationship between music and reading in beginning readers. *Educational Psychology, 13*(1), 19–27.

Larson, C., & Murtadha, K. (2002). Leadership for social justice. In J. Murphy (Ed.), *The educational leadership challenge: Redefining leadership for the 21st century* (pp. 134–161). Chicago, IL: National Society for the Study of Education.

Longo, A. M., Chmelka, B., & Curtis, M. B. (1997, April). *Teaching basic reading skills to adolescents with behavioral disorders.* Paper presented at the meeting of the Council for Exceptional Children Annual Convention, Salt Lake City, UT.

Mariotti, A., & Homan, S. (2005). Linking reading assessment to instruction: An application worktext for elementary classroom teachers (3rd ed.). Mahwah, NJ: Erlbaum.

Martindale, T., Pearson, C., Curda, L. K., & Pilcher, J. (2005). Effects of an online instructional application on reading and mathematics standardized test scores. *Journal of Research on Technology in Education, 37*(4), 349–360.

McCord, J., Spatz Widom, C., & Crowell, N. A. (Eds.), (2001). *Juvenile crime, juvenile justice. Panel on juvenile crime: Prevention, treatment, and control.* Washington, DC: National Academy Press.

Muse, F. M. (1998). A look at the benefits of individualized instruction in a juvenile training school setting: How continuous progress accelerates student performance. *Journal of Correctional Education, 49*(2), 73–79.

National Center on Education, Disability and Juvenile Justice (2001). *The case for quality education in juvenile correctional facilities*. Retrieved from http://www.edjj .org/focus/education/.

National Reading Panel Report. (2001). *National Institute of Child Health and Human Development*. Washington, DC: U.S. Department of Education.

Patel, A.D. (1998). Processing syntactic relations in language and music: An event related potential study. *The Journal of Cognitive Neuroscience, 10*, 717–733.

Rasinski, T., Homan, S., & Biggs, M. (2009). Teaching reading fluency to struggling readers: Method, materials, and evidence. *Reading and Writing Quarterly, 25*(2/3), 192–204.

Rasinski, T., Padak, N., & Fawcett, G. (2010). *Teaching children who find reading difficult* (4th ed.). New York: Allyn & Bacon.

Russo, L. A. (2007). *No child left behind principles as predictors of correctional youths academic performance scores*. Unpublished doctoral dissertation. City University of New York.

Samuels, S. J. (1979). The method of repeated readings. *The Reading Teacher, 41*, 756–760.

Shearer, A. (1982). *A psycholinguistic comparison of second grade readers and fourth grade good and poor readers on their oral reading miscues and standard and phoneme cloze responses*. Unpublished doctoral dissertation, University of South Florida, Tampa, Florida.

Shields, C. M. (2004). Dialogic leadership for social justice: Overcoming pathologies of silence. *Educational Administration Quarterly, 40*, 109–132.

CHAPTER 8

FINDINGS FROM THE FIRST AND ONLY NATIONAL DATABASE ON ELEMIDDLE AND MIDDLE SCHOOLS

(Executive Summary)

David L. Hough

Special Note: *In past issues, mention was made of the national database developed over a 2-year period between 2005 and 2007 from which reports would be forthcoming. This Executive Summary is the third report generated from the database and summarizes findings from the full report that will be submitted for review later this year. Preliminary findings were first reported to the National Forum to Accelerate Middle Grades Education in Long Beach, California, on February 7, 2008 (Hough, 2008), and then to the American Evaluation Association in Denver, Colorado, on November 6, 2008 (Hough, Hanson, & Schmitt, 2008).* Since those reports were made, 300+ additional middle grades schools have been added to the database.

Research Supporting Middle Grades Practice,
pp. 141–156

The study presented here is the first large-scale effort on a national level to examine the relationship between K–8 elemiddle schools and 6–8 middle schools. From a population of more than 2,000 middle grades schools in 49 public school districts across 26 states, a sample of 542 elemiddle and 506 middle schools was drawn. Both regression and discriminant analysis techniques were used to examine relationships, describe student and school characteristics, and predict outcomes. While students attending K–8 elemiddle schools were more likely to be of minority status, live in poverty, and attend an inner city or urban school; they were also more likely to have higher rates of attendance, fewer behavior referrals, and higher academic achievement than their 6–8 middle school counterparts.

BACKGROUND

Middle schools across America continue to face criticism. The critics site low academic achievement, poor attendance, discipline/behavior problems, waning parental involvement, and a perception that the middle school climate, in general, is not conducive to the types of student learning, self-esteem, or extrinsic motivation that compel students to persist in school through high school graduation. While these and other middle school issues have been at the fore of much national media attention over the past decade, until most recently they have not been studied comprehensively at the national level with respect to their relationship to different grade span configurations, specifically K–8 elemiddle and 6–8 middle school structures.

Drawing national attention to middle grades education are school districts throughout the country that have begun to scrutinize student- and school-level data, perhaps more closely and carefully than ever before, in concerted efforts to achieve Annual Yearly Progress (AYP) as mandated by the *No Child Left Behind Act* of 2001. Much of these data can now be aggregated across schools, districts, and states; and as a result, research studies can now be undertaken to identify and track hundreds of middle grades schools of all types in virtually every geographic location in the United States as they explore ways to improve education for young adolescent learners ten to fourteen years of age. Whether their middle grades schools are in urban, rural, inner-city, or suburban settings, school officials are turning in increasing numbers to the elemiddle school concept as an organizational structure to support student success in the middle grades. Unfortunately, and at the same time, middle schools are under attack, and their supporters most often blame the national trend towards establishment of K–8 elemiddles as one of the reasons.

The term "elemiddle school" was coined in 1991 to describe (not prescribe) an organizational structure beginning with kindergarten, pre-kindergarten, or first grade and ending after eighth grade in which age-appropriate promising or "best" pedagogical practices are implemented effectively over time to achieve positive student outcomes (Blair, 2008; Hough, 1991, 2005). As reported by Charles Gibson, ABC World News Tonight on October 7, 2007, "elemiddle" has now became woven into the fabric of the middle grades vernacular and educational jargon used by scholars, researchers, and school personnel nationwide (Banner, 2007).

Much of the attention is directed toward examination of types of educational experiences young adolescent learners encounter, along with the educational outcomes they achieve in PK–8/K–8/1–8 elemiddle schools as compared to those in 6–8/5–8/7–8 middle schools (Byrnes & Ruby, 2007; Cook, MacCoun, Muschkin, & Vigdor, 2008; Hough, 2003a, 2003b, 2004, 2005; Juvonen, Vi-Hhuan, Kaganoff, Augustine, & Constant, 2004; Weiss & Kipnes, 2006). Data used as the bases for comparisons to what has become perceived as failing middle schools most often consists of AYP status, state assessments, and other "indicators" of success such as attendance and behavior rates and subsequent dropout rates in high school (Bowler, 2004; Bradley, 1998; Cook et al., 2008; Granstrom, 1999; Harrington-Lueker, 2000; Hough, 2008; Look, 2001; Mizell, 2004; Pardini, 2002; Rumberger, 1995; Sanko, 1998; Yecke, 2005). While middle school devotees acknowledge shortcomings, they believe criticism of the middle school philosophy is unfair (Swaim, 2005)—a position that strikes an uncanny resemblance to attacks middle school advocates have levied against junior high schools over the past four to five decades, beginning in the late 1960s (National Middle School Association, 1982, 1995).

In an effort to frame the current debate and provide a national perspective regarding elemiddle and middle school education, I launched a 2-year data collection effort from 2005 to 2007 in an effort to examine similarities between elemiddle and middle schools. What resulted was the creation of a database consisting of 1,795 schools in 49 school districts across 26 states that house grades six, seven, and eight in either an elemiddle or middle school setting. This study is the first of its type and provides the only national perspective regarding relationships among demographic and descriptive variables to student outcomes commonly reported by these two different, often competing, grade span configurations.

THEORETICAL PERSPECTIVE

Throughout the 1970s and 1980s, a common approach for "researching" levels of implementation of programs associated with the expanding middle school movement focused almost exclusively on tracking the number of schools across the country that had adopted the 6–8 grade span config-uration and/or the middle school cognomen in lieu of "junior high school" grade spans and epithets. By the early 1990s, however, much mid-dle grades research had also begun to examine the efficacy of the middle school "signature" practices. Interestingly, many school districts now believe schools configured as PK–8 , K–8 , and 1–8 may be better able to implement middle grades "best" or "promising" programs, policies, and practices at higher levels than the 6–8 middle schools, per se, with which they were originally (and remain) most commonly associated (Hough, 2003a, 2004, 2005).

Counting the number of schools across the United States that have changed their grade span configurations and names has been an ongoing effort for a handful of scholars who have tracked the middle school educa-tion movement since the early 1970s. As Figure 8.1 indicates, these data collection efforts document rapid growth in the number of 6–8 middle schools subsequently "benchmarked" in 1982 with the publication of NMSA's first philosophy and position paper titled *This We Believe*. The number of K–8 schools dwindled during the middle school growth period and was accompanied by rapid elimination of K–6, 7–8, and 7–9 schools while 6–8 schools grew significantly until the mid to late 1990s, both in urban and rural areas throughout the United States. The last half of the 1990s and early 2000s, however, has seen a return to K–8 school struc-tures, surprisingly, not in rural America but in urban settings from coast to coast.

Conventional wisdom articulated by many school personnel is gener-ally supportive of the K–8 concept due to a number of observations noted by school personnel who work directly with young adolescents. Teachers and principals often report that parents tend to remain engaged in their child's education longer and that the school climate is more conducive for learning (as is often reflected by fewer behavior problems) when young adolescents are housed in K–8 elemiddle schools (Banner, 2007; Gewertz, 2004; Howard, 2005; McConnell-Schaarsmith, 2005; Nussbaum, 2004; Wolf, 2005). Parents tend to agree that the K–8 school climate provides a more nurturing environment than 6–8 or 7–8 middle schools, and many with multiple children attending pre-high school settings are quick to point out advantages of having their children in the same school. Princi-pals, teachers, and parents often refer to K–8 elemiddle schools as "fam-ily"-type environments where older siblings "look after" younger ones and feel compelled to set examples and model academic and social behaviors that are being observed by elementary students. When activi-ties, programs, and other functions occur in K–8 elemiddle schools, they are often attended by the entire family, not just by the students at a spe-cific grade level (Blair, 2008; Hough, 2003b, 2004, 2005).

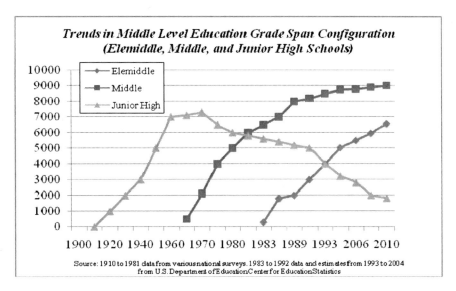

Trends in Middle Level Education Grade Span Configuration (Elemiddle, Middle, and Junior High Schools)

Source: 1910 to 1981 data from various national surveys. 1983 to 1992 data and estimates from 1993 to 2004 from U.S. Department of Education Center for Education Statistics

Note: Reprinted from: "Grade Span Does Make a Difference," by permission of the Institute for School Improvement.

Figure 8.1.   Trends in the growth and development of three different types of middle grades schools.

To examine this conventional wisdom now held by many middle grades educators and most recently spurred on by the No Child Left Behind Act (2001) with its requirements for schools to achieve Annual Yearly Progress (AYP), school systems across the United States have begun analyzing student outcome data more cautiously and critically than ever before in efforts to target grade level specific content areas in need of improvement. Among the findings many school systems are documenting is what can now be identified as a national phenomenon: young adolescent students attending 6–8 middle schools are our nation's "underperformers," not keeping pace with elementary and high school students in terms of academic achievement as measured by proficiency levels on state assessments (Balfanz, Herzog, & MacIver, 2007; Bedard & Do, 2005; Cook et al., 2008; Heller, Calderon, & Medrich, 2003; Juvonan et al., 2004; Lee & Smith, 1993; Mizell, 2004; Weiss & Kipnes, 2006). A noticeable "dip" in achievement during middle school has created alarm, along with other documented areas of concern: unacceptable rates of attendance, poor behavior, low self-esteem, parent and family disengagement from schooling, undesirable school climate, and an overall disinterest in school linked to subsequent high school dropout—concerns middle schools were designed to correct over four decades ago by replacing junior highs that were perceived to be experiencing many of the same problems (see Blair, 2008, for example).

To combat these problems in our nation's middle schools, officials in many public, private, parochial, charter, and magnet schools have turned (and continue to turn) to the elemiddle school approach in efforts to improve schooling for young adolescents. Despite some middle school advocates who oppose these districts' efforts, school officials continue to find their 6th, 7th, and 8th grade students in elemiddle schools outperforming their middle school counterparts and, as a result, continue to reconfigure their middle schools into elemiddles, citing a number of positive outcomes: higher academic achievement; better attendance; fewer behavior problems; higher self-esteem; more support and involvement from parents, families, and communities; improved school climate; and (subsequently) higher graduation rates (Banner, 2007; Blair, 2008; Brumble, 2006; Chaker, 2005; Cook et al., 2007; Delisio, 2007; Hough, 2004, 2008; Howard, 2005; Juvonen et al., 2004; Klump, 2006; Leech, 2007; Paglin & Fager, 1997; Viadero, 2008). In short, districts are turning to elemiddle schools to improve student performance and achieve other positive outcomes they hope will help their schools meet AYP.

Look (2001) identified a number of large, urban school districts, including Baltimore, Boston, Cincinnati, Cleveland, Denver, Detroit, Harrisburg, Hartford, Palm Beach, Philadelphia, and Phoenix, that examined K–8 elemiddle schools closely to determine the feasibility of converting to that type of organizational structure in an effort to improve schooling for young adolescents. Even school systems outside the United States have switched from middle to elemiddle schools. As of the development of this summary, Toronto, Canada, for example, is engaged in a study of the feasibility of converting to elemiddle schools throughout their system.

Many of these school districts opted to switch to the K–8 elemiddle model after studying their student outcome data (attendance, behavior, and academic achievement) and determining that a number of benefits could be achieved within the elemiddle school structure. Figure 8.2 shows the geographic location of many of these districts throughout the United States that have examined the K–8 elemiddle school issue, including those who, after examination, chose to implement the model in their district. Most recently, Portland, Oregon, began its conversion to K–8 elemiddle schools in 2006, for example, and Kansas City and

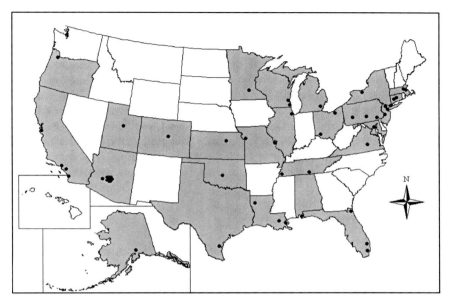

Figure 8.2.   Locations of school districts that have studied the feasibility of converting to K–8 elemiddle schools, and, as of September 2009 are implementing the model in one or more of their middle grades schools.

Detroit began their conversions in 2007. Both New York City Schools and the Denver, Colorado Public Schools are adopting this approach; St. Louis, Missouri, has been considered adopting the K–8 elemiddle model, as well.

While opponents of the current elemiddle school movement are quick to cite differences in student demographics, school size, and geographic location as factors impacting differences between 6–8 middle schools and K–8 elemiddle schools, their assumption that these factors work against 6–8 middle schools is not substantiated by data. In fact, most of the larger urban school districts converting to elemiddle schools are doing so in their inner city schools where the highest percentages of minorities as well as children and families living in poverty reside. Data presented in this study indicate more positive outcomes for students attending K–8 elemiddle schools in high poverty, minority, urban settings than in 6–8 middle schools with lower percentages of student "risk" factors. In addition, a significantly greater number of 6–8 middle schools studied herein are located in more affluent suburban settings albeit with larger student populations. All of these factors are considered in the analyses that follow.

METHODS

Four different sources of information were used to identify schools across the United States for potential inclusion in the national database: (1) school inquires, (2) popular media reports, (3) professional journal publications, and (4) the research literature. Each school identified was entered into a database for subsequent data collection to determine which schools were in a district that contained one or more PK–8, K–8 , or 1–8 school and one or more 5–8, 6–8, or 7–8 school and had examined the issue of grade configuration sometime between 1990 and 2006, whether or not they had made any changes in their school's grade span configuration.

School Inquires

Inquires from school personnel seeking information about middle school grade span configuration patterns and student outcomes made to the Principal Investigator (PI) between 2001 and 2006 were recorded in a contact log. The log developed from these inquiries was completed in 2007 and used for follow-up correspondence with schools to validate the status of efforts related to configuring or reconfiguring their schools.

Popular Media Reports

Popular media reports, most of which included interviews with the PI, were collected from 2000 to 2006. Most of these reports included interviews with school personnel and/or scholars/researchers who provided information related to research regarding grade span configurations. The media sources included national, regional, and local outlets—primarily newspapers and weekly or monthly magazines. Some reporters who contacted the PI were affiliated with radio or television stations / networks. Following is a list of these media sources: *Time* Magazine, *USA Today*, *Education Week*, *New York Times*, the *Boston Globe*, the *Wall Street Journal*, *ABC World News Tonight*, *St. Louis Post-Dispatch*, *Kansas City Star*, *Pittsburgh Gizette*, and *Miami Harold*.

Professional Journals

Professional journals that included studies published from 1999 to 2006 addressing middle and elemiddle school grade span issues were collected and examined to identify middle grades schools that had been studied by researchers. While an annotated bibliography focusing on professional journal grade span studies became a "living document" with continual updates through 2009, the identification of schools for consideration in this study was completed in 2007.

Research Literature

In addition to targeting professional journals, the broader research literature was also examined to obtain additional types of dissemination sources such as dissertations and research presentations made to professional organizations—for example, where grade span issues were addressed and specific schools, districts, or communities identified. The research literature focused on studies completed between 1999 and 2006 to be consistent with time frames associated with other data collection approaches. These sources were developed into an annotated bibliography, added to the database, and used for the purpose of school identification that was completed in 2007.

Sample

These four sources yielded over 2,000 middle grades schools nationally. Each school was entered into an Excel file, creating a master list of schools by name and geographic location. A web search was then conducted to obtain information specific to each school on the master list, beginning first with contact information, addresses, and affiliations with districts or other entities. All private, parochial, magnet, charter or otherwise "special" schools were eliminated, resulting in a population of 1,795 public schools. To focus specifically on the elemiddle v. middle school issue, all PK–8, K–8 , and 1–8 elemiddles and 6–8 middle schools in the data file were identified for inclusion in this study, producing a sample of 1,048 schools—542 elemiddle and 506 middle schools across 49 different school districts in 26 states. Additional schools added to this national database in 2008 by way of the *Schools to Watch* project and *Developmental Designs* program are not included in the analyses presented here. However, they are included in a comprehensive report to be submitted for review before the close of 2009.

Next, more specific school level data were obtained from a second web search with follow-up telephone calls to schools with incomplete, missing, or unclear information on their web sites. Common data across the sample schools included the following: grade span configuration, grade span adoption date, student population (grade level specific), number of certified teachers, per pupil expenditure, percent of children receiving free and reduced lunches, percent student ethnicity, attendance rates, behavioral referrals, in- and out-of-school suspensions, and AYP status.

The 542 elemiddle and 506 middle schools were then surveyed using a clustering technique by which each school received a packet of questionnaires designed for teachers, specialty personnel, and administrators. Almost 40% of these schools were represented by eight or more completed and returned survey questionnaires as of June 2008.

All data were transferred from Excel into SPSS 16.0 for analysis. Regression and discriminant analysis techniques were used to examine characteristics associated with both school types. Results from these approaches are detailed in the full report (forthcoming, fall 2009).

FINDINGS

Data from this study indicate that the average student enrollment in elemiddle schools is 647, ranging from 261 to 1,770; for middle schools, the average is 900 with a range of 264 to 2,557. Just over 70% of students attending elemiddle schools are receiving free/reduced lunches, compared to just under 68% of middle school students. Almost 83% of students attending the elemiddle schools studied here are non-White, compared to 81% in the middle schools.

In terms of outcomes, the average daily attendance rate for elemiddle school students is 94%, while that of middle school students is 92%; and 56% of elemiddle schools met AYP, compared to only 43% of middle schools. Average number of expulsions of elemiddle school students is .20 per year with ($\bar{X} = 77$) suspensions; while middle school student expulsions were 4.10 per year ($\bar{X} = 139$) suspensions. Table 8.1 indicates more specific descriptive and demographic data for the information provided above. All data in Table 8.1 that compare elemiddle schools to middle schools are statistically significant ($p < .05$).

Table 8.2 shows the most common responses from middle grades teachers, specialty personnel, and administrators when asked why their school is either a middle or elemiddle school. The most frequently cited reason by middle school personnel is because they want to be labeled a "middle school," while the most frequently cited reason by elemiddle school personnel is that they want to meet AYP, per NCLB (2001). When middle school personnel expressed their desire to provide more opportunities for students, they frequently mentioned accelerated classes such as Algebra as well as extra-curricular activities such as clubs, student government, and school dances. Elemiddle school personnel, on the other hand, expressed a desire to create smaller learning communities, if not smaller

Table 8.1.   Description of School Type

School Type	K–8 Elemiddle	6–8 Middle
Total Sample	(n = 542)	(n = 506)
(n = 1,048)		
Average School Size	646.8 (sd = 276.1)	900.4 (sd = 432.4)
(n = 1,048)	(n = 529)	(n = 425)
Average Daily Attendance	93.8% (sd = 2.3)	91.8% (sd = 4.2)
(n = 954)	(n = 529)	(n = 425)
% of Title 1 Schools	78.1%	71.8%
(n = 596)	96	340
Percent of Free/Reduced Lunch	70.2% (sd = 23.9)	67.6% (sd = 23.2)
(n = 653)	(n = 245)	(n = 408)
Ethnicity		
(n = 961)	(n = 517)	(n = 444)
White	16.9%	19.3%
African American	50.8%	41.2%
Hispanic	27.7%	30.6%
Asian/Pacific islander	3.6%	8.4%
American Indian/Alaskan Native	0.5%	0.8%
Other	0.9%	1.9%
Average # of Expulsions	0.26 (sd = .72)	4.1 (sd = 5.5)
(n = 253)	(n = 98)	(n = 155)
% Met AYP	56.4%	43.6%
(n = 993)	(n = 532)	(n = 461)

schools, altogether. Number three on the middle school personnel list is sports programs; a common response is that middle schools provide more interscholastic sports programs such as basketball, soccer, track, and football. Respondents from Texas, Georgia, and Florida (in particular) very frequently noted that schools in their states would "never" convert back to K–8 schools because they needed 6–8 or 7–8 or 7–9 middle schools to serve as "farm systems" for high school football. While statements that reflect this sentiment may not represent the majority opinion of educators in those states, they were nonetheless adamantly expressed in the data collected herein and, therefore, must be reported. Number three on the elemiddle school respondents' list is to improve school climate. These middle grades personnel note that elemiddle schools often contribute to the development of positive behavior traits among young adolescents who have younger siblings attending one of the elementary grades and/or feel compelled to exhibit "mature" behavior because younger children share the same building, if not the same hallways and commons areas.

**Table 8.2.   Five Most Common Responses on the
Middle Grades Survey Questionnaire to the Question:
"Why is Your School a 'Middle School'
or an 'Elemiddle School'"? (N = 2,847)**

Rank	6–8 Middle School Personnel	K–8 Elemiddle School Personnel
	(n = 1,288)	(n = 1,559)
1	Want to be called "Middle School"	To meet AYP
2	More opportunities for students	Create smaller learning communities
3	Sports programs	Improve school climate
4	Community demands it	Engage parents
5	Implement middle school practices	Implement best practices

Next on the list for middle school personnel is the fact that their communities demand they have "middle schools." Often noted here is that parents and school personnel are "in tune" with the middle school concept or philosophy and do not want to change to anything else. For elemiddle school personnel, this dimension takes a slightly different twist. They note that parents can be more easily and readily engaged in their young adolescents' learning because there is not any transition to another building, helping parents feel more connected to the school they have felt comfortable visiting in years prior. Again, parents of elemiddle school children often have children attending both elementary and middle grades. Rounding out the top five list for middle school personnel is their desire to implement so-call middle school "signature" practices such as team teaching, integrated curriculum and instruction, advisories, flexible schedules, common planning time, and other secondary structures associated with teaching and learning. The number five response from elemiddle school personnel is similar, yet different and couched as "best practices," rather than "middle school" practices. Here, elemiddle school personnel state that cross-age tutoring, parental involvement, and intramural sports programs can more easily be achieved with their school's structure. Much overlap with the middle school signature practices is common within responses label herein as "best practices," as well.

POSTSCRIPT

After creating the national database described herein, I took a sabbatical leave in 2009 to study (among other issues) 52 of the middle grades schools that had met AYP (26 elemiddles and 26 middles, one of each from the 26 states that included schools in the database). Site visits were conducted between August 2008 and July 2009 with a focus on the effects of poverty in these school settings. As a result of that work, along with new data from the *Schools to Watch* project and the *ORIGINS Developmental Designs* program evaluation, scores of additional middle grades schools are continually being added to the national database.

Over the past year and a half, I have received numerous requests from the research community and media to release information from the database. A full report will be submitted for review later this year containing a detailed description of the statistical techniques used to address the research questions. Implications for policy are given much attention in that report. While the findings presented here may be considered "preliminary," they do not differ from those contained in the full report; however, the latter provides greater depth of discussion of the data that support these (and other) findings. I thank all those who have expressed interest, support, and patience as an in-depth report is readied for release soon.

REFERENCES

Balfanz, R., Herzog, L., & Mac Iver, D.J. (2007). Preventing student disengagement and keeping students on the graduation track in high-poverty middle-grades schools: Early identification and effective interactions. *Educational Psychologist, 24*(4), 123-135.

Banner, J. (Executive Producer). (2007, September 6). *ABC World News Tonight with Charles Gibson* [Television broadcast]. New York, NY: Public Broadcasting Service.

Bedard, K., & Do, C. (2005). Are middle schools more effective? The impact of school structure on student outcomes. *The Journal of Human Resources, 40*(3), 660–682.

Blair, L. (2008, April). Back to the future: The shift to k–8 schools. *SEDL Letter, 1,* 14–19.

Bowler, M. (2004, June 2). Middle school goes the way of junior high. *Baltimore Sun.* Retrieved from http://www.baltimoresun.com/news/education

Bradley, A. (1998). *Muddle in the middle.* Retrieved from http://www.edweek.org./we/weprintstory.cfm/slug=31middle.h17

Brumble, M. (2006, July 7). Research on urban K–8 schools' performance offers mixed results. *The Shreveport Times.* Retrieved from http://www.shreveporttimes.com/apps/pbcs.dll/article?AID=/20060707/NEWS04/607070311/1002.

Byrnes, V., & Ruby, A. (2007). Comparing achievement between K–8 and middle schools: A large-scale empirical study. *American Journal of Education, 114,* 101–135.

Chaker, A. (2005, April 6). Middle school goes out of fashion—Amid evidence kids struggle with move to junior high, districts shift to K–8 model. *The Wall Street Journal*, p. D1.

Cook, P. J., MacCoun, R., Muschkin, C., & Vigdor, J. (2008). The negative impacts of starting middle school in sixth grade. *Journal of Policy Analysis and Management, 27*(1), 104–121.

Delisio, C. (2007). Is the time right for "Elemiddles?" *Education World*. Retrieved from http://www.education-world.com/a admin/admin/admin324.shtml.

Gewertz, C. (2004, May 19). City districts embracing K–8 schools. *Education Week, 23*(37), 1, 20.

Granstrom, N.L. (1999, May). A parent criticizes middle school theory. *Basic Education*. Retrieved from www.c-b-e.org/articles/parent.htm

Harrington-Lueker, D. (2000). The middle years. Are middle schools up to the task? *American School Board Journal*. Retrieved from http://www.asbj.com/ 2000 /10/1000coverstory.html

Heller, R., Calderon, S., & Medrich, E. (2003). *Academic achievement in the middle grades: What does research tell us?* Atlanta, GA: Southern Regional Educational Board. Retrieved from http://www.sreb.org

Hough, D. L. (1991, April). *A review of middle level organization*. Paper presented at the annual meeting of the American Educational Research Association, Chicago, IL.

Hough, D. L. (2003a). *R3 = research, rhetoric, and reality: A study of studies*. Westerville, OH: National Middle School Association.

Hough, D. L. (2003b). The case for the elemiddle school. *Middle Matters, 11*(2), 1–3.

Hough, D. L. (2004, December). *Grade span does make a difference (Policy Brief)*. Springfield, MO: Missouri State University, Institute for School Improvement.

Hough, D. L. (2005). The rise of the 'elemiddle' school. *The School Administrator, 3*(62), 10–14.

Hough, D. L. (2008, February). *The first ever national database for middle grades education*. Presentation made at the annual meeting of the National Forum to Accelerate Middle Grades Education, Long Beach, CA.

Hough, D. L., Hanson, C., and Schmitt, V. L. (2008, November). *Developing a national database to examine middle grades "grade span" [sic] configurations and student outcomes*. Paper presented at the annual meeting of the American Evaluation Association, Denver, CO.

Howard, T.L. (2005, May 25). City district will float idea of K–8 schools. *St. Louis Post-Dispatch*, p C2.

Juvonen, J., Vi-Hhuan, L., Kaganoff, T. Augustine, C., & Constant, L. (2004). *Focus on the wonder years; Challenges facing the American middle school*. Santa Monica, CA: RAND Corporation.

Klump, J. (2006). What the research says (or doesn't say): About K–8 versus middle school grade configurations. *Northwest Regional Education Laboratory, 11*(3). Retrieved from http://www.nwrel.org/nwedu/11-03/research

Lee, V.E., & Smith, J.B. (1993). The effects of school restructuring on the achievement and engagement of middle-grade students. *Sociology in Education, 66*(3), 164–187.

Leech, M. (2007). Birmingham schools keep K–8s in mind. *The Birmingham News.* Retrieved from http://www.al.com/birminghamnews/stories/index.ssf?/base/news/1177834604216990.xml&coll=2

Look, K. (2001). The great K–8 debate. *Philadelphia Public Schools Notebook.* Retrieved from http://www.philaedfund.org/notebook/TheGreatK8Debate.htm

McConnell-Schaarsmith, A. (2005, August 29). Great beginnings: Tough decisions—middle schools or K–8?. *Pittsburg Post-Gazette.* Retrieved from http://www.post-gazette.com/pg/05241/561897.stm.

Mizell, H. (2004). *Still crazy after all these years: Grade configuration and the education of young adolescents.* Keynote address at the National School Board Association's Council of Urban Boards of Education, San Antonio, TX.

National Middle School Association. (1982). *This we believe.* Columbus, OH: Author.

National Middle School Association. (1995). *This we believe: Developmentally responsive middle level schools.* Columbus, OH: Author.

National Middle School Association. (2003). *This we believe: Successful schools for young adolescents.* Westerville, OH: Author.

National Middle School Association. (n.d). *Research in support of middle level grade configuration* (Research Brief). Westerville, OH: Author.

Nussbaum, D. (2004, September 12). Why middle schools are being questioned. *The New York Times.* Retrieved from http://www.nytimes.com/2004/09/12/nyregion/12NJ.html?ei=5070&en=40b5559ca8907647&ex=1143349200&pagewanted=print&position=.

Paglin, C., & Fager J. (1997). *Grade configuration: Who goes where?* Northwest Regional Educational Laboratory & *Education World.* Retrieved from www.nwrel.org /request

Pardini, P. (2002). Revival of the K–8 school: Criticism of the middle school fuels renewed interest in a school configuration of yesteryear. *School Administrator, web edition.* Retrieved from www.aasa.org/publications/sa/2002_03/pardini.htm

Rumberger, R.W. (1995). Dropping out of middle school: A multilevel analysis of students and schools. *American Educational Research Journal, 32*(3), 583–625.

Sanko, J. (1998, December 10). Quit building middle schools? Top education official floats idea to legislators. *Rocky Mountain News.* Retrieved from www.middleweb.com/quitbuilding.html

Swaim, S. (2005). *It's about educating young adolescents.* Westerville, OH: National Middle School Association.

Viadero, D. (2008). Evidence for moving to K–8 model not airtight. *Education Week, 27*(19), 1, 12. Retrieved from http://www.edweek.org/ew/articles/2008/01/16/19k8.h27.html

Weiss, C.C., & Kipnes, L. (2006). Reexamining middle school effects: A Comparison of middle grades students in middle schools and K–8 schools. *American Journal of Education, 112*(2), 239–272.

Wolf, I. (2005, September 15). Experts say middle schools fail students, promote K–8 model. *Kansas City InfoZine.* Retrieved from http://www.infozine.com/news/stories/op/storiesView/sid/10274

Yecke, C. P. (2005). *Mayhem in the Middle; How middle schools have failed America—and how to make them work.* Washington, DC: The Thomas B. Fordham Institute.

CHAPTER 9

IMPACT OF ENVIRONMENT-BASED TEACHING ON STUDENT ACHIEVEMENT

A Study of Washington State Middle Schools

Oksana Bartosh, Margaret Tudor, Lynne Ferguson, and Catherine Taylor

This chapter reports on a project that investigates the impact of systemic environmental education (EE) programs on student achievement on EE-based integrated tests and standardized tests in math, language arts, and listening. Systemic environmental education programs are defined by curriculum designed to align and integrate subjects around real-world environmental contexts. To assess environmental literacy knowledge and skills, integrated EE-based tests for Grade 8 were administered to students in participating schools, and the results were compared to students' scores on standardized tests. Quantitative analysis shows correlations between EE scores and standardized scores in math, reading and writing, with students from EE schools performing higher on EE and state tests than students from schools with traditional curriculum. The project findings suggest that

Research Supporting Middle Grades Practice,
pp. 157–172

by providing a universal context for learning, environmental education could support schools' accountability efforts to integrate discipline standards and improve student performance.

INTRODUCTION AND RESEARCH OBJECTIVES

"I have to serve my masters. I have to cover all the curriculum. I have to make sure my students do well on the state tests. And all this doesn't leave much time for environmental education or other extra activities." "As an administrator I need to see evidence that these types of programs can help my school perform well on the WASL." The Pacific Education Institute (PEI) research group regularly encounters comments like these during research meetings, professional development workshops, and informal conversations with teachers and administrators from Washington State public schools. While those involved in environmental education strongly believe in its benefits for students and schools, teachers and administrators often need more than just words and emotions. They need evidence that proves EE's beneficial impact on students—evidence that would help them defend their choices of the curriculum activities and programs.

In Washington State, like in many other states and countries across the globe, environmental education is required to be taught in all grades and subjects. However, while most teachers and parents would like to see EE become a part of the school programs, environmental education designed to align subjects around real-world environmental contexts is still marginalized or absent from everyday school activities (Hart, 2003; Volk, Hungerford, & Tomera, 1984; U.S. Environmental Protection Agency, National Environmental Education Advisory Council, Environmental Education Division (EPA), 1996). As a result of the current accountability climate, schools in North America (and especially in the U.S.) continue to focus on the content that is measured on discipline-based standardized tests, marginalizing rich interdisciplinary activities and environments. While teachers and researchers in the field of environmental education call for more evidence that EE can be effective in improving student learning (see Angell, Ferguson, & Tudor, 2001), this research is still limited. The study presented here begins to address this need.

Our research project investigated the impact of high quality EE programs on student performance on the EE-based assessments and the state standardized tests. Specifically, we asked whether students involved in rigorous environmental education programs achieve at higher levels on standardized tests and/or on environmental literacy measures. This paper presents a summary of our findings.

THEORETICAL BACKGROUND

While EE practitioners have been observing the beneficial influence of EE on their students for years, there are a limited number of empirical research studies corroborating this fact.

One of the first groups that attempted to investigate the efficacy of environmental education in increasing student learning was the State Education and Environment Roundtable (Lieberman & Hoody, 1998). Their study, Closing the Achievement Gap: Using the Environment as an Integrating Context for Learning, analyzed student achievement at 40 schools with environment-based programs across the United States. The report suggests that students in classrooms with EE programs tend to have higher scores on standardized tests in math, reading, writing, science, and social sciences.

California Student Assessment Project, another study conducted by the SEER group, evaluated student achievement in 11 environmental schools in California and found that when compared to students from traditional (non-EE classes), EE students showed higher results in 101 (72%) out of 140 academic assessments in language arts, math, science, and social science (Lieberman, Hoody, & Lieberman, 2000).

In their study of the impact of EE on students' critical thinking, achievement and motivation, Athman and Monroe (2004) also found a strong positive correlation between participation in environmental education programs and higher achievement on state tests. The study compared students' scores on three tests that measure critical thinking and motivation (the Cornell Critical Thinking Test, the California Measure of Mental Motivation, the Achievement Motivation Inventory) and found that students in programs designed around an environmental context tended to score higher than students in the traditional classes.

Cheak, Hungerford, and Volk (2002), Billings, Plato, Anderson, and Wiley (1996), Monroe, Randall, and Crisp (2001), National Environmental Education and Training Foundation (2000), and National Environmental Education and Training Foundation and North American Association for Environmental Education (2001) also suggest that environmental education may improve student learning. According to these authors, achievement, student motivation and engagement tend to improve when students participate in environment-based programs. Unfortunately, some of the reports published to date on this issue present promising anecdotal "success stories" (e.g. NEETF & NAAEE, 2001) rather than rigorous empirical studies corroborating these findings.

The literature reviews conducted by Norman, Jennings, and Wahl (2006) and Wheeler, Thumlert, Glaser, Schoellhamer, and Bartosh (2007) support the claim of the lack of rigorous studies. Norman et al. (2006), who aimed to "to determine whether meaningful evidence exists that shows a connection between environmentally-based education programs and improvements in academic achievement" (p. i), reviewed 100 studies and identified only eight that were regarded as providing strong or supportive evidence of the positive impact of EE programs on student achievement, whereas 35 studies provided incomplete or unclear data and descriptions. Similarly, the review of the research conducted by Wheeler et al. (2007), which included 20 studies that address student achievement, found that while 18 papers and reports indicated a correlation between participation in environmental education and improved academic achievement, many of them did not provide sufficient description of the research methods and/or participants. Very few studies controlled for other factors such as gender, socioeconomic status, age, and level of achievement prior to participation in environmental education; some relied on small sample sizes and did not test for statistical and/or practical significance of the results. The existing research points to the complexity of understanding the impact of environmental education programs and illustrates a pressing need for more in-depth qualitative and quantitative studies of this issue.

In response both to these calls for more rigorous research and to the urgency of education reform, the Pacific Education Institute, a consortium of stakeholders interested in advancing student learning through curriculum designed around an environmental context, started a long-term research project that investigated the impact of EE on student achievement in Washington State. This consortium was initially called the Environmental Education Assessment Project and, in 2003, came under the umbrella of the Pacific Education Institute (PEI). Initially, the effort was co-sponsored by Project Learning Tree (PLT) and the Washington Forest Protection Association (WFPA), Project WILD and the Washington Department of Fish and Wildlife (WDFW), Project WET of the Washington State Department of Ecology (DOE), and the Washington State Office of the Superintendent of Public Instruction (OSPI). Today the participants in PEI include additional representatives from the business community, nonprofit education and environmental organizations, state agencies, national environmental education programs, residential environmental learning centers, school districts, and individual schools.

Since 2003, the Pacific Education Institute has conducted studies that explored the relationships between student achievement on the state tests and EE programs. The first study (Phase 1) compared the results of state standardized tests for 77 pairs of schools in Washington State: schools that have environmental programs and schools with traditional curriculum (Bartosh, Tudor, Taylor, & Ferguson, 2006). The Environmental Education Rubrics were used to select schools with well-developed environmental education programs for this study. Environmental Education Rubrics have been developed by representatives of several state agencies, business, and educational organizations including the Washington Department of Fish and Wildlife, the Washington Forest Protection Association, the University of Washington, and the Evergreen State College. Using these EE Rubrics, it was possible to evaluate a school's activities in six areas:

- School commitment to integrate environmental education into the curriculum (measures number of years in EE, number of students and teachers participating in EE programs, and frequency of EE programs or units)
- Curriculum development (evaluates how teachers design their curricula, whether they work alone or in a team, the type of curriculum, and the links to natural environment)
- Instruction used in the classrooms (determines whether teachers work in teams integrating different subjects together)
- Student learning (evaluates the way students learn and whether they are encouraged to construct their own knowledge)
- Assessment (determines whether students have an opportunity to make presentations and assess their own learning or if they are assessed through more traditional assessments)
- Community commitment (studies the ties between school curriculum and community).

Schools involved in the programs with environmental education were targeted initially and ranked on EE Rubrics in terms of level of involvement. The rankings were conducted by external EE providers and other EE and educational experts who work with the schools in Washington State and know how programs are implemented by the schools. For the study only the schools that have at least three years of practicing EE strategies and have 20% of teachers/classrooms and at least 33% of students involved have been selected as "environmental" schools. Table 9.1 presents characteristics of EE and comparison schools on the Rubric (Ferguson, Tudor, & Bartosh, 2005).

For each EE school a comparison school was identified using the U.S. census and other economic, demographic, and geographic criteria. Pairs were selected in the same location and where possible in the same school district and had similar ethnic composition, size, and the percentage of students receiving free/subsidized lunch. The study used Non-Equivalent

**Table 9.1. Characteristics of EE
and Comparison Schools On The EE Rubrics**

	EE	*Comparison*
Extent of EE Implementation • # of years in EE • % of students involved • % of teachers /classrooms involved	• At least 3 years • 20% or more • 33% or more	• less than 3 years • less than 20% (or none at all) • less than 33% (or none at all)
Curriculum	• Integration around EE • Links to natural areas	• No integration around EE • Stand-alone EE activities or none at all
Instruction	• Team teaching	• Individual teaching OR no teaming OR teams are only forming
Assessment	Best practices	• Traditional assessment practices
Student Learning	• Focus on activities allowing students to construct their own learning	• Traditional approach
Community	• Participation of community members in learning process	• Few community partners OR no participation of community members in learning process

Groups Design and, instead of random assignment to control and treatment groups, used economic, demographic, and geographic data to ensure comparability of the groups.

Bartosh et al.'s (2006) study showed that schools that undertake systemic environmental education programs consistently outperform "traditional" schools on state standardized tests in math, reading, writing, and listening. In 73 pairs (out of 77), environmental schools had higher scores in *at least* one subject. Furthermore, analysis of longitudinal data for the period of 1997–2002 showed that EE schools had higher mean percentages of students who met standards on the WASL every year. However, although the percentage of students who meet or are above standards on the state tests is higher for EE schools, the question remains: What does it mean for individual students? Will we observe the same trend if we look at individual student scores? The second stage of the project presented in this chapter explores that issue.

RESEARCH METHODOLOGY

Study Groups

Out of 77 pairs of schools participating in the first stage of the project, 10 schools were invited to participate in the second stage. Five of the selected schools had a long history of environmental education. The PEI staff have been working with the administrators and teachers of these schools for at least five years helping with development of programs and materials and providing professional development workshops. This close partnership allowed us to identify schools with exemplary environment-based programs and collect information about school wide initiatives and individual classroom activities.

In the first phase of the research, administrators and teachers at participating schools and external experts familiar with school programs, activities, and environment evaluated the schools' level of EE implementation using Environmental Education Rubric developed by PEI. Table 9.2 presents the comparison of scores on the EE Rubric for five pairs of schools selected for this second phase of the project and compares it to the scores of the 77 pairs of schools from the initial phase of the research. As seen from the table, the scores for the individual categories (implementation of EE programs, curriculum, instruction and assessment strategies, student learning and community involvement) are similar for the pairs of schools that participated in Phase 1 and Phase 2 of the study. The EE Rubric scores indicated that EE schools had higher level of EE implementation with more students and teachers being involved in environmental education for at least three years. Furthermore, curriculum of EE schools was integrated around environmental themes, had multiple links to outdoors and nature areas, and was designed and delivered by teams of teachers. The Rubric also showed that the groups of schools were similar with regard to their assessment strategies and student learning approaches.

For the second phase of the project, we have selected schools from the list of 77 pairs that participated in the first part of study, so the selected EE and non-EE schools were similar in their demographic and economic criteria. Table 9.3 presents the comparison of the demographic and economic data for EE and non-EE schools.

All participants of this study were students in the K–12 public school system in Grade 8 during the 2002–2003 school year. Between 30 and 50 students from each school participated. Students represented rural, suburban and urban populations as well as geographically diverse regions in

Table 9.2.   Comparison of EE Rubric Scores
for EE and Comparison Schools (Averages)

	Study of 77 Pairs of Schools (1 Phase)		Present Study of 10 Pairs of Schools (2 Phase)	
	EE	Comparison	EE	Comparison
Implementation	4	1	4	1
Curriculum	4	1	4	1
Instruction	4	2	4	2
Assessment	4	3	4	3
Student learning	4	3	4	3
Community involvement	4	2	4	1
Total rubric score	24	12	24	11

Table 9.3.   Demographic and Economic Comparison
of EE and Non-EE Schools (Averages)

	Study of 77 Pairs of Schools (1 Phase)		Present Study of 10 Pairs of Schools (2 Phase)	
	EE	Comparison	EE	Comparison
School Size	550	547	656	610
Free /reduced lunch %	27	27	24	23
Ethnicity				
White %	84	80	81	79
Black %	4	4	5	8
Native Americans %	3	3	3	2
Asian %	7	7	7	8
Hispanic %	6	6	4	4

Washington State. Grade 8 was selected for the testing because students at this level are tested in math, reading, writing, listening,[1] and science.

Research Instruments

To explore whether there is a difference in academic achievement of students in EE and non-EE schools, we used two measures: integrated EE-based assessments developed by the Pacific Education Institute and scores on the state standardized tests in math, reading, writing and listening.

Integrated EE-Based Tests

To assess environmental literacy knowledge and skills, students from participating schools were given three integrated EE-based tasks, one in each of the three areas: inquiry, systems, and civic participation. The Inquiry task assesses inquiry skills of students and their ability to design and describe steps of an inquiry process. Systems assessment focuses on students' understanding of environmental systems and the interplay between natural and social systems. Finally, the Civics assessment task evaluates students' civic participation skills that would allow them to play an effective citizenship role. The tests were developed by the Pacific Education Institute and refined from 1998 to 2003 (Taylor, Kurtz-Smith, Tudor, Ferguson, & Bartosh, 2005). These criterion referenced assessments are modeled on the Washington Assessment of Student Learning (WASL) test (standardized test in Washington State) in format and correlate with the state standards (Essential Academic Learning Requirements) that are consistent with and reflect National Standards. The WASL-like assessments integrate subject areas and allow assessment of student performance not only in environmental education but also in the process skills of language arts and mathematics and content knowledge of science and the social sciences (geography, civics, and economics). Each assessment has been pilot tested, and student work has been gathered to help ensure the validity of the tasks and the rubrics. The Office of Superintendent of Public Instruction (OSPI)'s personnel have worked with the assessments to ensure that the EE-based assessments remain close to the WASL tests in format.

Short-answer and extended (open-ended) response items of the EE WASL-like assessments were scored using rubrics similar to those used for the operational WASL assessments. They were scored by teachers trained to score standardized tests developed by NCS-Pearson, Washington State's scoring contractor. Three trained teachers (raters) scored each student's work, and the final student score was the average of the three raters' scores. If raters' item-level scores were discrepant by more than one point, a fourth rater scored student work to ensure accurate scores. Table 9.4 presents the number of students from both groups completed the tests.

Information About Standardized Tests

The second measure of achievement used in this study was student achievement data for the Washington Assessment of Student Learning test. This criterion-referenced achievement test is designed to measure whether students are achieving the Washington State standards in read-

**Table 9.4.   Number of Students in EE and
Non-EE Programs Completing WASL-Like Tests**

	Number of Students	
Task	EE program	Non-EE program
Inquiry	204	166
Systems	215	210
Civics	208	194

ing, writing, listening, mathematics, and science. These data were obtained from the WA OSPI database.

FINDINGS

Reliability and Validity of WASL-like Tasks

To obtain evidence of the reliability of the EE WASL-like assessment scores, two types of data have been analyzed: inter-judge agreement data (to look at reliability of raters using rubrics) and internal consistency data. In most cases, exact agreements and exact plus adjacent rater agreements (which looked at the percent of times a pair of raters give the same score to the same students' responses) for all Grade 8 items were high (70% and 90% respectively) suggesting that rater agreement was acceptable. Table 9.5 presents the inter-judge agreement data for the WASL-like items.

Similarly, the correlation between the total scores (sum of the item scores) given by a pair of raters (which illustrates the degree to which students would earn the same total score if scored by different raters) was high (~0.9). Table 9.6 presents the correlations between raters' final scores for one of the WASL-like tests. The complete reliability and validity data are published in the Technical Report #7 by Taylor et al. (2005), available for download through the PEI's website (www.pacificeducation-institute.org).

Comparison of State Test Scores
and WASL-Like Scores for EE and Non-EE Students

To investigate the differences in achievement for students in integrated EE programs and non-EE classes, two sets of scores were analyzed: scores on the WASL standardized tests and scores on the PEI's WASL-like EE-

Table 9.5. Agreement by Rater (R) Pairs for Grade 8 WASL-Like Tests

Test	Item	Points Possible	R1 & R2 Exact Agreement	R1 & R2 Exact + Adjacent Agreement	R1 & R3 Exact Agreement	R1 & R3 Exact + Adjacent Agreement	R2 & R3 Exact Agreement	R2 & R3 Exact + Adjacent Agreement
Inquiry	1	4	78.9%	98%	79.6%	99%	84.8%	~100%
Systems	1	4	72.5%	99%	70%	98%	75.3%	100%
	2	4	75.8%	98%	83.8%	97%	78.2%	97%
	3	4	68.5%	99%	78.1%	99%	69.2%	96%
	4	4	60.7%	89%	78.9%	97%	70.8%	90%
	5	4	61.7%	95%	77.4%	98%	64.7%	95%
Civics	1	4	75.7%	99%	76.3%	~100%	70.1%	~100%
	2	3	70.2%	~100%	74.7%	99%	74.4%	~100%
	3	4	66.7%	95%	66.9%	97%	63.5%	96%
	4	4	66.2%	97%	68.5%	95.8%	70.3%	98%
	5	4	77.4%	97%	65.2%	94%	69.2%	98%

**Table 9.6. Rater Score Agreement
for A WASL-Like Task: Pearson Correlation**

	Rater 1	Rater 2	Rater 3
Rater 1	1.000	.928	.883
Rater 2		1.000	.933
Rater 3			1.000

based assessments. Figure 9.1 presents the comparison of average scores for students from EE and non-EE schools on the WASL-like tests. According to individual sample t tests, students in EE schools tend to have higher scores on the Inquiry, System, and Civics WASL-like tests, and this difference was statically significant (p[inquiry] = 0.036; p[systems] = 0.001; and p[civics] = 0.000). This demonstrates that students in EE programs develop stronger environmental literacy skills and deeper understanding on environmental systems.

Similarly, analysis of the individual students' WASL test scores in math, reading, writing, and listening indicated that on average students from EE schools have higher scores on the WASL tests. Figure 9.2 presents the comparison of average test scores on the WASL tests. However, statistically this difference is significant for two tests (out of four)—for math and

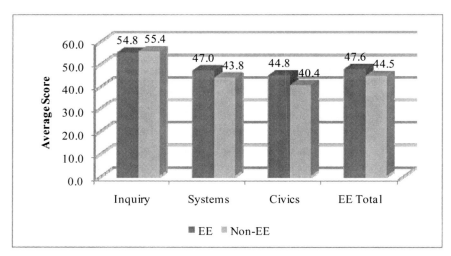

Figure 9.1. Middle school comparison of student achievement on WASL-like tests for EE And non-EE schools (presented as *T*-scores).

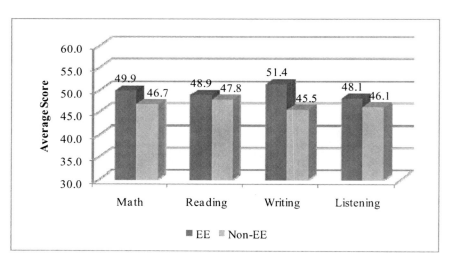

Figure 9.2. Middle school comparison of student achievement on WASL test scores for EE and non-EE schools (presented as T-scores).

writing. Although students from EE schools tend to outperform students from non-EE schools on reading and listening tests on the WASL, there is no significant difference in these areas with p values higher than 0.05 (0.24 for reading and 0.11 for listening).

Table 9.7.   Effect Sizes for Both EE Tasks and WASL Tests

Subject Area	Effect Size (d)
WASL	
Math	0.3
Writing	0.8
Reading	0.2
Listening	0.2
EE-Based Tasks	
Inquiry	−0.1
Systems	0.4
Civics	0.5
Total EE Score	0.3

Although statistical significance testing (the results of which are presented above) allows us to speculate about the possible effects of EE programs, it does not allow us to assess the magnitude of the observed effect. To explore the practical significance of our results and measure the magnitude of the treatment effect, the effect sizes were calculated as standardized difference between two means (Cohen's d) (Cohen, 1988; Hartung, Knapp, & Sinha, 2008). Cohen considered d that is equal or smaller than .2 as small, d around .5 as medium, and d equal or larger than .8 as large effect size. Table 9.7 presents effect sizes for both EE tasks and WASL tests.

As seen from the table, the largest effect is observed in WASL writing and civics, whereas inquiry, WASL reading, and listening have small effect sizes that cannot be considered as practically significant. At the same time, while the differences between EE and non-EE schools are not large, this finding has educational significance. Our study illustrates that students in EE programs can perform at least at the same level as students in non-EE classes and do well on the state tests, while learning things that go beyond the "three R" basics. EE students gain an understanding of environmental issues and concepts and develop skills that are crucial for our survival as a species in the age of current environmental crisis and degradation. They learn about natural systems and interactions of the environment and society; gain inquiry, problem solving, and decision-making skills; and develop an understanding of how they can participate in society as citizens. In other words, by doing environmental education, teachers can help their students become better readers, writers, and thinkers as well as develop awareness about environmental issues, sense of responsibility and care for the world and the environment.

DISCUSSION AND CONCLUSIONS

This study illustrates what many EE practitioners and supporters have anecdotally known for a long time: Students benefit from environmental education programs. Experiences outside the classroom with the opportunity to observe, explore, and wonder engage and motivate students and improve their attitude to school and learning and, as a result, their achievement and grades. Programs that use the environment as a context for learning provide space and time for students to make connections between school learning and real life.

In this study, we compared two groups of students: students participating in school-based environmental programs and students from traditional classrooms. The schools differed by the level and extent of environmental education programs and were assessed by internal and external experts. While we did not randomly assign students to control and treatment groups, we used demographic, economic, and geographic data to ensure the comparability of the groups. Furthermore, the five pairs of schools selected for the second phase of the project were similar in demographic parameters and level of EE implementation (according to the EE Rubric scores) to the 77 pairs of schools that participated in the first study. Using these procedures, we tried to control for some of the factors that may affect student achievement, such as school size and socioeconomic status. Because of the design of this study and our extensive knowledge of schools and teachers who participated in this project, we believe that our study indicates a correlation between student achievement and environmental education programs. However, we acknowledge that other factors (e.g., gender, parent educational background, internal and external motivations) may and often do influence student academic performance, and this study does not investigate the impact of those factors on student scores. Furthermore, as the purpose of this study was to explore if there was a difference in student scores on state and EE-based tests, the study does not analyze the specific reasons of why that difference occurs. To identify specific characteristics of EE programs that may lead to improved student test scores, there is a need for more in-depth research using qualitative and quantitative methods.

Overall, this study adds to the body of evidence that environmental education not only provides an opportunity to help students learn how to live sustainably but also helps schools to meet state standards and requirements. With the current focus on accountability and testing, studies like this support teachers who want to teach EE in their classrooms. Some educators critique these efforts of the EE community to find evidence of EE efficacy. Gruenewald (2004) believes that they shift the priorities from transformation of the society, culture, and educational system to being able to "satisfy problematic state learning goals" (p. 82). At the same time, these so-called "legitimatization" efforts can be seen as first steps to transformation of the educational system. Elements of the educational culture (as well as system of schooling) are closely interconnected, and a serious change in one of them might lead to changes in the others (Hargreaves, 1994; Sarason, 1990). As such, changing teaching requirements and guidelines, adopting more EE-friendly administrative and educational policies, and providing teachers with more empirical evidence could be the first steps in this process of systemic change. Changes in cultural values and practices take years to happen. Teachers and administrators need research to support their instructional choices. The research presented here supports anecdotal evidence known by those who believe in the benefits of EE for their students and provides statistical evidence of the impact of environmental education on students. Through environmental education programs we can provide learners with a richer, more comprehensive experience that ties learning to the real world, advances thinking abilities, and helps students to perform at high levels. Moreover, it allows us to educate citizens of the future who would have knowledge and skills to address the environmental problems the world is facing—the very skills and knowledge that we do want our children to know.

NOTE

1.   Listening has not been tested on the WASL since 2004. Science was not tested the year this study was conducted.

REFERENCES

Angell, T., Ferguson, L., & Tudor, M. (2001). Better test scores through environmental education? *Clearing, 110*, 20–22.

Athman, J., & Monroe, M. C. (2004). The effects of environment-based education on students' critical thinking skills and disposition toward critical thinking. *Environmental Education Research, 10*(4), 507–522.

Bartosh, O., Tudor, M., Taylor, C., & Ferguson, L. (2006). Improving WASL scores through environmental education: Is it possible? *Applied Environmental Education and Communication, 5*(3), 161–170.

Billings, J. A., Plato, K., Anderson, J., & Wiley, M. S. (1996). *Washington Environmental Education Model Schools Program. Environmental education in the school culture: A systemic approach. What did we do? What did we learn?* Olympia, WA: OSPI.

Cheak, M., Hungerford, H., & Volk, T. (2002). *Molokai: An investment in children, the community and the environment.* Carbondale, IL: Center for Instruction, Staff Development and Evaluation.

Cohen, J. (1988). *Statistical power analysis for the behavioral sciences* (2nd ed.). Mahwah, NJ: Erlbaum.

Ferguson, L., Tudor, M., & Bartosh, O. (2005). *Environmental education rubrics that assess level of EE implementation by school buildings and grades* (Technical Report 3). Olympia, WA: Pacific Education Institute.

Gruenewald, D. (2004). A Foucauldian analysis of environmental education: Toward the socioecological challenge of the Earth Charter. *Curriculum Inquiry, 34(1)*, 71–107.

Hargreaves, A. (1994). *Changing teachers, changing times: Teachers' work and culture in the postmodern age.* Toronto, Ontario, Canada: OISE Press.

Hart, P. (2003). *Teachers' thinking in environmental education.* New York, NY: Peter Lang.

Hartung, J., Knapp, G., & Sinha, B. K. (2008). *Statistical meta-analysis with application.* Hoboken, NJ: Wiley.

Lieberman, G. A., & Hoody, L. (1998). *Closing the achievement gap: Using the environment as an integrating context for learning.* San Diego, CA: State Education and Environment Roundtable.

Lieberman, G. A., Hoody, L., & Lieberman, G. M. (2000). *California student assessment project: The effects of environment-based education on student achievement.* San Diego, CA: State Education and Environment Roundtable.

Monroe, M. C., Randall, J. & Crisp, V. (2001). *Improving student achievement with environmental education.* Retrieved from http://edis.ifas.ufl.edu/ BODY_FR114

National Environmental Education & Training Foundation & North American Association for Environmental Education. (2001). *Using environment-based education to advance learning skills and character development.* Washington, DC: Author.

National Environmental Education and Training Foundation. (2000). *Environment-based education: Creating high performance schools and students.* Washington, DC: Author.

Norman, N., Jennings, A., & Wahl, L. (2006). *The impact of environmentally-related education on academic achievement: A literature survey.* Berkeley, CA: Community Resources for Science.

Sarason, S. (1990). *The predictable failure of educational reform.* San Francisco, CA: Jossey-Bass.

Taylor, C., Kurtz-Smith, K., Tudor, M., Ferguson, L., & Bartosh, O. (2005). *Demonstrating the efficacy of environmental education: Using criterion referenced tests to demonstrate student achievement on state discipline based exams* (Technical Report 7). Olympia, WA: Pacific Education Institute.

U.S. Environmental Protection Agency, National Environmental Education Advisory Council, Environmental Education Division. (1996). *Report assessing environmental education in the United States and the implementation of the national environmental education act of 1990.* Washington, DC: Author.

Volk, T. L., Hungerford, H., & Tomera, A. (1984). A national survey of curriculum needs as perceived by professional environmental educators. *The Journal of Environmental Education, 16*(1), 10.

Wheeler, G., Thumlert, C., Glaser, L., Schoellhamer, M., & Bartosh, O. (2007). *Environmental education report: Empirical evidence, exemplary models, and recommendations on the impact of environmental education on K–12 students.* Olympia, WA: Office of Superintendent of Public Instruction.

CHAPTER 10

HOPE AND ACHIEVEMENT GOALS AS PREDICTORS OF STUDENT BEHAVIOR AND ACHIEVEMENT IN A RURAL MIDDLE SCHOOL

**Christopher O. Walker, Tina D. Winn, Blakely N. Adams,
Misty R. Shepard, Chelsea D. Huddleston, and Kayce L. Godwin**

Relations among a set of cognitive-motivational variables were examined with the intent of assessing and clarifying the nature of their interconnections within a middle school sample. Student perception of hope, which includes perceptions of agency and pathways, was investigated, along with personal achievement goal orientation, as predictors of student willingness to seek help, student engagement in disruptive behaviors, and academic achievement. A sample of 314 participants (approximately 52% Native American, 22% Caucasian, 10% Hispanic, 8% African American, and 4% "Other") was obtained from a rural middle school in the Midwestern United States. Consistent with theoretical predictions, intercorrelations among measures of hope, achievement goal orientation, help seeking, disruptive behavior, and achievement were found. Additionally, regression analysis revealed that student perceptions of available pathways were the lone signif-

Research Supporting Middle Grades Practice,
pp. 173–187

icant contributor to the prediction of academic achievement, while mastery goals and pathways were predictive of student help-seeking behaviors. Finally, mastery goals and agency were found to be statistically significant predictors of disruptive behaviors. Implications relating to both theory and practice are discussed.

INTRODUCTION

Snyder (1995, 2002, 2006) has suggested that hope is a cognitive-motivational construct comprised of two primary components (*agency* and *pathways*) that are related yet distinct and both essential for "hopeful thinking" (Babyak, Snyder, & Yoshinobu, 1993; Snyder et al., 2002). *Agency* involves the cognitive willpower to internally motivate oneself to accomplish a task or goal, while *pathways* refers to the belief that an avenue exists that will allow success to be achieved (Snyder, 1995). According to Snyder (1995), hope is especially salient in situations where a person feels a strong sense of both agency and pathways. For example, students who express a strong interest in doing well academically (high agency) and simultaneously believe that they know ways of achieving their academic goals (high pathways thinking) are likely to be categorized as being hopeful. Conversely, if students are not motivated to accomplish a task or feel incompetent in their abilities to do so effectively (low agency) and/or do not perceive any available strategies that would allow them to be successful (low pathway), then their corresponding level of hope would be reduced. Again, it is the combination of the two subcomponents that results in an individual's level of hope. In other words, having a high level of one component and an absence of the other is perhaps beneficial (better to have a high level of at least one than none at all) but ultimately will be insufficient to achieve an optimal level of hope.

Previous research has indicated that personal perception of hope can not only have a positive impact on individual performance but can do so within multiple contexts. For example, Curry, Snyder, Cook, Ruby, and Rehm (1997) found that hope positively predicted athletic accomplishment, specifically improving running times in cross-country and track athletes beyond what was predicted by "natural ability" (p.1263). Irving and colleagues (2004) found that high-hope clients experienced greater benefit from all phases of individual psychotherapy than did their low-hope counterparts, while, in the academic realm, hope has been predictive of achievement test scores in grade school (McDermott & Snyder, 2000), high grade point averages in high school (Snyder et al., 1991), higher semester and overall grade point averages in college (Curry et al., 1997), and graduation vs. dismissal from college over a six-year time span

(Snyder et al., 2002). Finally, hope has been found to be positively correlated with perceived academic competence (Onwuegbuzie & Daley, 1999) and academic satisfaction (Chang, 1998).

While personal perceptions of hope have been found to be strong predictors of individual behavior, other frameworks exist that have an equally extensive literature base. More specifically, Elliott and Dweck (1988) argued that personally adopted achievement goals have a direct causal impact on individual behavior, especially within the context of academics. Achievement goals have commonly been defined as the underlying "purposes" of individual behavior (Ames, 1992; Midgley, Kaplan, & Middleton, 2001; Urdan, 2004). Early work involving achievement goals emphasized two common goal orientations, namely mastery and performance goals (Ames, 1992; Ames & Archer, 1987, 1988; Elliott & Harackiewicz, 1996). While referring to mastery goals as learning goals, Grant and Dweck (2003) define this mastery/learning orientation as emphasizing "understanding and growth," whereas students adopting performance goals seek to gain approval through successful task completion (performance-approach goals) or to avoid negative evaluations of ability (performance-avoidance goals).

Research has consistently linked the adoption of mastery goals to a host of positive academic behaviors such as effort and persistence while studying, willingness to seek help, and the use of meaningful cognitive processing strategies (Anderman, Griesinger, & Westerfield, 1998; Elliot & Harackiewicz, 1996), along with scholastic outcomes such as end-of-semester class grades, test grades, and achievement test scores (Greene & Miller, 1996; Kaplan & Maehr, 1999; Meece & Holt, 1993; Midgely & Urdan, 1995; Roeser, Midgely, & Urdan, 1996). Conversely, performance-avoidance and performance-approach goals have been linked to maladaptive behaviors such as procrastination and the use of self-handicapping strategies (Elliot & Church, 1997; Elliot & McGregor, 1999; Elliot & Sheldon, 1997).

The Current Study

Although Snyder (2002) proposed a theoretical link between hope and personal achievement goal orientations, this study will be one of the first to empirically examine that relationship. Therefore, the purpose of the current study was to examine the collective contribution of the two components of hope (agency and pathways) and personal achievement goals (mastery, performance-approach, and performance-avoidance) in predicting student behavior and achievement in middle school. While numerous studies have supported a link between hope and positive academic outcomes (e.g.,

Chang, 1998; Lopez, Pedrotti, Edwards, & Bouwkamp, 2000; McDermott & Snyder, 2000), this study adds to existing cognitive-motivational literature in two ways. First, this study is one of the few, if not the first, to examine how (or if) a personal perception of hope adds to the prediction of student behavior (i.e., help-seeking behavior and willingness to engage in disruptive behavior) beyond the variance accounted for by personal achievement goals. Furthermore, the current study will be one of the first to examine how (or if) personal perceptions of hope adds to the prediction of academic achievement (i.e., grade point average) beyond what is accounted for by one's achievement goal orientation.

Research Questions

Based on the theory and findings described above, we developed two research questions for the current study. The first question addressed correlations between the two components of hope and the three personal achievement goal orientations: How are personal achievement goals related to a student's perception of agency and pathways? The second question concerned the role of agency and pathways in the prediction of two behavioral- and one achievement-related outcome variables: Do agency and pathway scores add uniquely to the prediction of help-seeking, self-reported disruptive behavior, and grade point average when personal achievement goals are also involved in the prediction equation?

METHOD

Participants

A total of 314 participants from a rural middle school in the Midwestern United States completed three questionnaires for the current study. The average age of the participants was 12.4 years. Native Americans (American Indians) comprised approximately 52% of the sample, Caucasians 22%, African-Americans 8%, Hispanics 10%, and those self-identifying as "other" 4%. Males and females comprised 45% and 55% of the sample, respectively.

Instruments

Students completed a questionnaire packet containing three questionnaires and a demographics sheet. The demographic sheet was used to col-

Table 10.1.   Descriptive Statistics for All Scales and Subscales

	Subscale	Alpha	Mean	Min–Max	SD	N of Items
1.	Mastery goals	.86	5.15	1-6	.90	6
2.	Performance approach goals	.72	3.57	1-6	1.26	5
3.	Performance avoidance goals	.68	3.77	1-6	1.30	6
4.	Agency	.79	4.26	1-6	1.11	4
5.	Pathway	.72	4.99	1-6	.94	4
6.	Help-seeking	.88	4.47	1-6	.95	17
7.	Disruptive behavior	.90	3.21	1-6	1.55	5
8.	GPA		2.79	.43 - 4.0	.75	

Note: $N = 314$.

lect basic information including participant age, grade, gender, and race/ethnicity. Each questionnaire item required a response on a six-point Likert-style agreement scale ranging from Strongly Disagree (1) to Strongly Agree (6). Table 10.1 presents the descriptive data for each subscale on the questionnaires including the number of items per subscale.

Personal achievement goals and disruptive behavior were measured using the *Patterns of Adaptive Learning Survey* (PALS; Midgley et al., 2000). The PALS provides a three-factor 17-item goal orientation measure that includes subscales for mastery goals (6 items), performance-approach goals (5 items), and performance-avoidance goals (6 items). Examples of mastery goal items are "It's important to me that I learn a lot of new concepts this year" and "One of my goals is to learn as much as I can." Performance-approach items include, "It's important to me that other students at my school think I am good at my school work" and "One of my goals is to show others that school work is easy for me." Items used to assess performance-avoidance goals include, "One of my goals is to keep others from thinking I'm not smart." Disruptive behavior items include, "I sometimes behave in a way during class that annoys my teachers" and "I sometimes don't follow my teacher's directions during class."

Items used to assess attitudes toward help seeking were adapted from Newman's (1990) *Mathematics Learning in the Classroom Questionnaire* (MLCQ). For the purpose of the current study, references to mathematics or math class were removed and replaced with generic yet academic-related terms such as "school work" and "during class." The MLCQ is a single-factor 17-item questionnaire that includes items such as, "I will ask for help if I can't remember something that I need to know in order to do the assignment" and "I will ask for help if I don't understand the directions." There were also five reversed scored items including, "I feel scared about asking questions" and "I think the teacher might think I'm dumb when I ask a question."

Hope was measured via Snyder et al.'s (1991) dispositional hope scale. The hope scale is a two-factor 12-item questionnaire that includes subscales for agency (4 items) and pathways (4 items). The hope scale also includes four filler items that are not used in the final calculations of dispositional hope scores. Examples of agency items include, "I will be successful in life" and "I energetically pursue my goals." Pathway items include "I can think of ways to get the things that are important to me" and "There are lots of ways around any problem." Example filler items include, "I feel tired most of the time" and "I worry about my health."

Finally, student GPAs were provided by school administrators at the conclusion of the school year.

Procedure

Only students returning a signed parental permission form were eligible to complete the research packet. Questionnaires were distributed and completed during the students' morning classes at the conclusion of the spring semester. The classroom teachers were asked to read a set of instructions to their students who were then told to sign and date the student assent form if they wished to complete the research packet. Participants were instructed to read each item carefully and reflect upon their current experience in middle school as they answered each item. It took students approximately 30 minutes to complete the entire packet.

RESULTS

Instrument and Subscale Statistics

In order to provide evidence for internal consistency, Cronbach alpha reliability coefficients were calculated for each scale and subscale. Alpha reliability scores for each scale were found to be adequate and ranged from .68 to .90 (see Table 10.1). From examining the means, it can be seen that except for the two performance goal orientations and disruptive behavior, the means for personal mastery goals, both hope subscales and the help-seeking variable, were above a 4 on the 6-point scale, suggesting that students' motivation was relatively positive in this middle school sample.

Subscale Intercorrelations

To address the first research question, a correlation matrix was created that included all of the variables examined in the present study (see Table 10.2). Student sense of agency and pathways was found to have a significant positive relationship with each of the three personal achievement goal orientations, although the weakest correlations were with the two performance goal orientations. As was expected, both agency and pathways were positively correlated with help-seeking. Interestingly, of the two hope subscales, only the pathway variable yielded a statistically significant correlation with GPA, while, as can be seen from the table, agency was found to have a positive relationship with student engagement in disruptive behaviors. Among the outcome variables, disruptive behavior was negatively related to both help-seeking and GPA, while, as anticipated, student willingness to seek help was positively related to GPA

To address the second research question, three regression analyses were conducted with mastery goals, performance-approach goals, performance-avoidance goals, agency, and pathways serving as the five predictor variables with GPA, help-seeking, and disruptive behavior serving as the three outcome variables.

Table 10.2. Bivariate Correlations Among all Predictor and Outcome Variables

		1	2	3	4	5	6	7	8
1.	GPA	1	.10	−.10	−.13*	.23**	.09	−.22**	.25**
2.	Mastery goals		1	.28**	.22**	.67**	.37**	−.13*	.54**
3.	Performance approach goals			1	.72**	.22**	.29**	.04	.16**
4.	Performance avoidance goals				1	.12*	.23**	.05	.06
5.	Pathway					1	.46**	−.08	.48**
6.	Agency						1	.12*	.22**
7.	Disruptive behavior							1	−.21**
8.	Help-seek								1

Note: $*p < .05. **p < .01.$

Prediction of GPA

Hierarchical regression analysis was selected in order to determine whether student sense of agency and pathways contributes additional explained variance in GPA beyond variance accounted for by mastery goals, performance-approach and performance-avoidance goals. In order to determine whether student sense of agency and pathways would significantly add to the explained variance of GPA, each of the three achievement goal orientations were simultaneously entered in a first block with the agency and pathway variables entered in the second block. The initial regression equation with mastery goals, performance-approach, and performance-avoidance goals serving as the predictor variables yielded a significant R^2 ($R^2 = .029$, $F(3, 281) = 2.79$, $p < .05$), while the addition of agency and pathway into the model accounted for an additional 4.3% of variance that was also statistically significant, $F(2, 279) = 6.52$, $p < .01$. The final regression equation explained 7.2% of the variance ($R^2 = .072$, $F(5, 279) = 4.35$, $p < .001$). As can be seen in Table 10.3, once all five predictor variables were entered into the regression equation, only student perception of available pathways yielded a statistically significant Beta.

Prediction of Help-Seeking Scores

The second hierarchical regression was performed with student help-seeking scores serving as the outcome variable and mastery goals, perfor-

Table 10.3.   Summary of Hierarchical Regression Analysis for Variables Predicting Student GPA

Variable	B	SE B	β
Equation 1			
Mastery goals	.104	.049	.130*
Performance approach goals	−.022	.051	−.037
Performance avoidance goals	−.066	.048	−.118
Equation 2			
Mastery goals	−.040	.063	−.05
Performance approach goals	−.041	.051	−.07
Performance avoidance goals	−.053	.048	−.095
Pathway	.202	.063	.260**
Agency	.024	.043	.038

Note: $R^2 = .029$ for Step 1; $\Delta R^2 = .043$ ($p < .01$). *$p < .05$. **$p < .01$.

**Table 10.4.   Summary of Hierarchical Regression Analysis
for Variables Predicting Student Help-Seeking Behavior**

Variable	B	SE B	β
Equation 1			
Mastery goals	.570	.055	.541**
Performance approach goals	.095	.056	.125
Performance avoidance goals	−.116−	.053	−.158*
Equation 2			
Mastery goals	.435	.071	.413**
Performance approach goals	.078	.056	.103
Performance avoidance goals	−.099−	.053	−.134
Pathway	.208	.072	−.200**
Agency	−.007−	.048	−.008

Note: $R^2 = .307$ for Step 1; $\Delta R^2 = .021$ ($p < .05$). *$p < .05$. **$p < .01$.

mance-approach goals, performance-avoidance goals, agency and pathways serving as the predictor variables. As with the previous regression analysis, the three achievement goal orientations were entered simultaneously in the first block with agency and pathways being added separately in a second block. A statistically significant R^2 of .307 was obtained in step one ($F(3,282) = 41.59\ p = .0001$). The addition of agency and pathways resulted in a R^2 change of 2.1% ($F(2, 280) = 4.47, p = .012$). The final regression equation explained 32.8% of the variance in help-seeking scores ($F(5, 280) = 27.36, p = .0001$). As can be seen in Table 10.4, mastery goals and student perceptions of available pathways had statistically significant Beta values.

Prediction of Disruptive Behavior

The third hierarchical regression was performed with student-reported disruptive behavior scores serving as the outcome variable and mastery goals, performance-approach goals, performance-avoidance goals, agency and pathways serving as the predictor variables. As with the previous regression analyses, the three achievement goal orientations were entered simultaneously in the first block with agency and pathways being added separately in a second block. A statistically nonsignificant R^2 of .025 was obtained in step one ($F(3, 289) = 2.49\ p = .06$). The addition of agency and pathways resulted in a R^2 change of 2.9% ($F(2, 287) = 4.37$,

Table 10.5. Summary of Hierarchical Regression Analysis for Variables Predicting Self-Reported Disruptive Behavior

Variable	B	SE B	β
Equation 1			
Mastery goals	−.265	.104	−.154*
Performance approach goals	.063	.106	.052
Performance avoidance goals	.067	.100	.056
Equation 2			
Mastery goals	−.304	.134	−.177*
Performance approach goals	.022	.106	.018
Performance avoidance goals	.059	.100	.050
Pathway	−.096	.135	−.058
Agency	.271	.092	.196**

Note: $R^2 = .025$ for Step 1; $\Delta R^2 = .029$ ($p < .05$). *$p < .05$. **$p < .01$.

$p = .014$) resulting in the overall regression equation becoming statistically significant. The final regression equation explained 5.4% of the variance in disruptive behavior scores ($F(5, 287) = 3.28$, $p = .007$). As can be seen in Table 10.5, mastery goals and student perceptions of agency had statistically significant Beta values.

DISCUSSION

These findings emphasize the usefulness of both frameworks for predicting academic outcomes and support the contention that hope offers unique prediction beyond personal achievement goals with regard to several factors specific to the academic domain. In fact, the regression analyses revealed that at least one of the two components of hope added to the prediction of each outcome variable. These findings are significant in that the outcome variables used in the present study included both an adaptive and maladaptive behavior and achievement, indicating that the components of hope give insight into a broad range of student behaviors in middle school.

More specifically, the findings of the current study suggest that when students focus on the mastery of course content they are likely to simultaneously seek avenues through which their comprehension of material can be developed. Consequently, if the classroom teacher establishes an environment where questions are encouraged, the net result will likely be a perceived pathway to learning, which, as hope theory would suggest, is a critical motivating factor. Furthermore, the results of the present study suggest that a tangible benefit of this type of dynamic person/environment fit is improved academic performance and achievement.

These results support the work of researchers who have emphasized the importance of early adolescents perceiving a fit between their interests and desires and the opportunities present within a given environment. For example, Eccles and Midgley (1989) and Eccles et al. (1993) have proposed a person-environment fit theory that suggests that student behavior (specifically within middle school) is directly influenced by the perceived fit between the "psychological needs" of the student and the nature of the social environment (p. 91). In short, the greater the fit between individual needs and environmental realities, the more adaptive the student motivation and behavior is likely to be. The results of this study would support that contention, insofar as saying that if those students with a mastery goal orientation find themselves in an environment in which they feel free to seek help when needed, they are likely to experience a boost not only in their motivation but also in their academic achievement.

It should also be noted that the agency component of hope was found to be a positive predictor of self-reported disruptive behavior. While this finding may at first seem counterintuitive, it does support an ever increasing point-of-view regarding the role of self-esteem as a precursor for various forms of maladaptive behaviors. While theoretical distinctions may exist between agency and self-esteem, a common thread is that both constructs denote a level of value and confidence either in the self generally (as with self-esteem) or in one's ability to manage a given set of circumstances (as with agency; see Pajares & Schunk, 2001, for additional comment on this last point). Dawes (1994, 1998) and Baumeister, Smart, and Boden (1996) have noted that high levels of self-esteem can be found in gang leaders, terrorists, and racists. Furthermore, Baumeister et al. (1996) suggested that high self-esteem can also be related to risk-taking behaviors, acts of violence, and criminal behavior. This is not to suggest that high self-esteem (or a high sense of agency, for that matter) is uniformly bad or maladaptive, but simply to indicate that behaviors related to elevated levels of intrapersonal confidence may result in behaviors that are ultimately self-defeating. Regarding the current study, it could be argued that students with a heightened sense of agency may perceive themselves as superior or above the rules or may simply be over-confident in their academic abilities and believe that work is not required for them to be successful academically. In other words, why devote attention to their studies in class when they are confident that they have the ability to "catch up" later. Clearly, additional research must be done before any definitive argument can be made as to the overall role of agency in student disruptive behavior.

Limitations

As with any study, limitations exist that limit the scope and potential impact of the present study. First, the fact that this is a correlational study means that we were unable to study effects, but instead focused on relationships. Secondly, we did not collect data pertaining to the previous academic experiences and outcomes of the students. Future cognitive-motivational research would benefit from longitudinal studies that examine the stability of each of the aforementioned factors over time. It could very well be that a consistent and/or multi-faceted sense of agency (i.e., one that is based on multiple past successes in a variety of different domains) would reduce the likelihood of students engaging in disruptive behaviors when compared to students whose sense of agency is either erratic or low in complexity.

CONCLUSION

Covington (2000) stated that "many motives, not just one, operate in any achievement setting," and that educational researchers should work to advance models of "achievement behavior in its full richness and complexity" (p. 191). This study has been an attempt to capture at least a sliver of the complexity of student behavior by examining the joint relationship of two cognitive-motivational frameworks to an array of academically related outcomes. As the results of the present study have demonstrated, both the achievement goal and hope frameworks provide us with unique information relevant to our understanding of student motivation and achievement in middle school.

REFERENCES

Ames, C. (1992). Classrooms: Goals, structures, and student motivation. *Journal of Educational Psychology, 84*, 261–271.

Ames, C., & Archer, J. (1987). Mothers' beliefs about the role of ability and effort in school learning. *Journal of Educational Psychology, 79*, 409–414.

Ames, C., & Archer, J. (1988). Achievement goals in the classroom: Students' learning strategies and motivation processes. *Journal of Educational Psychology, 80*, 260–270.

Anderman, E. M., Griesinger, T., & Westerfield, G. (1998). Motivation and cheating during adolescence. *Journal of Educational Psychology, 90*, 84–93.

Babyak, M. A., Snyder, C. R., & Yoshinobu, L. (1993). Psychometric properties of the hope scale: A confirmatory factor analysis. *Journal of Research in Personality, 27*, 154–169.

Baumeister, R. F., Smart, L., & Boden, J. M. (1996). Relation of threatened egotism to violence and aggression: The dark side of high-self-esteem. *Psychological Review, 103*, 5–33.

Chang, E. C. (1998). Hope, problem-solving ability, and coping in a college student population: Some implications for theory and practice. *Journal of Clinical Psychology, 54*, 953–962.

Covington, M. V. (2000). Goal theory, motivation, and school achievement: An integrative review. *Annual Review of Psychology, 51*, 171–200.

Curry, L. A., Snyder, C. R., Cook, D. L., Ruby, B. C., & Rehm, M. (1997). Role of hope in academic and sport achievement. *Journal of Personality and Social Psychology, 73*, 1257–1267.

Dawes, R. M. (1994). *House of cards: Psychology and psychotherapy built on myth*. New York, NY: Free Press.

Dawes, R. M. (1998). Behavioral decision making and judgment. In D. T. Gilbert, S. Fisk, & G. Lindzey (Eds.), *The handbook of social psychology* (pp. 589-597). Boston, MA: McGraw-Hill.

Eccles, J. S., & Midgley, C. (1989). Stage/environment fit: Developmentally appropriate classrooms for early adolescents. In R. E. Ames & C. Ames (Eds.). *Research on motivation in education* (Vol. 3, pp. 139-186). New York, NY: Academic Press.

Eccles, J. S., Midgley, C., Wigfield, A., Miller-Buchanan, C., Reuman, D., Flanagan, C. & MacIver, D. (1993). Development during adolescence: The impact of stage-environment fit on young adolescents' experiences in schools and in families. *American Psychologist, 48*, 90–101.

Elliot, A., & Church, M. (1997). A hierarchical model of approach and avoidance achievement motivation. *Journal of Personality and Social Psychology, 72*, 218–232.

Elliott, E. S., & Dweck, C. S. (1988). Goals: An approach to motivation and achievement. *Journal of Personality and Social Psychology, 54*, 5–12.

Elliot, A., & Harackiewicz, J. (1996). Approach and avoidance achievement goals and intrinsic motivation: A mediational analysis. *Journal of Personality and Social Psychology, 70*, 968–980.

Elliot, A., & McGregor, H. A. (1999). Test anxiety and the hierarchical model of approach and avoidance achievement motivation. *Journal of Personality and Social Psychology, 76*, 628–644.

Elliot, A., & Sheldon, K. (1997). Avoidance achievement motivation: Personal goals analysis. *Journal of Personality and Social Psychology, 73*, 171–185.

Grant, H., & Dweck, C. S. (2003). Clarifying achievement goals and their impact. *Journal of Personality and Social Psychology, 85*, 541–553.

Greene, B. A., & Miller, R. B. (1996). Influences on achievement: Goals, perceived ability, and cognitive engagement. *Contemporary Educational Psychology, 21*, 181–192.

Irving, L. M., Snyder, C. R., Cheavens, J., Gravel, L., Hanke, J., Hilberg, P., & Nelson, N. (2004). The relationships between hope and outcomes at the pretreatment, beginning, and later phases of psychotherapy. *Journal of Psychotherapy Integration, 14,* 419–443.

Kaplan, A., & Maehr, M. L. (1999). Achievement goals and student well-being. *Contemporary Educational Psychology, 24,* 330–358.

Lopez, S. J., Pedrotti, J. P., Edwards, L. M., & Bouwkamp, J. C. (2000, October). *Making Hope Happen via brief interventions.* Symposium conducted at the 2nd Positive Psychology Summit, Washington, D.C.

McDermott, D., & Snyder, C. R. (2000). *The great big book of hope: Help your children achieve their dreams.* Oakland, CA: New Harbinger Publications.

Meece, J. L., & Holt, K. (1993). A pattern analysis of students' achievement goals. *Journal of Educational Psychology, 85,* 582–590.

Midgley, C., Kaplan, A., & Middleton, M. (2001). Performance-approach goals: Good for what, for whom, under what circumstances, and at what cost? *Journal of Educational Psychology, 93,* 77–86.

Midgley, C., Maehr, M. L., Hruda, L. Z., Anderman, E., Anderman, L., Freeman, et al. (2000). *Manual for the Patterns of Adaptive Learning Scales (PALS).* Ann Arbor, MI: University of Michigan.

Midgley, C., & Urdan, T. (1995). Predictors of middle school students' use of self-handicapping strategies. *Journal of Early Adolescence, 15,* 389–411.

Newman, R. S. (1990). Children's help-seeking in the classroom: The role of motivational factors and attitudes. *Journal of Educational Psychology, 82,* 71–80.

Onwuegbuzie, A. J., & Daley, C.E. (1999). Relation of hope to self-perception. *Perceptual and Motor Skills, 88,* 535–540.

Pajares, F., & Schunk, D. H. (2001). Self-beliefs and school success: Self-efficacy, self-concept, and school achievement. In R. Riding & S. Raynor (Eds.), *Perception* (pp. 239–266). Norwood, NJ: Ablex.

Roeser, R., Midgley, C., & Urdan, T.C. (1996). Perceptions of the school psychological environment and early adolescents' psychological and behavioral functioning in school: The mediating role of goals and belonging. *Journal of Educational Psychology, 88,* 408–422.

Snyder, C. R. (1995). Conceptualizing, measuring, and nurturing hope. *Journal of Counseling & Development, 73,* 355–360.

Snyder, C. R. (2002). Hope theory: Rainbows in the mind. *Psychological Inquiry, 13,*249–275.

Snyder, C. R. (2006). Measuring hope in children. *Adolescent & Family Health, 4,* 26–34.

Snyder, C. R., Harris, C., Anderson, J. R., Holleran, S. A., Irving, L. M., Sigmon, S. T., et al. (1991). The will and the ways: development and validation of an individual-differences measure of hope. *Journal of Personality and Social Psychology, 60,* 570–585.

Snyder, C. R., Shorey, H. S., Cheavens, J., Pulvers, K. M., Adams, V. H., & Wiklund, C. (2002). Hope and academic success in college. *Journal of Educational Psychology, 94,* 820–826.

Urdan, T. (2004). Predictors of academic self-handicapping and achievement: Examining achievement goals, classroom goal structures, and culture. *Journal of Educational Psychology, 96*, 251–264.

ABOUT THE CONTRIBUTORS

Blakely N. Adams is a 2007 graduate of the University of Science and Arts of Oklahoma and is currently pursuing her master's degree in social work at the University of Kansas and working as a therapy department intern at Crittenton Children's Center in Kansas City, Missouri.

Oksana Bartosh is a research analyst at the Directions Evidence and Policy Research Group. She holds master's degrees in environmental sciences and policy (Budapest, Hungary) and in environmental studies (Olympia, WA). She recently completed her PhD in curriculum and instruction at the University of British Columbia. Dr. Bartosh has over 10 years of research experience in the field of environmental education and has conducted qualitative and quantitative studies in the United States, Canada, and Europe. Her research interest is in environmental education, particularly in curriculum and policy development, assessment, and ways of integrating environmental education into school practices. Oksana has produced a number of peer-reviewed publications, book chapters on secondary and postsecondary education, policy analysis, environmental education, and informal learning and authored and coauthored reports for Parks Canada, the Okanagan Science Centre, the Pacific Education Institute, the Association of Fish and Wildlife Agencies and the Environmental Careers Organization Canada.

Susan Bennett is a doctoral candidate in the Department of Childhood Education and Literacy Studies at the University of South Florida where she teaches literacy and creative arts courses. From 2005 until 2009, she assisted Dr. Susan Homan with research that investigated the effect of an innovative intervention, Tune in to Reading, on reading achievement of students in elementary, middle, and high school and juvenile justice centers. Her research interests include culturally responsive teaching, writing instruction, and multiple literacies.

Mary Margaret Capraro is an assistant professor of mathematics education, in the Department of Teaching, Learning, and Culture at Texas A&M University. Her research interests include teacher preparation in mathematics education, problem solving, and cross-cultural studies. Prior to her doctoral studies at the University of Southern Mississippi, she was employed with the Miami Dade County Schools as both a teacher and an assistant principal. She has over 35 peer-reviewed publications, and 40 national and international presentations. Dr. Capraro works extensively with public schools and school districts planning professional developments and designing mathematics learning activities. She is coprincipal investigator on the Aggie Science, Technology, Engineering and Mathematics Center. Additionally Dr. Capraro is associate editor for the *School Science and Mathematics* journal. She is currently past president of the Southwest Education Research Association.

Cynthia Calderone has been an educator for 27 years. She is currently an adjunct professor at Florida Atlantic University. Her areas of expertise are in emergent and early literacy, instruction for struggling readers, teacher education, and authentic performance-based assessment. Her research interests include the relationship between music and reading, and neuroscience and reading. Dr. Calderone was an elementary classroom teacher for 17 years and has taught undergraduate and graduate courses at the college level for 9 years. She earned a BS in elementary and special education from Lesley College in Cambridge, MA in 1983, a MA in curriculum and instruction from National Louis University in 1992, and a PhD from the University of South Florida in 2007. Dr. Calderone taught for the Department of Defense Dependent Schools) for 13 years in Germany, England, and Korea. She has also taught graduate courses for the University of Phoenix in Belgium, England, and Germany. She has provided reading services to middle grade students through a Gear-up grant, supervised student interns, and collected and analyzed data in 2003 for the National Longitudinal Evaluation of Comprehensive School Reform, in cooperation with AIR and NORC. In 2007 she was coprincipal investigator and lead researcher for a study of Tune in to Reading with students in high school and in the juvenile justice system, which was funded by a grant from the Florida Department of Education. She has coauthored several articles and reports.

Robert M. Capraro is a professor of mathematics education at Texas A&M University. He is interested in how students learn mathematics and how mathematical representations influence learning, how teachers mediate the mathematics-learning environment and quantitative methods as they apply in mathematics education. He has earned more than 50 publications, including two books, and several chapters in edited volumes. He was invited to be a visiting scholar at the Educational Testing Service in Princeton NJ. In 2003, he received the Montague Scholar Award for undergraduate teaching; in 2004 he earned the post of associate editor for the *American Educational Research Journal* and associate editor of the *School Science and Mathematics* journal. Dr. Capraro was the college nominee for the Presidential Award of Excellence for Faculty Service to International Students and the Joann Treat Research Award Winner for the College of Education and Human Development. Dr. Capraro has earned more than $2 million to support his research. He was a faculty researcher and coprincipal investigator on several funded projects; a grant from the Inter-agency Educational Research Initiative, coprincipal investigator that established the Aggie STEM, founding principal investigator of the New Traditions Program. He was appointed to National Middle School Association's Research Advisory Board and was program chair and president of the Southwest Educational Research Association, and as served on several committees for the college and university. Dr. Capraro was a guest lecturer at Bogaziçi University in Turkey and a visiting scholar in Italy and China—invited by the Department of Education of China.

Anne Chatfield is a teacher at Randall Middle School in Tampa, Florida. She was the director of juvenile justice programs for the Hillsborough County School District in 2007, during the study of Tune in to Reading with the juvenile justice population.

Robert Dedrick is a professor of educational measurement and research at the University of South Florida. He specializes in the development and validation of psychological and educational measures, and teaches courses in measurement, research design, and multilevel modeling. He served as the statistical consultant for the grant from the Florida Department of Education that examined the effect of the intervention, Tune in to Reading, on the reading achievement of high school and juvenile justice populations. He is currently involved in a national study examining the development of children adopted from China.

L. Mickey Fenzel, is professor and associate dean of the School of Education at Loyola University Maryland. A former middle school and high school teacher, he earned his PhD in developmental psychology from

Cornell University where he began his research on the transition students make from elementary to middle school. His recent research has focused on the social and academic development of urban students in the middle school context. His recent book, *Improving Urban Middle Schools: Lessons from the Nativity Schools*, examines an effective alternative model of middle school education for urban children placed at risk. He has also published research on the effects of participating in service-learning and predictors and consequences of alcohol abuse among emerging adults. Dr. Fenzel also serves on the editorial board of the *Journal of Early Adolescence* and the board of directors of Sisters Academy of Baltimore, a NativityMiguel network school.

Lynne Ferguson is coexecutive director of the Pacific Education Institute along with Margaret Tudor (for the past 6 years). She is a former classroom teacher, and has been director of environmental Education for the Washington Forest Protection Association for over 20 years.   She administers statewide education programs involving school districts, forest products companies, state departments of natural resources, teachers, facilitators/instructors and community groups. Her specific expertise involves training teachers to use the out of doors to help their students learn science and math. Lynne is coauthor of several EE curriculum guides, a 25-year member of the WA Association of Supervision and Curriculum Development, a former chair of the State OSPI Environmental Education Council, and has received numerous state and national awards.

Jennifer Friend is an assistant professor in the urban leadership and policy studies in education program at the University of Missouri-Kansas City where she teaches school finance, governmental and legal aspects of education, cultural diversity in American education, and urban educational leadership coursework for graduate and doctoral candidates. She received her PhD in urban leadership and policy studies in education from UMKC, with dissertation research on same-gender grouping in eighth-grade science classes. Her work experience includes 13 years as a middle-level teacher and administrator in Kansas. Recent publications include journal articles in *Middle School Journal, American Educational History Journal, Journal of Research on Leadership Education,* and the *Middle Grades Research Journal*. Her research agenda focuses on equity issues related to urban education and educational leadership, middle-level education, and documentary film as research.

Courtney George received her PhD in culture, curriculum, and change from the School of Education at the University of North Carolina at Chapel Hill in 2008. She currently serves as a part-time clinical professor at

UNC Chapel Hill and teaches English as a Second Language in the public schools. Her research interests focus on teaching culturally and linguistically diverse students, critical multicultural education, ESL teacher education, and narrative inquiry.

Susan Homan is a professor of literacy at the University of South Florida in Tampa. Her areas of expertise include adolescent struggling readers, emergent literacy, and diagnosis. She has coauthored several books and published over 30 articles in the literacy education field. She was the codirector (with Dr. James King) of the Accelerated Literacy Learning Program (ALL), which she helped develop in 1991. From 1991 until 2003 over 2000 at-risk children are taught to read by teacher's trained in the ALL program. In 2003 she was the first recipient of the Florida Reading Association's Marguerite Cogoino Radeneich Award for Outstanding Teaching Education in Reading. Most recently she has been researching the relationship between music, singing, and struggling readers. In 2007 she received a $468,000 grant from the Florida Department of Education to investigate a specific innovative intervention, Tune in to Reading, with high school and juvenile justice populations.

David L. Hough earned a PhD in education from the University of California in 1991 and has focused his research agenda on middle grades issues since that time. He is professor of research and statistics, former College of Education dean, and founder of the Institute for School Improvement at Missouri State University. In addition, Dr. Hough is managing editor of the *Middle Grades Research Journal* which he founded in 2006 after having served 12 years as the editor of *Research in Middle Level Education* for the National Middle School Association, Westerville, Ohio. Dr. Hough has worked with school organizations throughout the United States, Canada, and Mexico. He specializes in the design, evaluation, and reporting of education—community partnerships and character education initiatives. He has evaluated more than 40 professional development programs for state departments of education, school districts, and community organizations over the past two decades and provides professional development focused on middle grades education, grade span configurations, school climate, leadership, and community engagement. Dr. Hough coined the term *Elemiddle School* in 1991 as featured on *ABC's World News Tonight* on October 7, 2008. He has presented more than 70 research papers to professional organizations, published 68 research and scholarly studies, 15 policy briefs, 6 monographs, and 5 books. In addition, he has provided interviews regarding his research on elemiddle schools to the *San Francisco Examiner, Boston Globe, Washington Post, Miami Herald, St. Louis Post-Dispatch, Wall Street Journal, Education Week, USA*

Today, and dozens of radio and television stations, including National Public Radio. Dr. Hough continues to serve as an elemiddle school consultant to schools and communities across the United States.

Kayce L. Godwin is a 2007 graduate of the University of Science and Arts of Oklahoma and is currently employed as a program analyst at Tinker Airforce Base in Oklahoma City, Oklahoma.

Chelsea D. Huddleston is a 2008 graduate of the University of Science and Arts of Oklahoma and is currently employed with the Target Corporation.

Ken McCrary is a doctoral student at the University of Missouri–Kansas City, where he received his bachelor's degree in elementary education. He received his master's degree in administration from the University of Central Missouri. He is an elementary school principal in the Belton School District, Belton Missouri. The focus of his doctoral dissertation is the effects of professional development on the teachers of English Language Learners.

Ryan Most completed his master's degree in curriculum and instruction with honors at the University of Kansas studying methods of motivating struggling readers. He completed his education specialist degree in educational administration at the University of Missouri-Kansas City, researching the development of creativity in students. He is now an administrator at a middle school in Kansas City, Kansas with an ever-increasing English Language Learner population. His current research interests include professional development for educators working with ELLs and the development of culturally responsive classrooms.

Vicki L. Schmitt is assistant professor of assessment and measurement in the Department of Educational Studies in Psychology, Research Methodology, and Counseling at the University of Alabama, Tuscaloosa. She earned her PhD in educational research and evaluation from the University of Kansas in 2005. Her research focuses on the relationship of classroom assessments to curriculum and student achievement, from which she has published numerous manuscripts in professional journals and presented over 30 papers to professional organizations. Dr. Schmitt provides professional development and assessment consultation to schools throughout the country and has conducted a number of evidence-based program evaluations for schools and community groups. She is a cofounder of the *Middle Grades Research Journal* and currently serves as its editor-in-chief. Over the past decade, Dr. Schmitt has worked in editorial offices and research laboratories in Kansas, Missouri, and Alabama. Her ability to demonstrate practical applications drawn from research-based findings for classroom teachers and school-/district-level administrators has placed her in high demand among schools utilizing professional learning community models focused on improving student outcomes. Dr. Schmitt's research on middle grades classroom assessments has been widely and prominently cited within the middle school research community and continues to guide policy and practice across many systems.

Misty R. Shepard is a 2006 graduate of the University of Science and Arts of Oklahoma and is currently pursuing her PhD in educational psychology at Oklahoma State University.

Catherine Taylor is a professor of educational psychology at the University of Washington in the College of Education. She teaches classroom assessment for preservice teachers as well as test development courses to graduate students in education, psychology, statistics, speech-hearing sciences, and nursing. Her research is focused on validity issues in standardized testing, policies and practices in large-scale assessment programs, and how to teach teachers appropriate classroom-based assessment strategies especially performance-based assessments and portfolio assessments. She is coauthor (with Professor Susan Nolen, also from UW) of a textbook entitled, *Classroom Assessment: Supporting Teaching and Learning in Real Classrooms* (2005, 2007) published by Merrill-Prentice-Hall.

Margaret Tudor started her career as a classroom science teacher. For 18 years she has served as the director of environmental education at the Washington Department of Fish & Wildlife (sponsor of Project WILD). She also serves as executive director of the Pacific Education Institute (PEI), a consortium of education and natural resource government and industry stakeholders dedicated to quality education that assists schools in setting up outdoor programs integrating outdoor learning with subject learning. Her specific expertise involves helping school districts integrate PEI's published "field investigation" models into their science inquiry programs. Her expertise includes program evaluation and assessment of student learning in environmental education. Dr. Tudor has coedited and written a book entitled *Environmental Problem-Solving: Theory, Practice and Possibilities in Environmental Education*. She received her PhD in education from the University of Wisconsin, Milwaukee in 1989. She is founder and K-20 education director of Nature Mapping, a citizen/data collection and monitoring wildlife program begun in Washington and now utilized in 10 other states. She serves on numerous committees and actively seeks to "raise the bar" in environmental education to match and exceed school district standards.

David C. Virtue is associate professor of middle level and social studies education in the Department of Instruction and Teacher Education at the University of South Carolina. His areas of scholarly interest include social studies instruction, English language learners in the middle grades, and middle level teacher education and certification. His recent publications have appeared in *Middle Grades Research Journal, Research in Middle Level Education Online, Middle School Journal, The Clearing House, The Social Studies, Journal of Social Studies Research,* and *Social Studies and the Young Learner.* Dr. Virtue has contributed to numerous edited volumes, including *Surviving the Storm: Creating Opportunities for Learning in Response to Hurricane Katrina, An International Look at Educating Young Adolescents, The Young Adolescent in the Middle School,* and *The Encyclopedia of Educational Reform and Dissent.* Dr. Virtue currently serves as editor of *Middle School Journal,* a publication of National Middle School Association, and he is the recipient of a 2010-2011 Fulbright Award to Norway, where he will serve as a "roving scholar" visiting ungdomsskoler (lower secondary schools) throughout the country

Christopher O. Walker is an associate professor of psychology and is currently chair of the Division of Business and Social Sciences at the University of Science and Arts of Oklahoma. His research typically examines environmental and personal factors that influence student perceptions of belonging, achievement motivation, and the adoption of achievement goals. Dr. Walker serves on the editorial board of the *Journal of Scientific Psychology* and has served as an ad hoc reviewer for the journal *Learning and Individual Differences.* He is a past recipient of his university's Regents Award for Scholarly Research and Regents Award for Superior Teaching.

Tina D. Winn is an associate professor of education at Oklahoma Christian University where she teaches courses related to human relations and educational issues. Her research interests include examining personality and cognitive factors that contribute to academic and personal success. Her scholarly publications include topics such as adolescence in the twenty-first century, factors related to forgiveness, and the role of hope in academic achievement. She twice received the Regents Award for Superior Teaching while at the University of Science and Arts of Oklahoma and was selected as the Alumnus of the Year for the School of Education at Oklahoma Christian University.

Guili Zhang is an assistant professor of research methodology in the Department of Curriculum and Instruction, East Carolina University. She received a PhD in research and evaluation methodology from the University of Florida. She currently serves as chair of the American Educational Research Association Quantitative Dissertation Award Committee and editor of *Journal of Curriculum and Instruction*. She is a recipient of the Frontiers in Education Benjamin J. Dasher Best Paper Award, the American Society for Engineering Education Best Paper Award, and the Edward C. Pomeroy Award for Outstanding Contributions to Teacher Education from the American Association of Colleges for Teacher Education. Her research interests involve applied quantitative research designs, categorical data analysis, longitudinal data management and analysis, large-scale data analysis, program assessment and evaluation, meta-analysis, and mixed-methods research.

LaVergne, TN USA
09 September 2010
196508LV00002B/10/P